Counting on Marilyn Waring

Counting on Marilyn Waring

New Advances in Feminist Economics
Second Edition

Edited by
Margunn Bjørnholt & Ailsa McKay

Demeter Press logo based on the sculpture "Demeter" by Maria-Luise Bodirsky <www.keramik-atelier.bodirsky.de>

Cover image by Shira Richter
Printed and Bound in Canada.

Library and Archives Canada Cataloguing in Publication

Counting on Marilyn Waring : new advances in feminist economics / edited by Margunn Bjørnholt and Ailsa McKay.

(Second Edition)

Includes bibliographical references.

ISBN 978-1-926452-02-9 (pbk.)

1. Feminist economics. 2. Waring, Marilyn, 1952-. I. McKay, Ailsa, 1963-2014 editor of compilation II. Bjørnholt, Margunn, 1958-, editor of compilation

HQ1381.C66 2014   330.082   C2013-908300-6

Demeter Press
140 Holland Street West
P. O. Box 13022
Bradford, ON L3Z 2Y5
Tel: (905) 775-9089
Email: info@demeterpress.org
Website: www.demeterpress.org

Table of Contents

TABLE OF CONTENTS

In Memory of Ailsa McKay

MARGUNN BJØRNHOLT AND MARILYN WARING

THE PUBLICATION of this book very sadly coincided with Ailsa McKay's untimely death. The joy at its favourable reception, leading to a second edition, is mixed with grief. Regrettably Ailsa is not with us to enjoy the positive response to the book and the interest it has generated in feminist economics in different parts of the world.

Ailsa often told the story of our meeting in Toronto, at a conference a few years ago. It was one of those occasions in life when you meet someone with whom you can talk in shorthand and not have to explain all the her-story of what goes into any comment at that moment, and this began a very special friendship. We both benefited in different ways from her generosity of spirit towards other academics. We loved her passion, her humour and her vision, her warmth and honesty, and her feisty nature, making conversations with her funny and cathartic and healing.

Ailsa made a remarkable contribution to the field of feminist economics, as well as to the Scottish society and to the world, literally making women count, through her combination of academic work and an active role in society. She was a founding member of the Scottish Women's Budget Group, which was founded around her kitchen table, later growing into an influential voice listened to by successive Scottish Finance Ministers and by others.

Ailsa taught us through her life that economics and politics are not separate. She was incessantly campaigning for including gender into economic models and analyses, as well as for welfare reform, properly funded free universal childcare, and a citizen's basic income for all – all as means to build a different and more caring world. Even in the last months, while enduring treatment and pain, Ailsa was working with her colleagues to provide the evidence to ensure that ignorance would no longer serve as an excuse of the gender pay gap and the heavy incidence of austerity and welfare cuts on women.

Her impressive record of influencing policy and practice include serving as a consultant to the Scottish Parliament, the Irish Government, the UK Treasury, and the United Nations Development Programme, and as an expert witness to governments. She was also a founding member of the European Gender Budget Network and a board member of the Jimmy Reid Foundation as well as a chairperson of the European chapter of the International Association for Feminist Economics (IAFFE).

We feel privileged that we got to know her and we feel honoured to have called her our colleague and friend.

Oslo and Auckland
Margunn Bjørnholt and Marilyn Waring
21 July 2014

Foreword

JULIE A. NELSON

IN 1988, when Marilyn Waring's groundbreaking book came out, I was a young Assistant Professor at a United States university. Just beginning my own work on "feminist economics," I could count on one hand the number of people I had found who had ever put those two words together in the same sentence. You can imagine how pleased I was to see that someone—on the other side of the world, no less—had authored a book on *If Women Counted: A New Feminist Economics.*

Marilyn Waring's work woke people up. She showed exactly how the unpaid work traditionally done by women has been made invisible within national accounting systems, and the damage this causes. Her book—as the present volume attests—encouraged and influenced a wide range of work on ways, both numerical and otherwise, of valuing, preserving, and rewarding the work of care that sustains our lives. By pointing to a similar neglect of the natural environment, she also issued a wake-up call to issues of ecological sustainability that have only grown more pressing over time. In recent decades, the field of feminist economics has broadened and widened to encompass these topics and more. Marilyn Waring received a standing ovation at the 2006 International Association for Feminist Economics conference in Sydney, Australia.

Is her work still relevant? Sadly, yes. I was vividly reminded of this just weeks ago when—now, as a considerably older economics professor—I was called to the bedside of my dying sister. A single dose of her last chemotherapy treatment cost about the same as a pretty nice new car, but, with powerful insurance and pharmaceutical companies running our U.S. healthcare system, her health plan paid this in full. On the other hand, the hospice care her health plan provided depends heavily on unpaid family caregivers to keep costs down, and carefully rations the provision of home health assistance to a few hours a day, and no more.

Chemicals still count in a way that care does not. We need the essays in the current volume to inspire further action to set things right.

Julie A. Nelson
Boston, Massachusetts
September 2012

Acknowledgements

WE ARE BOTH EXTREMELY grateful to all those who responded to the initial call for papers and we are only too sorry we could not include all the proposed contributions. We are especially grateful to MIRCI and Demeter Press for supporting this publication and indeed for the range of work they continue to support in the fields of unpaid care work and mothering. In finalising this collection for publication we found ourselves recounting our personal experiences of meeting with Marilyn and sharing conversations with her. For both of us a particularly memorable occasion was in October 2012. Colleagues of Marilyn's at AUT hosted and organised a celebratory event entitled "Women's Leadership: The Political, The Personal, The Passionate, and The Phenomenal. An Event to Celebrate Marilyn Waring's 60th Birthday." We were both fortunate enough to be invited to participate in that event providing testimony as to the influence of Marilyn's teachings and writings on the international academic community. We subsequently met with many of Marilyn's friends, colleagues and family, hearing first hand of her many attributes and personal qualities that reach beyond her academic endeavours. We even heard her sing. What struck us both is the energy and passion Marilyn displays for all that she does and the space she creates for others to develop the same. The varied chapters in this book indicate the many ways in which that space has provided opportunities for new and creative ways of viewing the world.

Introduction

MARGUNN BJØRNHOLT & AILSA MCKAY

I T IS AN INDISPUTABLE fact that there is no such thing as a free lunch.
That is, everything has a cost. We are constantly reminded of this by
evidence of the impact of our production and consumption activities
on our environment, news reports of the loss of human life due to random
acts of violence and/or armed conflict arising from political power struggles
and research reports that highlight growing global inequalities and increasing incidences of absolute poverty amidst plenty. However, whilst many
of these costs are felt by us all either directly or indirectly, their very nature makes them less tangible in terms of our national economic systems.
Thus, much of what *counts* in terms of promoting welfare, or perhaps more
crucially what counts in harming our environment; our livelihood and the
welfare of our communities remain largely invisible in the process of developing frameworks that indicate a nation's relative economic performance.

Marilyn Waring not only recognized this significant failure in the internationally accepted and universally applied system of national accounts,
but additionally took on the challenge of making sure the rest of us recognized it also. Her contribution to developing a shared understanding of the
failure of our mainstream economic systems, in accounting for the range
of unpaid work women engage in, in itself essential for reproducing and
sustaining, and the environmental impacts of a focus on securing growth
through increasing GDP is unparalleled. Through a combination of her

teaching, her writing and her activism Marilyn Waring has provided us all with the required foundation to challenge our dominant economic systems. By providing us with the confirmation of what really counts, Marilyn has effectively illuminated and expanded the possibilities for us all as individual women, and for our sisters, our mothers and our daughters.

However, everything has a cost. Preparing this collection we became aware of some of the costs associated with Marilyn's chosen political and academic career. Soon after the call for papers was issued, we received an e-mail from Marilyn's father, in which he wrote:

> Another side of Marilyn's life was as a soprano in St. Peter's Choir in Wellington NZ. Yes, she still has a good voice...Sadly for her Mum and Dad her entry into Politics did not give her time to achieve fully this gift.

As mothers, and in the particular case of one of us, the mother of musically gifted children who have chosen very different careers, this was a very poignant personal communication from Bill. Some days later we received another e-mail, this one from Marilyn's old choir–master, John Hawley. After describing Marilyn's leading role in the choir as a young student he concluded:

> It would not have surprised me if she had become a soloist in performances of Messiah and other oratorios in New Zealand. Likewise in opera and in radio broadcasts as one with "National Artist" status. Whether she'd have moved from national to international stature I wouldn't guess at. No one should. But she'd have given it a good shot. She had great powers of concentration and a very good voice. And the confidence of course. With the right coaching she might well have been one of the few who make the transition from "listen to me" to "listen to this."

When we later asked her about her "lost" singing career, Marilyn replied: "I couldn't see myself as a dying Desdemona." Let this be a challenge to writers of opera librettos! Luckily for the many women, carers, subsistence farmers, and other groups whose lives and work are undervalued, and for the field of feminist economics, Marilyn chose a different path. In pursuing this path she has gained both national and international stature and regularly ranks on exclusive lists of people who have made a real change to the world. By drawing attention to the systems that exclude much of the activity that sustains us as human beings and as a result leaves so many individuals and communities marginalized and undervalued she definitely made the transition from "listen to me" to "listen to them."

This collection of essays demonstrates how Waring's work has inspired scholars, activists and students across the globe, and how the field has evolved and matured over the quarter-century, since the publication of *If Women Counted*. A common theme emerging throughout the varied contributions is the continued need for, and relevance of, asking who, what and how to value. In this regard we all still count on Marilyn. By continuing to challenge our economic systems and by approaching relevant questions in new ways, Marilyn's contribution to feminist economics has allowed us all to transform our thinking, develop new meanings and indeed expand our sense of actual possibilities. Or, perhaps put more accurately by Marilyn herself, "the opportunity to be wicked."

THE STRUCTURE AND CHAPTERS

The book mirrors the wide-ranging impact and resonance of Waring's work in academia, policy-making, activism and the arts. The collection opens with a number of essays presenting advances in feminist economic thought from a range of perspectives (Bjørnholt and McKay; Aslaksen, Bragstad and Ås; O'Hara). The largest part of the book features elaborations, advances and critical reflections on the art of counting (Aslaksen and Koren; Varjonen and Kirjavainen; Casper and Simmons; Jülich; Fairbairn-Dunlop; Dobell with Walsh; Katzav and Richter). There are also chapters on care and care-work (Shivdas and Mukherjee; Peters, Hemingway, Vaillancourt and Fiske), policymaking and advocacy (Grace and Craig; Smith; Turnbull and Fridell), as well as teaching, and being taught by Marilyn Waring (Eichhorn; Webster). The chapters draw upon a number of country specific experiences/initiatives as well as a varied range of academic disciplines. Many of the chapters are either cross or inter-disciplinary, demonstrating the reach of Waring's academic work which is further evidenced by chapters that draw upon Marilyn Waring's writings to provide insights into the relationship between academia and art (Eichhorn; Katzav and Richter).

ADVANCES IN FEMINIST ECONOMICS PERSPECTIVES

Margunn Bjørnholt and Ailsa McKay introduce the collection by highlighting the relevance of Marilyn Waring's academic treatise on value, care and the economy in developing new perspectives on what counts in assessing economic progress in the context of crisis. Iulie Aslaksen, Torunn Bragstad and Berit Ås discuss the intersection of, and synergies between, feminist and ecological economics as contributions to exploring visions and political strategies for a sustainable future. In doing so they draw upon a further aspect of Marilyn Waring's philosophical position on the relationship between the survival of the planet and how we manage the economy, and perhaps more crucially how we practice economics.

Sabine O'Hara offers an expanded concept of economic production that accounts for the sustaining nature of care services offered outwith the formal economy; O'Hara invites a fundamental rethinking of the economic conceptions of care, and its value in the context of the future of market economies in the long run.

WHO, HOW AND WHAT TO COUNT?

Iulie Aslaksen and Charlotte Koren survey the history of statistical measurement of unpaid household work in Norway concluding that gross domestic product (GDP) measures overestimate growth in real consumption possibilities. They argue that measurement of women's unpaid work is important for improving knowledge on the discrepancy between women's economic contribution to society and women's control over economic resources. Johanna Varjonen and Leena Kirjavainen, describe how unpaid work was measured and how the media and various academic disciplines in Finland received the results.

Monica Casper and William Simmons analyze infant mortality rates in the context of the UN Millennium Development Goals (MDGs). Drawing on the Mexican experience, they show that the development field's current accounting system have mobilized infant mortality as justification for the expansion of neoliberal policies.

Shirley Jülich brings together equality, Stockholm syndrome and the economic costs of child sexual abuse, arguing for improved frameworks for justice that better accommodate the nature and costs of gender based inequalities.

Tagaloatele Peggy Fairbairn-Dunlop proposes that women's work in the Pacifics, which is predominantly family based and occurring in semi-subsistence communities, is highly valued for its alignment with cultural norms and for its contribution to family and community quality of life. This is particularly crucial in the context of sustainability given absence of government provided services.

Rod Dobell and Jodie Walsh problematize the imputation of monetary values for intangible services as a means of integrating social and environmental concerns within economic decisions. They argue for greater community control to improve our understanding, and treatment of, within our economic decision-making processes, the relationship between the social and the economic.

CARE AND CARE-WORK

Meena Shivdas and Anit Mukherjee's chapter is based on their research on unpaid HIV carers' rights, and privileges across diverse settings in order to articulate an alternative economic framework to answer questions on whose rights count when interventions are planned and implemented. Heather Peters, Dawn Hemingway, Anita Vaillancourt and Jo-Anne Fiske explore the experiences of women caregivers in four small, rural communities in northern British Columbia (BC) in Canada, arguing that the devaluing of women's work is exacerbated by a number of factors including northern isolation, rural lack of services, economic decline and neo-liberal restructuring involving a significant transfer of responsibility for care from the public to the private sector.

ADVOCACY AND ACTIVISM

Julie Smith traces the evolution in thinking on the economics of breast-feeding and the role of Waring's 1988 feminist critique of the national accounting treatment of mothers' milk and breastfeeding. It shows how this work inspired women's advocacy on breastfeeding and influenced policy that served in improving economic justice for women. Marty Grace and Lyn Craig recapture how Waring's early work was taken up by scholars, policy makers and ordinary Australians, and discusses the impact of Waring's work in Australia, with illustrations from the social policy areas of paid maternity leave and fair wages for care workers, and with a particular focus on time use scholarship.

Mara Fridell and Lorna Turnbull review the impact of Marilyn Waring's work on the formation of a feminist organization in Manitoba, Canada, that was devoted to promoting the Platform for Action developed at the Fourth World Conference on Women in Beijing in 1995. This group has effected change despite a political and economic climate hostile to women's equality.

TEACHING AND LEARNING

Jill Eichhorn describes how she, inspired by Waring's work, started to count students' production of *The Vagina Monologues* as part of their academic development arguing for counting embodied learning as legitimate, especially in the case of politically disenfranchised or marginalized groups. This chapter also demonstrates how art, personal growth, activism and academic work can be combined in the production of value. Karen Webster draws on the contributions of Marilyn's post-graduate researchers and describes how Marilyn contributed to their academic and personal growth and the contribution they are making to the world as a result of knowing her.

ACTIVISM, ACADEMIA AND ART

In their contribution Hadara Katzav and artist Shira Richter offer a joint multidisciplinary investigation of the history of Zionism, Israeli politics, national matrimonial law, motherhood in Israeli art and current day activism based on the artistic project Invisible Invaluables. The chapter also contains selected images from the project.

The breadth and range of topics and perspectives covered highlights both the impact and endurance of Waring's work, in the shaping of the discipline of feminist economics and in influencing women's lives across the globe. In the foreword to this collection Julie Nelson pointed out how Marilyn Waring's *If Women Counted* "encouraged and influenced a wide range of work on ways, both numerical and otherwise, of valuing, preserving, and rewarding the work of care that sustains our lives".

We hope this collection further expands and advances the field of feminist economics as well as further demonstrating the ever more urgent need as well as the tools to change the economics discipline and economic policies. The future of economics is feminist.

1.

Advances in Feminist Economics in Times of Economic Crisis

MARGUNN BJØRNHOLT & AILSA MCKAY

INTRODUCTION

W
E FEMINIST ECONOMISTS gathered in Barcelona on the occasion of the 21st Annual Conference of the International Association for Feminist Economics (IAFFE), considering that in the last decades neoliberalism has produced multiple crises, in different parts of the world, and this global crisis has moved from the periphery to the centre and is now hitting Europe.... We reject both the current mainstream explanations of the global crisis and the proposals for resolving it. We reject the economic strategies that continue to skew income and wealth distribution in favour of finance and large capital while depriving people of necessary care and the means for a sustainable life. We reject an economic system that exploits women's unpaid care work to keep the economic system going, relying on them to absorb the dramatic costs of the crisis. *Barcelona, June 28th, 2012*

The above extract, from a manifesto, signed by many participants in the IAFFE annual conference 2012, highlights the current frustration felt from within the feminist economics movement about the limitations of mainstream economic thinking. The economics discipline, as it is most commonly understood and practiced, failed to accurately forecast the outcomes of deregulated global financial markets or come up with an effective response to the crisis that followed the collapse of those markets. Indeed, rather than promote recovery, the favoured austerity measures, imposed across Europe in order to deal with the aftermath of bailing out failing banks, has led to further recession. At the time of writing, predictions of a triple dip recession dominate media headlines indicating little hope of economic recovery in the immediate future. It looks highly likely that more of the same will feature across the economies of Europe and the US—further job losses, greater incidences of personal bankruptcy, continued reductions in public spending and the associated contraction in public services. Thus the economic outlook, for women in particular, is pretty gloomy. Existing evidence tells us that women have borne the brunt of austerity measures to date. This is due primarily to the combined effect of their position in the labor market and their role as users and providers of key public services. It seems then that by continuing to absorb the dramatic costs of the crisis women will keep our economies afloat. However, with what impact, and is it a price worth paying?

Starting with the gendered impact of the current economic crisis, in this chapter, we point out the need for reshaping the economy and, the economics discipline, and highlight some promising theoretical and conceptual advances that can be part of such a necessary reshaping.

AN ECONOMY IN CRISIS—AN OPPORTUNITY FOR RESHAPING?

The bursting of a financial speculative bubble in 2008, that led to a crash in financial markets and the subsequent global banking crisis, provided an opportunity to learn from the apparent inherent failures in the system of financial capitalism. Perhaps even an opportunity to consider an alternative political economy trajectory that would better serve the needs of all citizens as opposed to a privileged minority. Instead, the chosen route was to follow a path that effectively rewarded our global financial institutions for behaviour that expanded our understanding of concepts such as speculation and risk to include actions that can only be described as reckless and irresponsible. This recklessness is embedded in the global financial architecture itself. Monopoly structures and cross-ownerships within the sector has led to extreme accumulation and globalization of systemic risk and an overwhelming concentration of power (Vitali et al.).

Bailing out failing banks, the common response to the crisis across Europe and the US, has been achieved at considerable cost. While government intervention to save failing private sector businesses is not unusual, what does distinguish the recent economic crisis from previous ones is not just the cost, but also the consequences of the intervention for the public finances. Once some stability had been restored to the financial system, governments, partly as a result of pressure from financial markets, became more concerned about the growing level of public sector debt. Subsequently their attention switched from saving the banking system to curbing public expenditure in order to reduce the level of government debt. As a result, the period since 2008 has been characterised by a major retrenchment of public services and employment.

Thus, the unique feature of this recession and associated recovery plans is that rather than serve as a buffer against the impact of the downturn, public spending has been the focus of an austerity policy with long lasting implications for the nature and purpose of the public sector in modern economies. It is this reconfiguration of the public sector that presents as a real crisis when we consider the impact on women and families:

> These crises have arisen out of gendered economic processes, in which women were virtually absent, from key sites of decision making in the financial sector: and in which neither private nor public finance was equitably distributed, and failed adequately to address the requirements of women as producers and as carers. The impact of this crisis is gendered too. (Elson 202)

Rapid fiscal consolidation, evidenced across Europe and the US, has led to significant retrenchment in policy areas that have been key in supporting greater rates of participation in the labor market amongst women, not least of which has been the significant reduction in public sector jobs. Patterns of gender based occupational segregation serve to protect women in times of economic recession where the impact of the downturn is normally felt in male dominated industries, such as manufacturing and construction. Ironically that same segregation is now exposing women to far greater risks than their male counterparts in the labor market.

Prolonged and deep-seated spending cuts will thus impact significantly on women as workers in the public sector but also as users of public services. This is mainly a result of the very different positions they occupy within both the paid and unpaid sectors of the economy, and the design and delivery of state welfare provision. They all combine to ensure women, throughout the course of their lives, are more vulnerable to the risk of poverty. Thus, women are less able to withstand the impact of recession.

Cuts in state support of care services, alongside restrictions in benefit entitlement, pay and recruitment freezes in the public sector, and pension reform have dominated the policy agenda since at least 2009. The combined effect has been to expose women to greater risks of job losses and real reductions in income over the longer term. The gendered impact of the current economic recession, and subsequent recovery packages, highlights how women are now disproportionately absorbing the costs.

Although this impact remains largely invisible in the context of mainstream economic analysis, there are signs that an understanding is working its way into economic institutions. In a working paper released in January 2013, IMF's chief economist Olivier Blanchard admitted they had grossly misjudged the effects of budget cuts on public revenue (the fiscal multiplier) (Blanchard and Leigh), thus illustrating the inadequacy of the chosen solutions and a crisis in the understanding and workings of the economic system.

The lack of understanding with regard to the effects of budget cuts are partly the result of a lack of understanding of the role of the public sector and care in wealth creation. Salimah Valiani provides quantitative and qualitative data from the Canadian province of Ontario that demonstrates the centrality, and indeed the superiority, of public sector expenditure and the care sector in supporting economic and human development. Spending cuts to public health care, education, and other public services are subsequently shown to have a strong negative effect on overall economic performance.

Therefore, as opposed to providing a justification for cutting public spending, the crisis in the economy may provide us with an opportunity to justify public sector investment in key areas that support the well being of families and wider communities, and the development of human capital in individuals as well as societies. If we improve upon our economic models in ways that incorporate care as a capital investment rather than resource expenditure then the economic impact of the lack of adequate care resources will be more transparent. This, however would require a fundamental shift in the way we think about and do economics.

A DISCIPLINE IN CRISIS?

The economics discipline is traditionally associated with a particular focus, and range of methods, that can be criticized for being androcentric. This particular view has effectively served to influence both theory and practice to the extent that it has emerged as dominant and indeed superior to all other views. Feminist economists have sought to reshape their discipline to be more inclusive, and to reorient the approach to study in a more gender-sensitive fashion. In doing so, much progress has been made in establishing a feminist economics perspective as a credible field within the economics discipline. However, as the feminist economists (quoted above) highlighted, given the continued dominance of mainstream approaches in informing economic policy and the very gendered consequences of such, perhaps now more than ever we are in need of this reshaping.

The economics profession failed to predict the most recent and catastrophic global financial crisis. Possibly more concerning is the subsequent failure of the profession to come up with suitable and effective remedies to counteract the effects of the most widespread and significant economic slump since the Second World War. Robert Skidelsky, leading scholar of Keynes's life and works, highlights the relationship between the financial crisis and the crisis in ideas within the mainstream economics profession:

> To understand the crisis we need to get beyond the blame game. For at the root of the crisis was not a failure of characters or competence, but a failure of ideas...the present crisis is to a large extent the fruit of the intellectual failure of the economics profession. (28)

Thus the current economic crisis and the crisis in economics presents as an opportunity to generate new ideas—reshape the discipline. What would that reshaping look like? Given the evidence emerging relating to the very gendered impact of the economic crisis (Bettio et al.; Seguino; and Smith) it would seem that any attempt to render the economics discipline more effective as a tool for predicting, analysing and responding to economic phenomena should incorporate a gender perspective. That is, what is required is a more useful framework for understanding the complexities of human activity, the life experiences of all individuals, women in particular, and a widening of the debate to include the whole range of factors that contribute to human well-being.

Feminist economists have criticized the assumptions of human nature, associated with the central character in mainstream economics:

> The subject of the economist's model is an individual who is self-interested, autonomous, rational and whose active choices are the focus of interest, as opposed to one who would be social, other interested, dependent, emotional and directed by an intrinsic nature. (Nelson 22-23)

Thus human beings are not unrelated and self-interested individuals, as assumed in Hobbes' "state of nature". Rather, they have been nurtured and cared for and subsequently socialized; they are part of communities, depending on each other and adhering to social norms, morals and other social structures (McCloskey). The state of nature is not one of isolation and competition, but one of care and cooperation. This capacity for coop-eration, for good and for bad, also explains why there is no such thing as a free market without the regulatory framework of states and institutions.

The unrealistic assumption of human nature and societies underlying the "homo-economicus" thesis, however, remains the cornerstone of main-stream economic theory. This biased view results in limiting and biased eco-nomic models, which lead to biased and poorly targeted policies. We need to build economic theory, as well as policies informed by those theories on a more realistic assumption of human nature and human agency—taking "homo-socius" rather than "homo-economicus" as our starting point. As-suming that people are genuinely social, provides a more optimistic view of human capacities to build and maintain institutions and to pursue the com-mon good. Mobilizing these human capacities is crucial in order to address the huge and manifold challenges of our time.

CHALLENGING THE NORM?

Feminist economics is but one approach in a strong tradition of challenges to the dominance of mainstream economics. However, despite the exis-tence of varied approaches or traditions, captured under the umbrella term "heteredox economics" the policy world remains influenced by orthodox theory and practice. Furthermore, in its mainstream form, the economics discipline is a very powerful and persuasive feature of the public policy making process. As Keynes, so eloquently argued:

> The ideas of economists and political philosophers, both when they are wrong and when they are right are more powerful than is commonly understood. Indeed the world is ruled by little else. Practical men, who believe themselves to be quite exempt from any intellectual influence, are usually the slaves of some defunct economist. (383)

In considering how the "world is ruled by little else" in the context of creating space for new ideas that will more accurately acknowledge and account for the role of women in the economy, it is particularly worth noting that the dominant discipline continues to be a male dominated discipline. In 2010 women represented 22% of all academic staff in UK University Economics Departments and only 10% of full Professors (Blanco and Mumford, 2010). In the US the picture is strikingly similar. In 2011 women made up just over 22% of all faculty in PhD granting University Economics Departments and only 12.6% of full Professors were women (American Economics Association, 2011). In 2009 Professor Elinor Ostrom became the first, and to date only, woman, to be awarded the Nobel Memorial Price in Economic Sciences since it was established in 1968.

The marginalization of women throughout the economics profession has effectively rendered the discipline impractical. This bias and exclusion is particularly pertinent when considering the impact of current austerity measures. Policy measures directed at reducing state deficits by slashing public spending have involved both a transfer of responsibility for the production of certain goods and services from the public to the private sector and an absolute cut in particular areas of service provision. The consequences of such measures will have an impact on overall economic performance as well as individual welfare. Thus assessing the effectiveness of the cuts will require reference to standard market based indicators including the change in public expenditure, output levels and prices. This will provide quantifiable data on how effective the shift in emphasis from public to private provision, within a public policy context, has been in reducing state deficits. However, the exclusive reliance on such data will fail to account for the distributional consequences of the cuts and is therefore a very limiting approach to policy analysis.

State intervention in the provision of public goods and services is it-self a response to an identified market failure. That is, the private market will fail to provide certain goods and services, such as health care, education and care services, in sufficient quantities due to the nature of such goods. The very significant social benefits, as opposed to private or individual ben-efits, associated with the consumption of "merit goods" such as education and health care are not accounted for in private market transactions, and thus the free market will not supply a level of goods deemed to be socially efficient. Hence, the justification for public provision, either directly or through state supported subsidies. The shift from public provision to a greater reliance on the private sector should thus be assessed with reference to the impact on the overall level of provision and any subsequent third party or "spill-over" effects. These effects tend to be gendered in that the shift from public to private has knock-on effects for the functioning of the domestic or household economy.

Much of what takes place within the household economy is unpaid and thus invisible in terms of market-based criteria. However, this unpaid ac-tivity, primarily undertaken by women, is crucial to the efficient function-ing of market based economies. Significant and prolonged public spending cuts, involving the withdrawal of key public services, is taking place within a framework that provides little guarantee of the private sector stepping in to fill the gap. Questions remain as to who will fill the gap, how this will be sourced and the impact on individuals and communities.

Analysing the impact of deflationary fiscal policy should therefore in-clude an examination of patterns of distribution both within and across households; an assessment of how a lack of affordable care services impacts on access to the formal labor market and an evaluation of how patterns of social reproduction are affected by a process of economic restructuring that transfers costs from the formal paid economy to the unpaid household economy. That is, policy analysis should consider more than standard mar-ket based indicators and should include a closer examination of the impact of policy change on the household and the interaction between the paid and unpaid economies. Assessing policy within such a framework would serve to incorporate a range of relevant social outcomes into the policy process and would facilitate a more inclusive approach to economic management.

CHANGING DIRECTION—WHAT COUNTS?

The question then is how feminist economics and other critical perspectives inside of and outside of the economics discipline can come to make a real change? The crisis in the economy and the discipline provide strong arguments for bringing critical and heterodox perspectives into the core of the discipline as well as into politics. In order to achieve change, it is necessary to draw on multiple approaches, acknowledging the overlap, inter-connection and cross-fertilization between feminist economics, feminist legal theory, theorizations of care, care-work and dependency, in philosophy as well as in comparative welfare state research, and the reinvigoration and new theorizations of human rights. A common denominator is concern about how some activities, people and groups are valued and privileged whilst other groups are undervalued and marginalized.

Thus we need to reshape the discipline in the context of a rethink about what counts. What do we value and perhaps more importantly what do we not value in the context of evaluating the performance of any economy? In responding to crisis, both in the economy and in the ideas of mainstream economists we are drawn to three particular approaches that provide us with insights into how to rethink the relationship between the economy and all humans.

VULNERABILITY AND THE HUMAN CONDITION

Martha Fineman's vulnerability approach aims at "Anchoring Equality in the Human Condition." It builds on and expands on her previous work in feminist legal theory and the theorization of care and dependency. The vulnerability approach is a reconceptualization of the human rights trope, emphasizing the human side, drawing attention to social institutions, distribution, resources and resilience, and the relations between the individual and the state, rather than individual rights. According to Fineman, vulnerability is constant, inevitable and universal, and stems from our embodiment, and she uses the concept to "define the meaning of what it means to be human" ("The Vulnerable Subject" 28). Vulnerability is constant as it "carries with it the imminent or ever present possibility of harm, injury, or misfortune," through external and internal forces, including the passing of time and eventually death. While universal and constant, vulnerability is also particular and is experienced differently, depending on our positions "within webs of economic and institutional relationships" and "the quality and quantity of resources we possess or can command" (31). Vulnerability is complex, and one harm may unleash accompanying harms, such as illness leading to unemployment and poverty. The implications of harm for the affected person, or group, depends on societal institutions, which are at the core of the vulnerability approach. Resilience comes from "having some means with which to address and confront misfortune" (32) and these means are to a large extent provided by societal institutions. Drawing on and expanding Peadar Kirby, Fineman lists five kinds of assets or resources that provide resilience: physical resources, human resources, social assets or resources, ecological resources and existential resources. Institutions play a core role in allocating resources, and are pivotal in the production of privilege and disadvantage.

ECONOMIC POLICY AND HUMAN RIGHTS—HOLDING GOVERNMENTS TO ACCOUNT

Also employing a human rights framework, feminist economists Radhika Balakrishnan and Diane Elson have recently created a useful and practicable framework for a legal and moral social containment of the economy using human rights as a tool for evaluation of macro-economic policies and for holding governments to account. Their work represents a promising further step from feminist economists' and activists' work on gender budgeting. In considering the economy as a whole they argue for an evaluation of the macro-economic policy of governments according to the human rights framework, including all relevant human, economic, social, political, civil and cultural rights. Their framework of analysis is based on the following key human rights principles: the requirement for progressive realization and the use of maximum available resources, the avoidance of retrogression, the satisfaction of minimum essential levels of economic and social rights, non-discrimination and equality, participation, transparency and accountability. Armed with this framework, the human rights dimensions and implications of macro-economic structures and processes such as fiscal and monetary policy and the right to work, public expenditure, taxation and economic and social rights, trade policy and pension reforms would feature more prominently in the evaluation process.

GOVERNING THE COMMONS—THE CASE FOR REASONABLE AND COOPERATIVE (WO)MAN

Starting with the assumption of social, reasonable and cooperative (wo)men leads us to Elinor Ostrom's important work on governing the commons. Her work provides hope of a more caring and responsible management of the economy including our common living space on Earth. Contrary to the widely accepted idea of the inevitable "tragedy of the commons" as described in Hardin's famous article from 1968—a purely theoretical work based on the assumption of unrelated and self-interested individuals—Ostrom has formulated the basic principles of how to govern common resources in sustainable ways. Backed by the evidence from studies of real societies from different parts of the world, Ostrom has formulated the following key principles for sustainable management of common pool resources: 1) Group boundaries clearly defined. 2) Rules governing the use of collective goods, well matched to local needs and conditions. 3) Most individuals affected by these rules can participate in modifying the rules. 4) The rights of community members to devise their own rules are respected by external authorities. 5) A system for monitoring member's behaviour exists; the community members themselves undertake this monitoring. 6) A graduated system of sanctions is used. 7) Community members have access to low-cost conflict resolution mechanisms. 8) For common pool resources that are parts of larger systems: appropriation, provision, monitoring, enforcement, conflict resolution, and governance activities are organized in multiple layers of nested enterprises. In a recent paper for the World Bank, *A Polycentric Approach*, Ostrom took issue with climate change. In *Working Together*, Ostrom and colleagues develop a collaborative, multi-method research approach to collective action and the commons, outlining a revised theory of collective action that includes three elements: individual decision making, micro-situational conditions, and features of the broader social-ecological context (Poteete et al.).

Ostrom's studies are encouraging in showing that people and societies are indeed able to achieve agreements and to establish and maintain institutions which make it possible to act responsibly and care for the replenishment of a common resource over generations. In view of the huge challenges to the climate and to common living space, it's time to use this human capacity to build the institutions necessary for sustainable governance of the common earth systems that we all depend upon.

CONCLUSION

We set out to discuss how the contemporary crisis in the economy and in the economics discipline forms the basis of arguments for a reshaping of how we think about the economy, what counts and how we practice economics. In doing so we drew attention to the apparent crisis in ideas within the mainstream economics discipline and the need to build upon current feminist critiques of that discipline to provide the required conceptual tools and frameworks for the kind of reshaping we call for. In considering the double crisis we have highlighted three distinct approaches that build upon our understanding of what counts and how we frame our institutions to support and value that activity. Common to these advances, is that they transcend gender. They also share a common emphasis on institutions: Fineman, arguing that universal vulnerability demands a "responsible state," focusing on the allocation of resources that provide resilience; Balakrishnan and Elson pointing out that building and maintaining adequate institutions for raising and allocating necessary resources may be part of governments' human rights responsibilities; Ostrom focuses on institutions, although her emphasis is not the state, but rather the capacity of communities and groups of people—and of enlightened individuals, too, to act responsibly and to construct and maintain the necessary institutions for self-government and common action.

All three approaches start from an assumption of reasonable, responsible, socially embedded and governable people. These perspectives, alone and in combination can serve to develop further our understanding of the bias inherent within our current economic institutions and systems and provide us with very convincing theoretical propositions in support of a more equitable and sustainable world view. The insights provided by these scholars are invaluable in nudging us along the transformative path. They provide us with the new ideas and provide a basis for rethinking the economy along the lines of "economics for humans."

Let us not forget though that change will not come itself and in reminding ourselves of our role in orchestrating change we again count on Marilyn Waring:

> But no liberal minded male is waiting onstage to change the institutionalized value of women's work. That becomes the task for each of us in all that we do....we women are visible and valuable to each other, and we must now in our billions

proclaim that visibility and that worth. (*If Women Counted* 325-326)

Perhaps this crisis provides us with an opportunity to proclaim our visibility as our worth—all of us.

WORKS CITED

American Economics Association. 2011. *Report of the Committee on the Status of Women in the Economics Profession.* Web 16. August. 2013.

Balakrishnan, Radhika and Diane Elson. *Economic Policy and Human Rights: Holding Governments to Account.* London, New York: Zed Books. 2011. Print.

Bettio, Francesca, Marcella Corsi, Carlo D'Ippoliti, Antigone Lyberaki, Manuela Samek Lodovici and Alina Verashchagin. *The Impact of the Economic Crisis on the Situation of Women and Men and on Gender Equality Policies.* November 2012. Web 5. February 2013.

Blanchard, Olivier and Daniel Growth Leigh. "Forecast Errors and Fiscal Multipliers." Working Paper 13/1 (2013) *International Monetary Fund* 03.01.2013 Web. 12. January. 2013.

Blanco, Laura C. and Karen Mumford. 2010. *Royal Economics Society Women's Committee Survey on the Gender and Ethnic Balance of Academic Economics 2010.* Web 16. August. 2013.

Elson, Diane. "Gender and the Global Economic Crisis in Developing Countries; a Framework for Analysis," *Gender and Development* 18.2 (2010): 201-212. Web. 4. February. 2013.

Fineman, Martha Albertson. "The Vulnerable Subject: Anchoring Equality in the Human Condition." *Yale Journal of Law & Feminism* 20.1 (2008): 1-23. Web. 4. February. 2013.

— "The Vulnerable Subject and the Responsive State." *Emory Law Journal* 60.2 (2010): 251-277. Web. 4. 2013.

Keynes, John Maynard. *The General Theory of Employment Interest and Money.* 1936. Basingstoke, Hampshire: Palgrave Macmillan, 2007. Print.

Kirby, Peadar. *Vulnerability and Violence: The Impact of Globalisation.* 2006. London: Pluto Press.

McCloskey, Deidre. "The Demoralization of Economics: Can We Recover from Bentham and Return to Smith?" *Feminism Confronts Homo Eco-*

nomicus: Gender, Law & Society. Eds. Fineman, Martha Albertson and Terence Dougherty. Ithaca: Cornell University Press. 2005.

Nelson, Julie. *Feminism, Objectivity and Economics.* London and New York: Routledge, 1996. Print.

Ostrom, Elinor. *Governing the Commons: The Evolution of Institutions for Collective Action.* Cambridge University Press, 1990. Print.

Ostrom, Elinor. *A Polycentric Approach for Coping with Climate Change.* Policy Research Working Paper, WPS 5095. World Bank. Web. 8. February. 2013.

Poteete, Amy, Marco Janssen, and Elinor Ostrom. *Working Together: Collective Action, the Commons, and Multiple Methods in Practice.* 2010. Princeton, NJ: Princeton University Press. Print.

Seguino, Stephanie. "The Global Economic Crisis, Its Gender and Ethnic Implications, and Policy Responses." *Gender and Development.* 18:2 (2010) 179-199. Web 5. February. 2013.

Skidelsky, Robert. *Keynes The Return of the Master.* London: Penguin Books, 2010. Print.

Smith, Mark. *Gender Equality and Recession: Analysis Note.* Grenoble: Ecole de Management. May 2009. Web 5. February. 2013.

Valiani, Salimah. "Easy to Take for Granted—The role of the public sector & carework in wealth creation". Research paper 4 October 11, 2012 Ontario Nurses' Association. Web. 5 February. 2013.

Vitali, Stefania, James B. Glattfelder, and Stefano Battiston. "The Network of Global Corporate Control." *PLoS ONE 6.10.* e25995 (2011) Web 4. February. 2013.

Waring, Marilyn. *If Women Counted: A New Feminist Economics.* London: Macmillan, 1989. Print.

2.

Feminist Economics as Vision for a Sustainable Future

IULIE ASLAKSEN, TORUNN BRAGSTAD & BERIT ÅS

INTRODUCTION

FEMINIST PHILOSOPHY and eco-feminism have drawn attention to the devastating social and ecological consequences of the devaluation of feminine values and values of nature in society and the economy (Merchant; Mies and Shiva; Plumwood; Shiva *Staying Alive*). Marilyn Waring's book *If Women Counted* has been a source of inspiration for feminist economics and politics, by pointing out the economic invisibility of women's unpaid household work as well as the similar invisibility of women's unpaid work and nature's gifts in re-creating life (Waring). The critical perspectives of feminist and ecological economics have both drawn attention to the limitations of mainstream economics in providing visions and strategies of a sustainable future. Some feminist and ecological economists, however, have pointed out the parallel invisibility of nature and women's unpaid work and argued for the importance of considering those values within the same context (Nelson "Feminism;" Mellor; Perkins; Waring). In this chapter we argue that despite recent efforts, there is a prevalent invisibility of women's economic contribution in ecological economics and of nature's value in feminist economics, and that potential synergies between the approaches of feminist economics and ecological economics need to be identified in order to explore and strengthen visions and political strategies for a sustainable future.

In recent decades, economic globalization has continued to increase concentration of power and wealth, social polarization, and environmental devastation (Batra; Klein; George). Extensive deregulation of financial markets, followed by the financial crisis, has had serious economic, social and environmental consequences (Prins; Huffington; Bakan). Policies to protect nature, alleviate poverty and obtain social justice seem difficult to achieve within the current political context of modern capitalist societies and rising inequalities. The main reasons are clearly related to the shorttermism—the short-term thinking—inherent in attitudes and actions at all levels of society. Philosopher Hannah Arendt warned against the erosion of the community and solidarity of the public sphere, as a consequence of the relentless pursuit of short-term individual economic interests. Her concept of *earth alienation* captures how the technological dominance of the modern age has lead to loss of nature and to profound transformation of the natural environment as well as of our relationship to nature. The vision of sustainability we explore in this chapter, with critical feminist and ecological perspectives, inspired by eco-feminism, is that a sustainable society is based on an economy embedded within the ecological limits of the planet, ensuring the basis for re-creation of life, while supporting relationships of autonomy, respect and interconnectedness among people and between human beings and nature, and securing democratic participation and social responsibility. A sustainable society supports equitable economic development for women, for the general population, as well as for unprivileged groups in rich and poor countries, for young people struggling to enter the labour market, for subsistence farmers in poor countries, and for indigenous people. Our point of departure is the eco-feminist vision for a sustainable future proposed by Maria Mies and Vandana Shiva: "The aim of economic activity is not to produce an ever-growing mountain of commodities and money (wages or profit) for an anonymous market but the creation and re-creation of life" (319).

While it is clearly the economic and political forces and institutions of society that drive the current development, we argue that also the framing of the societal and political problems at stake is of importance for making the issue of sustainable development more visible on the policy agenda and in public debate. In order to explore and strengthen visions and political strategies for an ecologically sustainable and equitable future, the critical perspectives provided by feminist and ecological economics may have a role to contribute, and more so if they realize the synergy in their approaches to expressing the importance of invisible values, by taking into account women's economic and societal role in the ecological discourse and nature's importance in the feminist discourse.

FEMINIST AND ECOLOGICAL ECONOMICS—A SHARED VISION

Feminist economists point out the economic and political invisibility of women's unpaid household work when accounting for production in society. Ecological economists point out the invisibility of nature as an ethical concern when values of nature predominantly are expressed in economic and monetary terms. While some feminist and ecological economists, along with eco-feminists, have pointed out the importance of considering the invisible values of nature and women's unpaid household work, there is a need to strengthen the discussion of potential synergies between these approaches. The narratives of feminist economics, eco-feminism and ecological economics are similar in their call for a sustainable future, but their approaches take place in different spheres, prescribing different aspects of the "cure" for unsustainable development. Yet their arguments are similar and both contribute to pointing out consequences of the current economic development that threaten sustainability. We argue that the vision for a sustainable future would be strengthened if the critical approaches of these narratives would to a larger extent converge, in order to express a more comprehensive perspective on society and thus attain a larger impact on mainstream economics and policy.

The critical perspectives of feminist and ecological economics have developed in parallel, with their own international conferences and journals *Ecological Economics* and *Feminist Economics*. In the purpose statement of one journal, the feminist vision is expressed as follows: "*Feminist Economics* provides an open forum for dialogue and debate about feminist economic perspectives. By opening new areas of economic inquiry, welcoming diverse voices, and encouraging critical exchanges, the journal enlarges and enriches economic discourse. The goal of *Feminist Economics* is not just to develop more illuminating theories, but to improve the conditions of living for all children, women, and men". *Ecological Economics—The Transdisciplinary Journal of the International Society for Ecological Economics*—expresses its purpose statement as follows: "The journal is concerned with extending and integrating the study and management of nature's household (ecology) and humankind's household (economics). This integration is necessary because conceptual and professional isolation have led to economic and environmental policies which are mutually destructive rather than reinforcing in the long term. The journal is transdisciplinary in spirit and methodologically open."

At the 2012 conference of the International Society for Ecological Economics in Rio, a special session presented feminist perspectives on ecological economics, in itself a promising sign of future interdisciplinary cooperation. At that session, the following Figure 1 was presented, as a point of departure for discussing differences and similarities between the narratives of feminist and ecological economics, illustrated by some core issues characterizing these approaches. Figure 1 displays a "radar diagram" that tentatively suggests the priorities of feminist and ecological economics, respectively, given to core issues in their critique of the limitations of mainstream economics. While a radar diagram is a standard tool for displaying multi-dimensional quantitative information, the use of radar diagrams in our context—for indicating the relative importance given to various issues— is inspired by the discussion in Garnåsjordet et al and the references therein (Garnåsjordet et al 325). The following discussion is based on this comparison of feminist and ecological economics, in order to identify potential synergies in the critical perspectives on mainstream economics as offered by these approaches.

The priorities indicated by Figure 1 are only meant to be suggestive, intended to illustrate some over-arching points that may serve as reminders for the need to strengthen the common narrative of feminist and ecological economics, seen together as a vision for sustainable development. In the following, we discuss some important points in connection with each of the four quadrants in Figure 1.

CARE WORK: WOMEN'S WORK AND LIFE SITUATION

The United Nations report *The World's Women 2010* points to some main findings about women and poverty: Lone mothers with young children are more likely to be poor than lone fathers with young children, women are more likely than men to be poor when living in one-person households, and women are overrepresented among the older poor in the more developed regions. In poor as well as in rich countries, women persistently have lower incomes than men. Worldwide feminization of poverty is related to

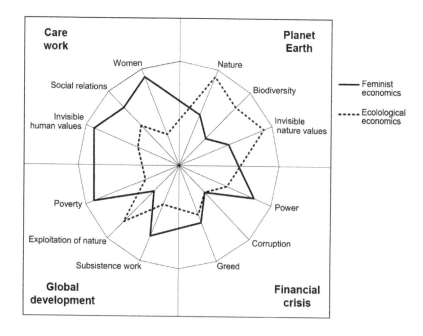

Figure 1: Narratives of Feminist and Ecological Economics

women's issues as well as class issues, the difficulty in living on one income, and increased pressure on labour rights and social security benefits.

An important topic in feminist economics is the invisibility of women's unpaid household work in measurements of economic value (Waring). Understanding the role of unpaid household and subsistence work is crucial for understanding what contributes to economic value, production, consumption possibilities, income distribution, taxation, social welfare and human well-being (Aslaksen and Koren). Feminist economists focus on the importance of social relations, care, rationality of care, and invisible human values (Nelson "Gender"; Folbre and Nelson). Ecological economics expresses the importance of the study of *oikos*—the household—and needs to more explicitly consider actual households, women's role in keeping home and household and family, and the relationship between care and stewardship of the household and the planetary household.

The vision of women's liberation in the 1960s and 1970s was that the economy would adapt to the needs of families, and that "feminine values" of care would be given more prominence in society, with the possibility of shorter working days. The outcome has, rather, been a gender mainstreaming, securing higher incomes and economic independence for some women, while an increasing number of women, disprivileged groups, and increasingly the general population, have suffered from the rising inequalities. Even in a rich country like Norway, a large share of women will only have minimum pension in the future. Although leisure has been increasing historically, increasing time pressure puts a double burden on many women.

PLANET EARTH: ECOLOGICAL VALUES

Mainstream economics takes market values as its point of departure, thus creating a boundary between the economic sphere and the ecological and social spheres that have led to a neglect of unpaid care work and nature. To represent values outside the market sphere, economists have suggested using monetary values of similar goods or estimates of what people are willing to pay. Ecological economists have pointed out the fundamental ethical concern over giving visibility to nature by expressing values of nature predominantly in economic and monetary terms (O'Neill; Soma; Spash). It is difficult to make loss of nature visible to policy makers. The language of power has become the language of economics. Values of nature and social equity become invisible when public policy is increasingly framed in terms of economic growth and financial markets. Many values of nature—like other human values—are incommensurable with an economic scale of measurement: "If the valued goods that give richness to our lives are reduced to commodities, then what makes those lives meaningful is itself betrayed" (Funtowicz and Ravetz 197). Nature's priceless qualities are overshadowed by the call of a resource-hungry world. Despite widespread understanding of the dramatic ecological consequences of loss of nature, humanity has chosen this path because it leads to higher material standard of living in the very short term.

The ecological chain of life was made visible to the public by the path-breaking work of Rachel Carson, warning the world of the imminent threats to our ecosystems from the widespread use of pesticides and the loss of ecological resilience from monocultures: "We realize that the poisons used in the name of production kill so many birds in the forest that it is soon silent. The chemical war is never won, and all life is caught in its violent crossfire" (Carson 25). "Single-crop farming does not take advantage of the principle by which nature works; it is agriculture as an engineer might conceive it to be" (Carson 27).

Ecological economics criticises the perspective emphasizing the possibilities of technology substituting nature, suggesting a redundancy of nature in light of other more valued human demands. This approach can be criticised for neglecting the limits to and uncertainty of substitution and the critical vulnerability of nature as a limiting factor on human activity. Public policy needs to take into account the risks society takes by destroying and degrading the richness of nature and to reconsider the importance of natural systems as a fundamental basis for the survival and health of humanity. Resonating with feminist economics and eco-feminism, ecological economics takes as its point of departure that the economy is embedded in society which is embedded in ecological systems: "Apt though we are to lose sight of the fact, the primary objective of economic activity is the self-preservation of the human species" (Georgescu-Roegen 93).

A feminist contribution is to point out that the understanding of human identity in our culture is based on separation from nature, rather than by the relationship between humans and nature (Plumwood). Loss of beloved nature has been argued to lead to a psychological state of denial of that loss (Nicholson). Modern environmental philosophy has been suggested to resonate with knowledge present in ancient cultures, of how core elements of our humanity are shaped by the natural world (Abram). A transformative approach, encompassing feminist and ecological perspectives, is called for by feminist philosopher Karen Warren:

> A transformative feminism would involve a psychological restructuring of our attitudes and beliefs about ourselves and 'our world' (including the non-human world), and a philosophical rethinking of the notion of the self such that we see ourselves as both co-members of an ecological community and yet different from other members of it. (19)

FINANCIAL CRISIS: REGULATIONS RECONSIDERED

Neither feminist nor ecological economics have sufficiently addressed the issues of power, corruption and greed and how they are expressed in the current financial crisis. Mainstream macroeconomics has to a large extent abandoned its previous reliance on the fundamental importance of regulatory frameworks. Both feminist and ecological economics need to more clearly address the need for strengthened public policy and regulation of the financial sector and corporate power as key strategy for a sustainable future.

During the current financial crisis, many families have lost the economic security they previously took for granted. The fact that the poor get poorer and the rich get richer may hide the fact that the majority of those who were poor from the beginning were women. Despite gender mainstreaming worldwide during the recent decades, large disparities remain between the economic conditions of men and women, both in less developed and developed regions of the world. Paola Melchiori points out the neo-patriarchal trend of society—when society is changing, patriarchy finds new ways to exploit women, undermining women's achieved progress. Regardless of economic system, women still bear a double burden. Neoliberal thinking has fostered a widespread suspicion to public regulation and eroded the "social contract" of modern Western societies and the understanding that efficient markets require public regulation in order to function. In many countries, the financial crisis has lead to severe reductions in pensions and other public benefits. Yet at the same time it is striking how the large extent of unpaid care and household work needed for the reproduction of labor is simply taken for granted and not accounted for in public economics and policy debate (Koren).

Political attention in Western democracies is primarily focused on individual rights—not the least the rights of the economic elite—and there is overwhelming resistance to envisioning collective priorities for our future life in ecological and social balance on this planet. There is similar resistance to implementing regulation of financial markets that could ensure a more sustainable economic development and help avoid devastating social and ecological consequences. While regulations of the financial sector and globalized industry are impaired by an unlimited belief in free markets by politicians, there is also an ongoing process which initiates and accumulates a critical counterculture and attempts to organize new groups from the exploited and underprivileged worldwide, not the least women.

GLOBAL DEVELOPMENT: WOMEN'S ECONOMIC CONTRIBUTION

Women's economic contributions are crucial for the rural economy in all developing countries (United Nations, *World's Women*). Women's subsistence work in agriculture provides a large share of food for the household. Esther Boserup showed that development aid did not necessarily help women. The intensification of the global economy has continued to exploit women workers in poor countries. The United Nations *Human Develop-*

ment Report documents that women consistently have less access than men to the resources and opportunities they need to sustain the livelihood for their families. In community forest management, increased participation of women enhances women's economic and social conditions and contributes to ecological sustainability. Increasing women's access to land, livestock, education, financial services, extension, technology and rural employment would generate gains in terms of agricultural production, food security, economic growth and social welfare. Making women's voices heard as equal partners for sustainable development, achieving gender equality and empowering women in agriculture is not only the right thing to do for women, it is also crucial for agricultural development and food security (United Nations, *Human Development Report*).

The First World Conference on Women in Mexico in 1975 and the ensuing United Nations Decade of Women 1976-1985 recognized the feminization of poverty as a global problem (UN, *Outcomes on Gender*). A panel of social scientists at the 1975 conference predicted that women's share of total workload would continue to increase and women's share of income and wealth would continue to deteriorate. The United Nations report *The World's Women 2010* documents recent trends in women's vulnerability to poverty. Laws limit women's access to land in most countries in Africa and half the countries in Asia. Fewer women than men have cash income in the less developed regions. Married women from the less developed regions do not fully participate in intra-household decision-making on spending. Also in rich countries, women persistently have lower incomes than men. Even in a highly developed country like Norway, women were not entitled to inherit agricultural land until 1974. The United Nations report *The World's Women 2010* documents relationships between women's situation and the environment: More than half of rural households and about a quarter of urban households in sub-Saharan Africa lack easy access to sources of drinking water, and most of the burden of water collection falls on women. The majority of households in sub-Saharan Africa and in Southern and South-Eastern Asia use solid fuels when cooking on open fires or traditional stoves, disproportionately affecting the health of women. Fewer women than men participate in high-level decision-making related to the environment.

Since the Green Revolution, food security has largely been framed in a policy context dominated by the agro-industrial complex, with strong drives towards GMO crops, and the call for integration of agricultural and environmental policies and socio-economic consequences is marginalized (IAASTD; Ray and Katzenstein). Agricultural innovations of the future need to be based more on local experience and knowledge if societies are to meet the global challenges of food security, poverty alleviation, and ecological sustainability (IAASTD). Women have been the local experts on food and health, a local traditional ecological knowledge that to a large extent has been lost and needs to be reclaimed (Shiva, *Earth Democracy*). The ecological and feminist perspectives need to be brought together in order to strengthen the basis for policy for sustainable development (Mellor; Nelson "Gender"; Waring).

THE ECONOMIC AGENCY OF SELF-INTEREST AND GREED: FROM PSYCHOLOGY TO POLITICS

Feminist scholarship originating from Carolyn Merchant's work on nature and gender has suggested that the cultural split between reason and emotion, science and nature, and mind and body has been expressed as hierarchical dualisms associated with a value dimension and a gender dimension—with a masculine/feminine association and a superior/inferior association as if these were the only two possibilities. One method for thinking beyond these hierarchical dualisms, addressing both the feminist and economic critiques of economic agency, has been suggested by feminist economist Julie Nelson ("Gender"). Her approach involves replacing the dualism by a so-called gender-value compass, in which the split between the stereotypically masculine-positive and feminine-negative associations could be replaced by a complementarity between masculine-positive and feminine-positive qualities. The feminist scholarship that Nelson draws upon does not necessarily claim that there is some intrinsic link between certain cultural values and being female, or being male; it claims that the perceived links between values and gender are part of the social gender construction, shaping how our thinking about cultural value tends to have powerful cognitive associations with gender.

The gender-value compass, illustrated in Figure 2, leads us to see the possibility of behaviour that combines the masculine-positive and feminine-positive aspects. The mainstream model of economic behaviour, embodied as *Homo economicus*, has been criticized from different perspectives (Doherty and Fineman eds.). While it is based on standard assumptions of self-interest, rationality and agency, it has a blind spot in its neglect of greed as a negative side of self-interest. At the same time, excessive self-interest may be seen as the only alternative to self-sacrifice, and the capacity for generosity may be overshadowed. A person who is able to develop a complementarity between the masculine-positive and feminine-positive aspects represents a possibility for a more generous, but not overly self-sacrificing, human being as an actor in economic affairs.

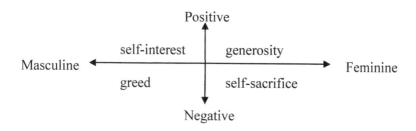

Figure 2: Gender-value Compass: From Greed to Generosity (Source: Aslaksen)

Generosity may be perceived as having feminine-positive associations, with its emphasis on a rationality of care. However, a generosity that does not pay attention to the proper self-interest and, to use economic terminology, the budget constraint, is not viable. The complementarity of the masculine-positive "self-interest" and the feminine-positive "generosity" requires balanced attention to both maintenance and flux, to both the scarcity that requires prudence, and the creative flow and empowerment that abundantly enriches life (Aslaksen). Understanding and overcoming the drive towards greed can strengthen the capacity for solidarity and acting on the basis of doing what is right and called for. The psychological insights of the roots of greed may give a deeper understanding of the political issues of self-interest as a driving force of the economy and of the need to balance the pursuit of self-interest with strengthened regulatory frameworks to achieve a sustainable and equitable economy. The origins and consequences of greed and excessive consumption are largely disregarded in mainstream economics. Economic growth is fuelled by the consumer culture of Western societies, strengthened by the advertisement industry and the social rat race, implying that ever-increasing consumption is the goal of life (Whybrow). The short-termism inherent in private greed and excessive pursuit of profit is exacerbated by public policies that reflect the prevailing consumer culture—without furthering alternative voices and objectives, or securing the required regulations of financial institutions. Feminist and ecological economics have the potential to strengthen their common agenda in pointing to the unsustainable consequences of this development.

Feminist and ecological perspectives on the economy challenge the technocratic view of the environmental crisis, based on the illusion of mastery over nature (Nelson, "Feminism"). Mainstream economics has a strong assumption that technological development shall solve all problems, while on the other hand, the technological promises are not always delivered, and technological development may have unwanted ethical consequences, for the human being and the environment. While nature and biodiversity continue to be destroyed at an alarming pace, there is an increasing pressure for technologies of substitution, from genetic engineering to synthetic biology. As long as the problems of food security and the future of agricultural livelihoods are framed as technological and economic, rather than ecological, social, behavioral or political, innovation will be directed toward top down technological solutions without due consideration of the institutional context for technological progress (van den Hove et al.). Different types of uncertainties are compounded (Taleb). Technology development and science-policy institutions need to be guided by a more humble attitude to the unforeseen and "unknown unknowns" (Ås). Proposed solutions can often create new problems of ecological risks, social vulnerability and lack of democratic governance. Global energy networks, called for in the name of sustainability, may lead to centralized control replacing democratic decisions (Wood).

President Eisenhower's "Farewell Address" from 1961 is known and remembered for its warning of "the military industrial complex." Still there is a second warning, where the president drew attention to how the intertwining of science, technology and politics may overshadow the freedom of science, with the danger that "public policy should itself become the captive of a scientific-technological elite." Sadly, this echoes that the most profitable industries globally are weapons, drugs, trafficking in women, and pharmaceuticals. We may raise the question of where economists find themselves in the picture of power and economics—just following the "technoscience"—or contributing towards a critical tradition than can identify research that is useful for sustainable development for the human being and the environment?

CONCLUSION

Our discussion of how to bring feminist and ecological economics together in a common vision, as proposed by eco-feminism, has pointed out a number of issues that need stronger attention in public policy and debate: acknowledge the importance of care work, consider the possibility of a shorter working day, provide mechanisms for stronger stewardship of nature, strengthen regulation of financial markets in view of rising inequalities and concentration of power as threats to social rights and ecological sustainability, and consider women's issue as integral to global development. Democratic policies need to be revitalized. The political challenge is for society to foster a more inclusive democratic participation and develop a culture of community and solidarity. The struggle to change the current erosion of the public sphere has the potential for addressing the need to deal with environmental threats and improve the human condition, for the general population, while not forgetting women lacking privilege. The path to sustainability requires a transition to a more healthy system of governance, conditioned by public regulatory frameworks which ensure economic, social and ecological responsibility. Feminist and ecological economics can together contribute to challenge the technocratic view of the environmental crisis, and explore visions and political strategies for a sustainable future.

WORKS CITED

Ås, Berit. "Usikkerhet om framtiden og vår handlingsevne." In: Stenseth and Hertzberg (eds). *Ikke bare si det – men gjøre det!* Oslo: Universitetsforlaget, 1992. 103-114. Print.

Abram, David. *The Spell of the Sensuous: Perception and Language in a More-Than Human World.* New York: Vintage Books, 1996. Print.

Arendt, Hannah. *The Human Condition.* Chicago: University of Chicago Press, 1958. Print.

Aslaksen, Iulie and Charlotte Koren, "Reflections on Unpaid Household Work, Economic Growth, and Consumption Possibilities." In: Bjørnholt, M. and McKay, A. *Counting on Marilyn Waring.* Demeter Press. 2013. Print.

Aslaksen, Iulie. "Gender Constructions and the Possibility of a Generous Economic Actor." *Hypatia* 17 (2002): 118-132.

Bakan, Joel. *The Corporation: The Pathological Pursuit of Profit and Power.* New York: Free Press, 2004. Print.

Batra, Ravi. *The Myth of Free Trade.* New York: Touchstone, 1993. Print.

Boserup, Esther.*Woman's Role in Economic Development.* London: Earthscan, 1970. Print.

Carson, Rachel. *Silent Spring.* London: Penguin. 1962. Print.

Doherty, Terrance and Martha Fineman (eds). *Feminism Confronts Homo Economicus: Gender, Law, and Society.* Cornell University Press. 2005. Print.

Ecological Economics. Journal Home Page. Web.

Eisenhower's Farewell Address to the Nation, January 17, 1961. Web 21 August 2013.

Feminist Economics. Journal Home Page. Web

Folbre, Nancy and Julie A. Nelson. "For Love or Money – Or Both?" *Journal of Economic Perspectives.* 14 (2000): 123-140. Print.

Funtowicz, Silvio O. and Jerome R. Ravetz. "The worth of a songbird: Ecological economics as a post-normal science." Ecological Economics 10 (1994): 197-207. Print.

Garnåsjordet, Per Arild, Iulie Aslaksen, Mario Giampietro, Silvio Funtowicz and Torgeir. Ericson. "Sustainable Development Indicators: From Statistics to Policy." *Environmental Policy and Governance* 22 (2012): 322–336. Print.

George, Susan. *Whose Crisis, Whose Future?* Cambridge: Polity Press, 2010. Print.

Georgescu-Roegen, N. *Analytical Economics.* Cambridge: Cambridge University Press, 1966. Print.

Huffington, Arianna. *Pigs at the Trough.* New York: Crown Publishers, 2003. Print.

IAASTD. International Assessment of Agricultural Knowledge, Science and Technology for Development. Agriculture at a Crossroad. Global Report 2008. Web 21 Aug 2013.

Klein, Naomi. *The Shock Doctrine.* New York: Metropolitan Books. 2007. Print.

Koren, Charlotte. *Kvinnenes rolle i norsk økonomi.* Oslo: Universitetsforlaget. 2012. Print.

Melchiori, Paola. "Towards Neo-Patriarchy?" *The Rule of Mars: The Origins, History and Impact of Patriarchy*, Cristina Biaggi (ed). Manchester: Knowledge, Ideas & Trends, 2006. Print.

Mellor, M. "Ecofeminist Political Economy." *Feminist Economics* 11 (2005): 120-126. Print.

Merchant, Carolyn. *The Death of Nature.* San Francisco: Harper & Row, 1980. Print.

Mies, Maria and Vandana Shiva. *Ecofeminism.* Halifax: Fernwood, 1993. Print.

Nelson, Julie A. "Gender, Metaphor and the Definition of Economics." *Journal of Economic Philosophy* 8 (1992): 103-125. Print.

Nelson, Julie A. "Feminism, Ecology and the Philosophy of Economics." *Ecological Economics* 20 (1997): 155-162. Print.

Nicholson, Shierry W. *The Love of Nature and the End of the World.* Cambridge: MIT Press, 2002. Print.

O'Neill, John F. *Ecology, Policy and Politics: Human Well-Being and the Natural World.* London: Routledge, 1993. Print.

Perkins, Patricia E. "Feminist Ecological Economics and Sustainability." *Journal of Bioeconomics* 9 (2007): 227-244. Print.

Plumwood, V. *Feminism and the Mastery of Nature.* London: Routledge, 1993. Print.

Prins, Nomi. *It Takes a Pillage.* New York: Wiley, 2009. Print.

Ray, Raka and Mary Fainsod Katzenstein (eds.). *Social Movements In India: Poverty, Power, And Politics.* Rowman & Littlefield, 2005. Print.

Shiva, Vandana. *Staying Alive: Women, Ecology and Development.* London: Zed Books, 1988. Print.

Shiva, Vandana. *Earth Democracy. Justice, Sustainability, and Peace.* London: Zed Books, 2006. Print.

Soma, K. "Natura Economica in Environmental Valuation." *Environmental Values* 15 (2006): 31-50. Print.

Spash, Clive L. "The Political Economy of Nature." *Review of Political Economy* 7 (1995): 279-293. Print.

Taleb, Nassim Nicholas. *The Black Swan.* Random House, 2007. Print.

United Nations. *Human Development Report 2011: Sustainability and Equity.* New York: United Nations, 2011. Print.

United Nations. *The World's Women 2010.* New York: United Nations, 2010. Print.

United Nations. *Outcomes on Gender and Equality.* 2005. Web 21 August 2013.

van den Hove, Sybille, J McGlade, P Mottet, M.H Depledge. "The Innovation Union." *Environmental Science and Policy,* 12: (2012): 73-80.Print.

Waring, Marilyn. *If Women Counted: A New Feminist Economics.* London: Macmillan, 1989. Print.

Warren, Karen. "Feminism and Ecology: Making connections." *Environmental Ethics* 9 (1989): 3-20. Print.

Whybrow, Peter C. *American Mania - When More is Not Enough.* New York: W.W. Norton and Company Inc., 2005. Print.

Wood, P. "Technocracy, Carbon Currency and Smart Grids." *Nexus,* August-September (2011): 23-30. Print.

3.

Everything Needs Care

Toward a Context-Based Economy

SABINE O'HARA

INTRODUCTION

THE NOTION THAT everything needs care seems rather trivial. Humans are one of the most care-intensive species especially at the beginning and end of life. In addition, virtually everything we humans use requires care—our homes, gardens, pets, resource supplies, energy needs, and even our inanimate gadgets require at least some degree of care. It is therefore surprising how little attention the field of economics has paid to the concept of care and its value. Economic valuation is instead concerned with high value output. According to mainline economic theory high value is attached to those activities and resources that create high monetary value output while those activities that sustain high value output go largely unnoticed. An exception is feminist economics. Forerunners in this field, like Marilyn Waring, Maria Mies and Hazel Henderson, have long pointed to the need to consider the underlying fabric of economic activity and those who provide and sustain it. The scope of these activities includes reproductive services, care-taking services, and supportive services that often take on gendered and cultured biases rather than being provided in a flexible and skills-based manner.

This chapter builds on the work of these early feminist economists and adds an ecological perspective. Its premise is that care is not only indispensable to the economic process, it first makes economic activity possible.

Three concepts of care are considered. They are (1) rest, (2) restoration, and (3) recreation. It is argued that the first is associated with all types of productive and value creating resources (inputs) whether animate or inanimate; the second is associated particularly strongly with ecological/biological resources; and the third is associated primarily with human resources that are unique in their ability to use their creative and innovative capacity. All three types of care stress the need to consider the social, cultural and environmental context of economic activity rather than focusing solely on the economic process itself. The chapter further introduces an expanded concept of production, and by extension of economic activity, that takes context based care functions into account and moves them from the periphery to the center of the economic process. By inviting feminist and ecological economists to further explore and define the context-based care services that first undergird economic activity, persistent distortions of standard economic valuation can be corrected.

WHY IS CARE INDISPENSABLE?

Economic activity encompasses more than what meets the eye. When inputs are transformed into output and when consumer goods are utilized, emissions and waste are generated in addition to the purported goals of production and consumption. The unintended consequences associated with the allocation of inputs, the production of goods and services, and their consumption, have been examined by scholars in a range of fields including labor economics, ecological economics, sociology, gender studies, psychology and political science. The general consensus is that the unintended consequences of economic activity are costly. Depending on their extent and impact, these negative externalities must therefore be avoided, reduced, or cleaned up. Such avoidance and cleanup efforts are costly and do not simply happen without intentional effort and political will.

Much of environmental and ecological economics has framed these issues in terms of accounting for negative externalities, internalizing external costs, and full-cost accounting. There is by now a sizeable body of knowledge about what to count, what valuation methods to employ and how to determine the costs of negative externalities and the various strategies to reduce or avoid them. While this is a step in the right direction, it is not enough. A host of other considerations demand attention: for example, what are the social implications of various clean up or prevention strategies? There is clearly a difference between pollution prevention and remediation, yet different remediation strategies too may have different consequences, pose different time demands, cause different levels of stress, and exacerbate inequalities to a different degree. This points to the immense complexity of negative externalities and their attendant environmental and social impacts.

Feminist scholars have long focused on the direct and indirect social implications and valuation biases of economic activity, and its solutions to the externality problem. Starting with the ground-breaking work of Marilyn Waring, these scholars have argued that all human activity, economic and non-economic, draws upon a web of services provided in households, communities, ecosystems and physical/spatial contexts that we typically call 'the environment' (Mellor "Ecofeminism"; Aslaksen et.al.; Ferber and Nelson). All productive inputs (especially labor), the capacity to process them, and even the capacity to utilize outputs of final goods and services depend on care, regeneration and reproduction. Without these care-services creativity, innovation, muscle power and the ability to process inputs and produce and consume goods and services cannot be sustained. In short, all economic activity depends on a web of social, cultural and environmental functions that sustain it in the long term (O'Hara, "Feminist").

The burden of supplying these care-services is not distributed evenly. It is disproportionately carried by nature, by women, by the young, the old, the poor and those without power. Those providing them frequently also lack marketable skills or chose not to utilize their skills in the marketplace; they receive little or no remuneration for their services; and they have fewer options to shift their burden. The loss of care-services translates into reduced absorptive capacities, exhausted buffers, longer commutes, more stress, less time to socialize, less engagement in democratic institutions, and ultimately declining health.

The valuation biases that cause the neglect, overuse, and degradation of those context systems that supply needed care-services, assert that marketable output has value and satisfies consumer demand while non-market or un-used goods and services do not. Likewise, inputs invested in the production of marketable goods and services have value while conserved inputs or those dedicated to the production of non-marketable households, subsistence and informal sector goods are considered valueless. These valuation biases undermine the provision of care-services: high paying jobs are valuable—subsistence work is not; marketable services are valuable— unused services are not; extracted and processed resources are valuable— conserved resources are not. The result is that those less able to shift their services into the marketplace, and those whose contributions receive low remuneration, pay the highest price for the deteriorating social and environmental contexts. Mary Mellor writes: "If payment is not made in economic terms someone will pay in other ways: they will die before their time, sleep on the street, be nursed by a relative, go without shoes, walk miles to the well." (Materialist Communal Politics 3).

Care-services also point to the unalterable fact that some processes are time-dependent and irreversible (Prigogine). Consequently, productivity increases and efficiency gains have their limit. Many of the biological, physiological and social services that sustain human labor and ecosystems services are characterized by time-dependence. People have to rest, eat, be clothed, sheltered, affirmed and motivated. And ecosystems too must rest and be tended in order to sustain their productive, absorptive and buffering capacity.

The real economic process then is quite different than that portrayed in standard economic theory. As non-renewable resources are used up and renewable resources are replenished at a lower rate than their rate of extraction, all resource allocation must necessarily become less optimal since it takes place within an ever-shrinking stock of resources. And as restorative and reproductive capacities are impaired, efficiency levels cannot be sustained without ever increasing investments. The results are self-evident. Half of the world's wetlands, temperate and tropical forests are gone; more than half of all arable land is suffering some degree of deterioration and desertification; oceans are dying and 75% of marine fisheries are either overfished or fished to capacity; the US Environmental Protection Agency estimates that $335 billion is needed to fix deteriorating drinking water systems, and overall infrastructure repairs are estimated at over $2 trillion.

INTEGRATING CARE

The costs associated with the neglect and deterioration of care-services raises questions about the conceptual framework that underlies the standard approach of internalizing externalities. Why would one want to assign value to negative externalities in order to internalize them back into the very conceptual framework that caused their neglect, overuse and deterioration in the first place (O'Hara, "Discursive Ethics")? What is called for instead, are efforts that move beyond a focus on internalization toward a reconceptualization of the economic process itself. This reconceptualization must acknowledge that all economic activity is sustained by the social, cultural and environmental contexts within which it takes place. The task thus is not

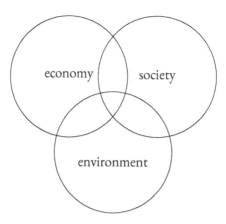

Figure 1: Intersectional Framework

to internalize externalities, but to internalize the economy into its social, cultural and environmental context.

This new conceptual framework moves well beyond the Venn diagram that has so often been cited as a basis for sustainability. According to this framework, sustainability is described by the intersection of the economy, society and the environment—the sweet spot at the center of the diagram (Fig. 1).

The work of feminist scholars suggests instead that all economic activity is a part of a set of nested systems or spheres. There is no economic activity that is situated outside of its social and environmental context. Environmental context, including location, climate, biological, ecological characteristics, influences economic activity. Social context too, including customs, agreements, institutional arrangements, perceptions, influences economic activity (Fig. 2).

These considerations are not new. The Romanian born economist Nicolai Georgescu-Roegen distinguished between two types of productive inputs: stocks and flows versus funds and services ("Feasible Recipes"). A stock is a type of productive input that may be used at any given rate of throughput. A fund is a type of input that can be used only at a certain rate. For example, seven tons of coal can be burned in one day or one ton can be burned every day for seven days; yet one laborer can only dig one ditch a day for a week, but cannot dig seven ditches in one day. A stock is capable of producing a flow at any desired rate, but a fund is capable of producing a service only at a given rate. It is subject to the constraints of biological

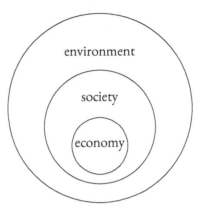

Figure 2: Social, Environmental and Economic Context

time and physical context. The substitution of economic activity and its context therefore has consequences: production and care, the valuable and seemingly valueless, are inseparably linked [1]. The social and environmental context systems of economic activity do not simply feed the economic machine (Fig. 3); the machine itself is connected to its context through multiple linkages and feedback loops (Fig. 4). As Georgescu-Roegen observed:

> In every enterprise, in every household, a substantial amount of labor-time and material are steadily devoted to keeping the buildings, the machines, the durable goods, in a useful, workable state....Undoubtedly, when a worker leaves a process, he is a tired individual. But when the same individual returns to work the next day he is again a rested worker after being restored in an adjacent household. ("Feasible Recipes" 24)

The focus of the analysis must therefore shift from the center to the margins and from economic activity to that which sustains it. This requires further consideration of the kinds of care that sustain both economic and context activity. The following section introduces a possible classification scheme.

WHAT KIND OF CARE?

The neglect of the care-services that make economic activity possible in the first place is no accident. As has been previously argued, it is the result of

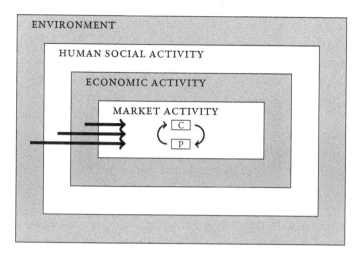

Figure 3: Activity

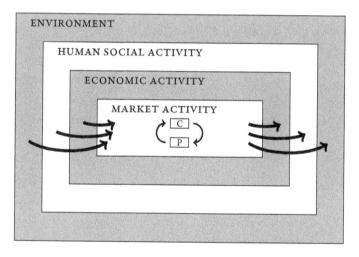

Figure 4: Activity in Context

underlying valuation biases that have shaped the prioritization of use over preservation, work over leisure, markets over households and communities, culture over nature, ratio over emotion. The underlying ethical framework associated with these same biases is a utilitarian ethic that has shaped prevailing more-is-better and use-it-or-lose-it mentalities.

In contrast, the ethic of care, which has its roots in Carol Gilligan's research on Kohlberg's stages of moral development, questioned the general applicability of a male model of moral development. Gilligan's distinction became known as the relation-based ethic of responsibility (female) versus the rules-based ethic of justice (male). Those critical of the ethic of care have questioned the usefulness of an ethical framework that reinforces stereotypical gender divides—especially if they are associated with white, middle class women. These divides associate the private sphere, subsistence work, reproduction and care with the female and the public spheres, market work, production and utility with the male (O'Hara "Toward").

Yet the ethics of care cuts across various marginalized groups, some described by gender, others by race, ethnicity, class, religion or culture (Cannon; Cortese). Studies of African Americans, for example, found that solutions to ethical dilemmas were both rules and care based (Stack); similar findings are described for West Africans (Jackson); and Kohlberg himself pointed to class differences in his research. Care provided in the marketplace too reflects the valuation biases associated with non-market care. Human service sector wages, for example, are among the lowest and reinforce stereotypical gender and ethnic roles. 97% of childcare workers and 94% of domestic workers in the United States are women; 37% of them are African American and 15% are Hispanic.

Contrary to these biased associations of care, care is not an option. It simply is. As the framework offered in figures 2 and 4 suggests, the care necessary to support and maintain the services that undergird economic activity are not optional. Care is instead an essential part of who we are as human beings. Fisher and Tronto write:

> On the most general level, we suggest that caring be viewed as a species activity that includes everything that we do to maintain, contain, and repair our 'world' so that we can live in it as well as possible. That world includes our bodies, our selves, and our environment, all of which we seek to interweave in a complex, life-sustaining web. (40)

The lives of those whose care work ensures the provision of services that sustain economic activity must therefore become just as visible as the work of those who ensure the provision of inputs for market production[2]. Following Tronto's definition, care must have four dimensions: 1) Caring About: this dimension recognizes that care is an indispensable fact of life that cannot be reduced to notions of helplessness and inferiority. 2) Taking Care Of: since care is indispensable we must establish a "flexible notion of responsibility" (Tronto) that is publicly negotiated rather than accepting inflexible, socio-culturally based practices of obligation. 3) Care-Giving: the actual work of care must be based on competence that recognizes the value of care and views a lack of competence in care-giving as morally unacceptable. 4) Care-Receiving: this dimension recognizes that those in need of care may be vulnerable, yet quite articulate about their needs; the care receiver's response to care and not only the competencies of the care-giver, must therefore form the basis for the valuation of care (Tronto).

All four dimensions recognize the complementarity of economic (productive) and care (sustaining) activities and suggest an assignment of value that goes beyond markets and includes a political commitment to the careservices provided in households, communities and ecosystems. This suggests the need for a renewed focus on the intersection between work and family, and on care policies and organizational models of paid care that move beyond familiar biases (Oliker). What is particularly important is a better understanding of the policies, institutional arrangements, and organizational structures that support more equitable and flexible models of paid care work. The work of Gornick and Meyers for example, explores institutional and policy arrangements that support flexible notions of careresponsibilities. Yet rather than focusing on paid care work their focus includes flexible and symmetrical models of paid market work and unpaid care-work that cut across gender lines. Their blueprint for an earner–carer society suggests three dimensions of reconciling care-needs: paid familyleave provisions, working-time regulations, and early childhood education and care. The proposed policies draw on some of the innovative arrangements of European countries whose policies appear to be more care conscious than U.S. policies.

And not only the young, but the elderly too place growing demands on care-services. Care for the elderly is one of the fastest growing sectors in the U.S. economy as the informal sector of households and communities can no longer absorb the needs of an aging population. As human longevity continues to rise, the need for long-term care is expected to grow as well; and the longer people live, the more likely they fall victim to chronic ailments along with the standard decline associated with the aging process. As Tong argues, this places growing pressures on governments, individuals, and families and requires the collaboration of all parties. The more successful a country is in overcoming inflexible assignments of care, the more effective it will be in meeting the care needs of its elderly and other vulnerable populations.

These considerations suggest that a more generally applicable typology of care is needed that cuts across demographically defined subsets of age and ethnicity. Moreover, such a typology of care must be relevant to both the human and non-human sphere and must include both animate and inanimate context factors. I submit three types of care: (1) Rest, (2) Restoration and (3) Recreation. While all three are relevant to all context spheres, the first one is most closely associated with the economy and the labor and capital inputs that sustain it. The second one is associated particularly strongly with ecological and biological context factors. And the third type of care is associated most strongly with human social and cultural contexts and the specific demands of the post-industrial knowledge economy.

(1) Rest: The need for rest is almost ubiquitous. It is difficult to imagine any process that does not require at least some degree of rest. Even machines must be turned off some time for maintenance. Rest thus reminds us of the biological and physiological realities that inescapably tie us as humans to our environmental context. This fact seems rather difficult for us to accept—maybe especially in the U.S. with its culture of perpetual youth. The denial of physical and biological limits associated with perpetual youth places human activity outside of the constraints of biological time and spatial contexts. Rest in fact has negative connotations especially in the economic sphere with its expectations of ongoing productivity increases, round the clock activity and ideals of not-wasting-time. The expectations of rest-less productivity are especially evident in such devices as smart phones, pagers, i-pads and laptops[3]. The overt and covert expectations communicated through these gadgets is that we are to reduce rest, work faster, and be accessible any time day or night. Non-human systems and materials too are subject to the expectations of limitless productivity. While fallow periods or cover crops to counteract the overuse of soils used to be a common feature in crop rotations, the practice has become all but extinct. Yet the fallacy of a notion of productivity that denies biological and physical limits is all around us. Reports of collapsing bridges, water main breaks, and burned out circuits are on the rise; lack of sleep now appears to be the top cause of commuter traffic accidents in the U.S.; and risk rises when flight controllers or medical personnel nod off from sheer exhaustion. Rest reminds us that we need to feed our bodies and recharge our batteries in order to sustain our capacity to work.

The caring work of rest is typically associated with individual responsibility and with the private sphere of households, personal space, and a close circle of family and friends. Yet personal responsibility and private space cannot be neatly separated from their larger social and cultural context. As noise levels increase and the intrusion of mobile devices becomes almost ubiquitous, it is increasingly difficult to carve out private and quiet space to rest. An estimated 75% of the adult population in the U.S. experience some sleep disorder symptoms at least one night per week. Rest thus does not simply happen. It demands attention and deliberate effort to allocate the time and space necessary to meet its requirements.

(2) Restoration: Restoration becomes necessary when signs of overuse, stress and decline are already evident. The care-work of restoration requires more than rest; it requires deliberate efforts to renew the capacity to absorb, process and buffer the stressors and emissions that impair our individual, communal and ecosystems health and capacity. As ecosystems have taught us, some of the lost absorptive, buffering and filtration capacity can be restored—albeit typically not to its original level. For example, it is possible to restore ecosystems, such as coastal wetlands, albeit at considerable cost; and successful restoration requires knowledge both about how absorptive and restorative capacities work, and about the complex networks of relationship that support and sustain them.

Similarities between the restoration of ecosystems health and human health are readily apparent. For example, activities associated with the restoration of human physical and emotional health can be viewed as care activities of restoration. These include health care, therapy, exercise and other health and wellness related activities. Less formal health restoration activities such as social connections, communal activities, support networks and civic engagement too are important contributors to human health and wellbeing. The care of restoration must therefore be about maintaining and strengthening the people, places and communities where such restoring connections can flourish. Sadly, the time pressures associated with the growing demands of the market economy and its productivity definitions tend to undermine rather than strengthen such networks of relationships. For example, most families do not have the option of having a stay-at-home caregiver who provides physical, emotional and mental restoration. While the flexible notion of responsibility Tronto calls for in her qualities of care may support an expansion of restorative care, a care-wage or civic-engagement-wage may also be an important element of encouraging and accounting for restorative care.

In addition, restorative care activities must be considered a minimum at best. Preventive care too must be considered a part of restoration so that the deterioration of human and ecosystems health can be avoided rather than requiring restoration. The tremendous costs of restoration are becoming increasingly evident in the form of defensive expenditures associated with lost ecosystems functions, desertification, water treatment, aging infrastructure (especially in dense urban environments) and the renovation of deteriorated buildings, including cultural icons.

(3) Recreation: recreation, the third type of caring work, implies more than restoring the status quo. It implies care that increases the capacity to be creative, to think new thoughts, and to innovate. Supporting the caring work of recreation is not only desirable, but essential, especially in the new knowledge economy. And it may also be a uniquely human need. Creativity and innovation have been the drivers behind the human capacity to improve energy efficiency, health, and the ability to feed, clothe and shelter a growing world population.

At first blush, the U.S. tends to be comparatively inapt at the care of recreation. U.S. workers have fewer paid vacation days than their counterparts in other developed economies. And yet the U.S. economy has maintained a remarkably high level of productivity and innovation. This points to a more complex notion of recreation that implies more than time away from the office or from a familiar environment. It implies instead the ability to make room for renewal, and for stepping out of routine tasks and patterns that prevent new thinking and new behavior. For some, this may mean room for solitude; for others, being close to nature; for others expanding and diversifying communities and relationships; or exploring new places. Invariably, it implies learning and questioning the way things have always been.

One factor that may positively impact recreation may be diversity and the resulting proclivity to question any one perspective and its claims. This is clearly a trait of U.S. society. Another factor may be the energy and personal initiative characteristic of a can-do attitude. Exposure to nature, music, the arts, and physical activity may support this aspect of the care of recreation. Providing and accessing such care requires deliberate effort and deliberate action that goes beyond considerations of a shorter work-week or comfortable vacations. Real recreation may be both counterintuitive and challenging in today's fast paced, over-stimulated world. Bill McKibben, for example, challenges the recreation associated with a three-day television marathon versus a three-day hike in the Adirondack Mountains. Access to the care of recreation may thus be as much a matter of understanding the attributes of real recreation, as it is a matter of understanding the role gender, race, and socio-economic status play in access or exclusion.

MODELING A CONTEXT-BASED ECONOMY OF CARE

What might a model of the economy look like that takes the reality of care and its complexities seriously? Much has been written in recent years about the need to revise the model of the individual interest maximizing, rationally acting consumer. Newer models include social considerations, altruism, collective decision-making, and collaboration versus competition. The production side of the economic model has been less examined. I offer a new framework as depicted in Figure 5 (see O'Hara, *Production in Context*). Each quadrant is a schematic representation of the processes associated with a systems component of the overall process of economic output and value production. The model does not claim to be comprehensive. It simply serves as a schematic summary of a context-based process that builds on the familiar schematic description of economic production and expands it to account for neglected care-services (see Figure 5).

The first quadrant of Figure 5 depicts the common formulation of production (output q) as a function of input flows including labor (l), capital (k) and natural resources (n) summarized as inputs i with $q = f(i)$. The input vector (i) reflects the technology, labor, material and energy resources necessary to generate output, including management practices and know-how.

The function underneath in the second quadrant of Figure 5 depicts the emission function corresponding to the described production process whereby emission e is a function of the input vector i or $e = f(i)$. E describes the common conception of negative externalities. As technology changes, the relationship between inputs and outputs will change, as do the emissions generated in the production process. In some cases technological change may reduce both inputs and emissions; in other cases it may lead to a shift in emissions, but not necessarily to their reduction.

Quadrant three of Figure 5 describes the processes associated with the care-services of rest, restoration and recreation. They take place between the emission source and the social and environmental context to which the emissions are released. The social, cultural and environmental processing capacities that transform emissions, waste and stressors between their entry and their state in situ are a function of multifaceted and complex factors, conditions and interactions. This is where much of the research on care and its impact must focus. Better information is urgently needed to understand the processes at work including the multiple gendered relationships between human/social care and nature/ecosystems care. For example, groundwater quality is not simply a function of emission levels, but also of soil type, aquifer condition, precipitation patterns, cultivation and land-use patterns. Similarly, labor quality is not simply a function of education and physiology, but also of rest, care, recreation, self-esteem, social connections, meaning and much more. Emission levels e in situ are therefore a function of complex sustaining functions s or $e = f(s)$. As care deteriorates, the functional relationship between sustaining environmental and social care-services (s) and emission levels (e) will be impaired; as a result, the ability of environmental and social systems to ameliorate the effects of waste, physical exhaustion, and emotional stress will be reduced.

A more complex picture of output production thus emerges where q is a function of sustaining services s or $q = f(s)$. A process of output generation that qualifies as sustaining production will maintain or improve sustaining care-services (s). A process that will reduce or undermine them is unsustainable. A non-sustainable process will not be able to maintain output levels without further investments in compensatory services.

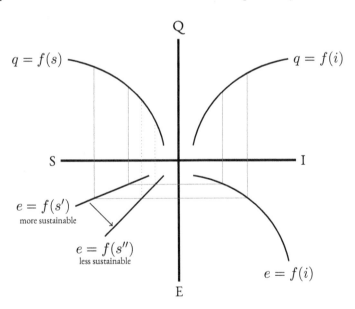

Figure 5: Sustaining Production Concept

While this model is a rather crude graphical depiction, it points to the complex relationships operative in an integrated model of the economy that moves beyond individual systems components. The project of defining productive funds and the functions necessary to maintain them is no trivial task. As Georgescu-Roegen pointed out—while an alternative model is necessary to escape the "save-invest-grow cycle....one should not overlook the gigantic problem of applying the model to actual situations." ("Feasible Recipes" 28).

CONCLUSION

Feminist scholars have long pointed out that addressing the root assumptions of mainline economic theory is imperative to achieving a more realistic, just, and sustainable economy. What is especially problematic about prevailing views of economics is the lack of focus on the very context systems that first make economic activity possible, but that are typically viewed as 'external'. All too often, these context systems are associated with gendered notions of care and support, as opposed to production and livelihood. To account for the sustaining care-services that first make economic activity possible requires an expanded acuity of what sustains productivity and the steady stream of productive inputs as well as the capacity to process them at ever-higher levels of efficiency. This requires a fundamental rethinking of economic conceptions of value from market-based to subsistence-based, and use-based to conservation-based.

When the complexities of social, cultural and environmental systems are added, what may seem sound from one temporal or spatial perspective may not be sound from a longer time frame or a larger spatial scale. This does neither imply the exclusion of usefulness nor of reason. Instead it places them into a larger context that recognizes that usefulness and reason are defined by multiple layers of relationships and systems conditions.

Three types of care are especially relevant to a context-based view of the economy. They are (1) Rest, (2) Restoration, and (3) Recreation. The characteristics of an economy that takes these fundamental notions of care into account are reminiscent of Georgescu-Roegen's work on production (*Entropy*); yet it expands them to include both social/cultural and environmental context systems. Such an economy is both viable and feasible, it sustains context (outside of the economy) and process (inside), its value is derived from both use and conservation (un-used), and its decision mode is both individual and social/ecological. Much research remains to better understand the relational links and systems connections between complex economic, social/ culture and environmental systems and processes. Understanding and properly accounting for them may well be vital to our future.

[1] See also Herman Daly and others who have argued that the notion that capital offers a substitute for land and labor without consequences or limits is deeply flawed

[2] This differs considerably from some of the recent innovations in consumer theory that include altruism in a more enlightened concept of individual utility maximization.

[3] For earlier work on the deceptiveness of time-saving devises see for example Juliet Schor.

WORKS CITED

Aslaksen, Iulie, Ane Flaatten and Charlotte Koren. "Introduction: Quality of Life Indicators." *Feminist Economics* 5.2 (1991): 79-82. Print.

Bohtlingk, Louis, Ernie Robson and Hazel Henderson. *Dare to Care: A Love-Based Foundation for Money and Finance.* San Francisco: Cosimo Books, (2011). Print.

Cannon, K.G. *Black Womanist Ethics.* Atlanta: Scholar's Press, (1988). Print.

Cortese, A. J. *Ethnic Ethic: The Restructuring of Moral Theory.* Albany: SUNY Press, (1990). Print.

Daly, Herman. *Ecological Economics and Sustainable Development: Advances in Ecological Economics.* College Park: Edward Elgar Publishing, (2007). Print.

Ferber, Marianne, and Julie Nelson. *Beyond Economic Man: Feminist Theory and Economics.* Chicago: University of Chicago Press, (1993). Print.

Fisher, Betty and Joan Tronto. "Toward a Feminist Theory of Care." Ed. E. Able and M. Nelson. *Circles of Care: Work and Identity in Women's Lives.* Albany, SUNY Press, (1991). Print.

Georgescu-Roegen, Nicolai. *The Entropy Law and the Economic Process.* Cambridge: Harvard University Press, (1971). Print.

Georgescu-Roegen, Nicolai. "Feasible Recipes Versus Viable Technologies." *Atlantic Economic Journal* 12 (1984): 21-31. Print.

Gilligan, Carol. *In a Different Voice: Psychological Theory and Women's Development.* Cambridge: Harvard University Press, (1982). Print.

Gornick, Janet and Marcia Meyers. "Creating Gender Egalitarian Societies: An Agenda for Reform." *Politics & Society* 36.3 (2008): 313-349. Web. 21

August 2013.

Henderson, Hazel. *Creating Alternative Futures: The End of Economics.* San Francisco: Berkley Publishing Corporation, (1979). Print.

Henderson, Hazel. *Paradigms in Progress.* San Francisco: Berrett-Koehler Publishing, (1995). Print.

Hekman, Sandra. *Gender and Knowledge. Elements of a Postmodern Feminism.* Boston: Northeastern University Press, (1992). Print.

Jackson, G.G. "Black Psychology: an Avenue to the Study of Afro-Americans as an Emerging Point of View." *Journal of Black Studies.* 12 (1982): 41-60. Print.

Kohlberg, L. *Essays in Moral Development.* New York: Harper and Row, (1981). Print.

Mellor, Mary. "Ecofeminism and Ecosocialism: Dilemmas of Essentialism and Materialism". *Capitalism, Nature, Socialism.* 3 (1992): 2. Print.

Mellor, Mary. *Materialist Communal Politics: Getting from There to Here.* San Jose, Costa Rica. Oct. 24 1994. ISEE Conference lecture.

Mies, Maria. *Patriarchy and Accumulation on a World Scale.* London: Zed Books, 1986. Print.

Nobles, William. "Extended Self: Rethinking the So-Called Negro Self-Concept." *Journal of Black Psychology* (1976): 15-24. Web 21.Aug 2013.

O'Hara, Sabine. *Production in Context: The Concept of Sustaining Production.* Festschrift for Herman Daly. Ed. J. Farley Burlington: University of Vermont Press, (2012). Electronic.

O'Hara, Sabine. "Feminist Ecological Economics in Theory and Practice." *Eco-Sufficiency & Global Justice – Women Write Political Ecology.* Ed. A. Selleh. London, England and New York: Pluto Press, (2009). Print.

O' Hara, Sabine. "Economics, Ecology and Quality of Life: Who Evaluates?" *Feminist Economics.* 5.2 (1999): 83-89. Print.

O' Hara, Sabine. "Toward a Sustaining Production Theory." *Ecological Economics.* 20.2 (1997): 141-154. Print.

O' Hara, Sabine. "Discursive Ethics in Ecosystems Valuation and Environmental Policy." *Ecological Economics.* 16.2 (1996): 95-107. Print.

Oliker, Stacey. "Sociology and the Status of Gender, Caregiving, and Equality." *Sociology Compass.* 5.11 (2011): 968-983. Web. 2 July 2012.

Prigogine, Ilya. *The End of Certainty.* Paris, New York: Simon & Schuster, (1997). Print.

Schor, Juliet. *The Overworked American: The Unexpected Decline of Leisure*. New York: NY Basic Books, (1991). Print.

Stack, C.B. "Different Voices, Different Visions: Gender, Culture, and Moral Reasoning." in: (ed.) *Uncertain Terms: Negotiating Gender in American Culture*. Ed. Faye Ginsburg and Anna Lowenhaupt. Boston, Beacon Press, (1990). Print.

Tong, Rosemarie. "Long-term Care for the Elderly Worldwide: Whose Responsibility is it?" *International Journal of Feminist Approaches to Bioethics* 2.2. (2009): 5-30. Web. 2 July 2012.

Tronto, Joan. *Moral Boundaries. A Political Argument for an Ethic of Care*. Routledge. London, New York, (1993). Print.

Waring, Marilyn. *If Women Counted*. London: Macmillan, (1989). Print.

4.

Reflections on Unpaid Household Work, Economic Growth, and Consumption Possibilities

IULIE ASLAKSEN & CHARLOTTE KOREN

INTRODUCTION

ARILYN WARING'S BOOK *If Women Counted* brought attention to the invisibility of women's unpaid work in official measurements of economic value. Despite their larger contribution to total economic production, women have less access to money, measured as own income and assets, less wealth, and less control over the economic processes they have contributed to (United Nations *Human Development Report* 1995). Increased awareness of the economic importance of unpaid household work, and of women's work in general, has led to more widespread acceptance that statistical measurements should be expanded to include unpaid work. Measurement of unpaid household work is important in order to better understand income distribution as well as to give visibility to women's work and achieve more comprehensive estimates of the level of economic activity. Although this may seem to be a new perspective, it was developed long ago, particularly by the pioneering work of Charlotte

Perkins Gilman and Margaret Reid. The renewed interest in women's economic contribution is reflected in new feminist perspectives on economics, from Marianne Ferber and Julie Nelson in their book *Beyond Economic Man* and Nelson "Gender".

Recent social and political discussions have proposed a number of measures to ameliorate the discrepancy between women's economic contribution to society and their control over economic resources. Such policy measures require knowledge of not only the magnitude of unpaid work but also its distribution and composition. This suggests that an analysis of unpaid household work should be approached from different perspectives. Supplementary, or satellite, accounts should be combined with conventional measures of national income to give a more complete picture of total production and economic activity in society (United Nations *System of National Accounts* 1993; United Nations *Updates*). Income statistics should provide a more comprehensive concept (extended income) of the consumption possibilities available to a household.

In this chapter, we first discuss household work in the context of economic growth. Then we provide a brief survey of efforts to measure unpaid household work in the Norwegian national accounts. We review the use of time budget surveys as data sources for unpaid household work. Finally, we focus on distributional aspects of unpaid household work. We consider extended income, defined as the sum of income and the value of household work, as a more complete measure of the consumption possibilities of a household. We find that extended income in Norway appears to be more evenly distributed than money income, although this result is somewhat sensitive to our choice of estimation method (Aslaksen and Koren).

HOUSEHOLD WORK AND ECONOMIC GROWTH

Despite the invisibility of women's unpaid work in the general economic approach and in policy, the measurement of the contribution of unpaid household work has had a long statistical history, e.g. in the measurement of income in the United States in the 1920s, see Mitchell et al., and has received renewed attention in recent years. The importance of measuring household work in relation to the national economy is expressed by Robert Eisner in 1989:

The problem is not merely the extent of understatement of total output of the economy; it includes the measurement of rates of growth and major policy issues. Thus, more and more women have gone to work in the market. Home cooking is being replaced with TV dinners and restaurants. Maternal home nurture of children is being replaced with day-care centers. [...] These shifts and the privatization of government activity entail moves between non-market and market output and across the conventional line separating final and intermediate product. Non-market output of households and government is generally harder to measure, without the concrete numbers from market transactions. But we need comprehensive measures of output of all sectors, market and non-market, if we are to get a meaningful picture of what is happening to the economy and what we should be doing to make it better. We may not want to pursue policies that bring increases in market output accompanied by greater decreases in non-market output, and we need measures to inform us. (7-8)

This was pointed out already in 1937 by Lindahl, Dahlgren, and Kock in their study of national income in Sweden:

The question, whether the value of unpaid domestic work should be included or not, remains to be answered. Taking the whole field of domestic services into consideration, it is evident that in such a long period of great changes in the economic structure of the country as that under revie , the transfer of processing work from the homes to the factories must have been of great importance. An income estimate in which the value of domestic work, paid or unpaid, is not included, would thus show a more rapid increase that had actually taken place. (738-739)

A large part of economic growth in the Scandinavian countries over the last forty years is a result of increased labour market participation by women, mainly in public provision of care and other services. Yet many of the care-taking services were previously provided by unpaid household work, as pointed out by Koren. As gross domestic product (GDP) does not include goods and services produced in the household, conventional GDP growth rates overestimate growth in real consumption possibilities in time periods when women have transferred a large part of household production to the market sectors, as discussed by Nordhaus and Tobin, Jorgenson and Fraumeni, Devereux and Locay, Wagman and Folbre, Ohlsson, Fuess and van den Berg, and Ironmonger.

GDP growth can be decomposed into productivity gains and reallocation gains. In this context we extend the notion of reallocation gain to include the (potential) economic gain in the transition from unpaid household production to the labour market, as well as reallocation gains within the unpaid household sector. Reallocation gains depend on growth in real wages, the wage structure of the service sector, prices of market substitutes for household production, tax wedges, productivity growth differences, as well as choice of valuation method for unpaid household production.

The *counterfactual* GDP is assessed by a calculation of what GDP would have been if the transition of service production from household to market had taken place at a slower rate. We interpret counterfactual GDP as a measure of pure productivity gain in the economy, i.e. the difference between observed GDP and the "reallocation" gain from women transferring their work from household activities to market activities. In other words, we assert that observed GDP can be decomposed into a reallocation term that represents the transition from unpaid to paid work, and a productivity term that represents the "real" GDP growth, in the sense that GDP growth is corrected for the fictitious growth component.

The switch of care-taking services from unpaid to paid work has resulted in an overestimation of growth in production by national account figures. In Norway, GDP increased in real terms by 84 per cent from 1972 to 1990. Adding unpaid household work implies that growth in "extended" GDP was only 66 per cent. This means that growth in real consumption possibilities over this period may have been overestimated by more than 20 per cent when we apply a traditional measure of GDP without adjusting for the transition from unpaid to paid production of goods and services (Aslaksen and Koren).

In practice, the real economy is not unaffected by the transition of care-taking services from home production to market and public sector. In particular, over time there will be productivity gains in all sectors, including household production. However, there is clearly a limit to productivity growth in labour-intensive work such as caring for children, the sick and elderly, where part of the work just consists in providing a hand to hold (Nelson "Markets"). This illustrates the theoretical discussion of substitutability between home produced and market produced goods. Although there has been substantial reallocation gains from transferring women's work from home to market, the substitution of market work for non-market work may be approaching a limit, and future reallocation gains may be considerably less than in the past.

Neglecting unpaid household work has large policy implications. In his analysis of the welfare state in Sweden, Rosen concluded that "the welfare state encourages excessive production of household goods and discourages production of material goods," and "... the high marginal tax rates required to finance current welfare state policy almost certainly results in losses in aggregate output and per capita welfare in Sweden today" (731;739). Rosen assumed that welfare and future production possibilities depend only on market produced goods, not taking into account that per capita welfare depends on the goods and services produced both in the market and non-market sectors of the economy. The transition of women from household to markets, has led to a substantial bias in growth rates for actual output. With regard to the future welfare state, policies will need to explicitly address the allocation of time between paid and unpaid provision of care work.

HISTORY OF UNPAID HOUSEHOLD WORK IN THE NATIONAL ACCOUNTS IN NORWAY

Counting household work in the national accounts has a long history in Norway. As early as in 1892 and 1893, and again in 1912, the first estimates of unpaid household work were compiled by Anders N. Kiær, then director of Statistics Norway. Kiær's calculations were quite elaborate. Estimates for the value of unpaid household work for married women were based on average wage income for unmarried women and widows in various age groups. To these figures were added 10 per cent of the husband's income, representing the housewife's responsibility for organizing the home, as well as a compensation for child care. The resulting numbers seemed somewhat high, according to Kiær, and they were slightly downscaled. The value of housewives' unpaid work was estimated at 15 per cent of national income.

After World War II national accounts for the years 1935-43 were compiled, and these estimates included the value of unpaid household work. For 1943 the value of unpaid household work in Norway was estimated to be 15 per cent of the national product, in fact the same percentage as in 1912. The estimates include "only housework done by women, since housework done by men is insignificant in Norway. Not only paid housework (domestic servants) is calculated. Also unpaid housework done by the housewives and daughters living at home is tentatively estimated" (Statistics Norway *National Income in Norway*).

Similar estimates were also calculated in the other Scandinavian countries. In Sweden, unpaid housework was 22 per cent of national income in 1861 and 20 per cent in 1930 (Lindahl; Dahlgren and Kock).

At this time the only data source on women's unpaid work was the national census. The methodology for measuring the value of unpaid work was simpler than that used in the 1912 calculations. The number of housewives and daughters living at home was multiplied by the average wage rate for domestic servants, differentiating between urban and rural wage rates. This approach corresponds to the method of Mitchell et al. in their pioneering study of the value of unpaid household work in the United States.

Statistics Norway (*National Income in Norway*) mentioned that the figures are underestimated, "especially in the case of the housewives. On the other hand they are perhaps overestimated for the daughters, but are altogether on the low side. Lacking other data, they are still used. They will at least indicate changes over time" (82). In the national budget for Norway from 1946 to 1949, estimates for unpaid housework were included, based on the national account figures from 1943.

The purpose of including the value of unpaid household work in the national accounts was to provide a comprehensive picture of the economic activity in society. Despite the apparent undervaluation as compared to recent estimates (see Table 1 below), they represented a pioneering effort to record women's economic contribution to society. The Scandinavian economic tradition of the 1930s was characterized by its clear distinction between the real economy (production of goods and services) and the monetary economy. According to this view, the goods and services produced by unpaid household work clearly belong within the production boundary, regardless of whether money changes hands or not. (Petter Jakob Bjerve, former director of Statistics Norway, private communication).

In contrast, the first international standard for national accounts from 1953 came to be based on a market approach, where only goods and services that were traded or could be traded should be included. Goods and services produced by unpaid household work were excluded by this choice of production boundary (United Nations *A System of National Accounts and Supporting Tables*). Concern for internationally comparable national account figures led Norway in 1950 to omit unpaid housework from the national accounts and national budgets.

TIME BUDGET SURVEYS AND SATELLITE ACCOUNTS

The time budget surveys, conducted 1971, 1980, 1990, 2000, and 2010, provided a new consciousness of unpaid work. These surveys are based on diaries filled out by the respondents over a period of two days. The main activity in each quarter of an hour is recorded. The 2010 survey questioned 3,975 people, ages 9-79, and was designed to ensure consistency in comparisons over time and international comparisons. Both paid work and unpaid household work were recorded. Household work included the following activities: housework, maintenance, care, shopping for goods and services, travels related to household work, and other activities (Haraldsen and Kitterød). Time budget surveys thus describe the individual's allocation of time between paid and unpaid work, whereby consumption needs are covered either by goods and services bought for money or by home-produced goods and services.

It is difficult to distinguish between household work, personal care, and leisure. As Marilyn Waring reminds us, for time to qualify as leisure, "The mind must be free of guilt feelings and ready to pursue any number of activities, with the sole purpose of enjoyment for its own sake, and not feeling that you should be doing something else" (161).

Time budget surveys apply the criterion that if an activity can be performed by someone else, it should be considered household work, (the "third person criterion" as originally defined by Reid in 1934), in contrast to leisure activities and personal care. You can hire someone to do the cooking and cleaning, but not the jogging and reading for you. But the dividing line is not obvious; leisure is a subjective perception, and leisure activities may range from being "productive" to "personal," as exemplified by child care and gardening. These are complex activities that contain elements of work that can be done by others as well as elements of pleasure that renders them personal activities.

Figure 1 shows some results from the Norwegian time budget surveys. The length of an average work day, the total number of work hours in both paid and unpaid work, is about the same for men and women, and has been surprisingly stable through 40 years.

Time use in unpaid household work has declined considerably, in particular between 1970 and 1980. The gap between the length of men's and women's total workdays has narrowed, but distinctively gendered patterns remain. Men do more household work today than 40 years ago. Women have reduced their household work considerably, but they still do more

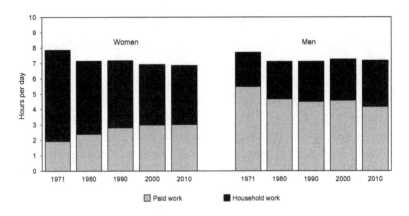

Figure 1: Time spent on work 1971, 1980, 1990, 2000, and 2010

than men. The time budget surveys indicate that men and women still have distinctly different responsibilities in the household; while the daily housework chores primarily remain women's responsibility, men spend more time in repair and maintenance. Caretaking, comprising all child care, including reading and helping with school work, as well as care for sick and disabled persons, amounts to a larger share of household work now than in 1970.

The value of unpaid work can be estimated from time budget data. Table 1 shows the main figures from the national account estimates by Statistics Norway (Brathaug, Dahle and Kitterød). The "wage rate" for unpaid household work is set equal to the wage of a home help (a municipally provided substitute in case of mother's illness or hospitalization). Two alternative methods use the wage rate of specialized workers (gardener's wage for gardening time, cook's wage for cooking time, etc.), or the opportunity costs corresponding to the individual's wage rate in the labour market. The results obtained from all three methods are surprisingly similar, yielding an estimate roughly equivalent to the average market wage rate for women. Goldschmidt-Clermont discusses the choice of wage rate. A comparison of time budget surveys and valuation of unpaid household work in fourteen countries is provided in Goldschmidt-Clermont and Pagnossin-Aligisakis.

Table 1 shows that unpaid household work around 1970 amounted to about 40 per cent of GDP. Its share of the national product has been declining over the last decades, in particular during the 1970s. This reduction is

	1972	1981	1990	2000	2010
All	43	35	33	24	26
Women	32	23	22	15	14
Men	11	12	11	9	11

Table 1: Source: Reiakvam and Skoglund, Statistics Norway *The Value of Unpaid Work* and Brathaug and Westberg, Statistics Norway *The value of unpaid household work*. Percentages do not add up due to rounding.

solely due to a decline in the hours spent in unpaid household work, as the imputation method does not capture changes in productivity in the household. However, general productivity growth in the economy is reflected in wage growth over the period. Today, men's relative share of total household work is one third, compared to one fourth in the early 1970s. In 2000 the value added in household production was 24 per cent of GDP, larger than in the petroleum activities of Norway.

These estimates ignore the value of household capital, which has grown substantially over the period due to large investments in homes and household equipment. In the satellite accounts for Norway in 1990 it is assumed that all household capital goods are consumed when purchased, so that depreciation and income from capital can be disregarded. With this simplification, value added in unpaid household production equals imputed wage cost.

HOUSEHOLD WORK AND INCOME DISTRIBUTION

Not only in national accounting, but also in income statistics, estimates of household work will give a better understanding of the links between market and non-market activities. Income as recorded by income statistics may underestimate the real consumption possibilities of the household. Unpaid household work gives rise to consumption possibilities beyond the purchasing power of disposable income. Since household work has decreased over the last 40 years, income statistics thus overestimate the growth in household consumption possibilities, assuming that household productivity has not grown any faster than productivity in the market sector. The distribution of income between households is substantially influenced when the value of unpaid household work is introduced as an additional income component.

One might argue that married women receive a higher share of family income than suggested by their individual income. On the other hand, it is important to have an income of one's own and household production is not a perfect substitute for cash income, which provides far greater flexibility. Also, access to money income probably increases women's bargaining power in the family. Considering household work in the context of income distribution raises a number of questions, such as the division of work and responsibility between men and women, income distribution within the household, who decides how income is spent, who benefits from the home produced goods, and differences between men and women as to how income security is attained, as discussed by Marilyn Waring, Tove Dahl, and Duncan Ironmonger.

Although household work obviously increases the consumption possibilities of a household, it nonetheless is a family-specific investment that cannot always be capitalized outside a given family situation. Unpaid household work hardly counts towards social security entitlements, although the care credits introduced in 1992 in Norway are a first step towards recognizing the economic value created by unpaid household work as a basis for future income security. Women who change between phases of full-time and part-time employment, and unpaid housework and care, may find that the earning of social security entitlements is not sufficient to replace income loss in the event of single parenthood, divorce, death of spouse, illness, disability or unemployment. This is referred to as the social risk of unpaid household work, the term borrowed from Bea Cantillon. Despite the relevance of differences in individual income, however, most households are income-pooling units, and it is important to look at differences in household income. In addition to money income, the consumption possibilities of a household depend on the goods and services produced within the household. Income data need to be supplemented by assessments of the economic contribution from activities such as looking after children, cooking and cleaning, as well as repair and maintenance of clothes, household equipment and dwellings.

Using data from the time budget survey, we have calculated the value of unpaid household work for selected household types: single women, single men, married couples without children, married couples with two children and one, one-and-a-half, and two full-time incomes (see Aslaksen and Koren). Figures for average time in unpaid household work are multiplied by the average wage rate for men and women. Thus, we apply a methodology similar to that used in national income accounts estimates. We define extended income as the sum of income after tax (disposable income) and the value of goods and services from unpaid household production.

Whether household work has an equalizing effect on consumption possibilities is a complex issue. Our data show that on average high money incomes are correlated with large household production. On the other hand, extended income is much more evenly distributed than disposable income for families with children. Families with a breadwinner and a homemaker compensate for parts of the foregone money income through their larger value of household work as compared to the two-income family. Also for single parents, inequality is reduced when the value of child care is taken into account.

We found that extended income is thus more evenly distributed than money income. In fact, the redistributional effect of adding household work is larger than the redistributional effect of the tax system. The reduction in inequality is larger for couples with children than for other groups, reflecting the long workday of mothers, whether in paid jobs or in household work.

CONCLUSION

Unpaid household work amounts to a substantial portion of economic value, in developed and developing countries alike. In times of changing employment patterns for women, when families differ considerably in their choice of paid and unpaid work, information on the extent and distribution of unpaid work will give us a more complete picture of the economic welfare of households. Goods and services produced in the household are economic values that represent income for households, regardless of actual choices between market and non-market time allocation.

A number of important questions remain for future research. More disaggregated analysis should focus on the following issues: How does inequality in extended income differ across age groups, between families with small and large children, and between families with full-time and part-time labour market participation? Such a detailed analysis might provide results that are more directly applicable in social policies. Future reforms in family taxation and social security policies should take into account the contribution from unpaid work to the household economy. Further research on time use and income could provide valuable insights into issues of distribution and consumption within the family.

Women's unpaid work needs to be made more visible, for a number of reasons, to show the extent and the importance of care for the children, and to show the unequal distribution of economic resources between spouses that make women more vulnerable if divorced.

It is probably a misguided view that everyone is supposed to live equal lives in order to have equal rights. A civilized society should support women and men in their expressions of a diversity of individual choice. Counting for women's unpaid work should induce the public sectors to consider equity over the entire life span rather than exerting pressure to make women and men live equal lives at all times. Recognizing the importance of care work involves considering a larger picture of equal pay, shorter work day, and improving unequal outcomes for divorced women, rather than merely adopting an approach of gender mainstreaming.

The economic concepts of value need to reflect the human values of care and provision. "Apt though we are to lose sight of the fact, the primary objective of economic activity is the self-preservation of the human species" (Georgescu-Roegen 93).

WORKS CITED

Aslaksen, I. and C. Koren. "Unpaid Household Work and the Distribution of Extended Income: The Norwegian Experience." *Feminist Economics* 2 (1996): 65-80. Print.

Brathaug, Ann-Lisbet. "Verdiskapning i husholdningene." (Value Added in Households.) *Økonomiske Analyser* 3/1990. Oslo: Statistics Norway. Print.

Brathaug, Ann-Lisbet and Nina Bruvik Westberg. "Verdien av ulønnet husholdsarbeid. Oppvask, oppussing og barnepass – hva hvis noen andre hadde gjort det i stedet? (The value of unpaid household work. Dishwashing, maintenance and child care – what if someone else had done it?)" *Samfunnsspeilet* 26.4 (2012): 70-74. Oslo: Statistics Norway. Print.

Cantillon, Bea. "Socio-demographic Changes and Social Security. Social Security and Changing Family Structures." *Studies and Research* 29 (1992). Geneva: International Social Security Association. Print.

Dahl, Tove Stang. *Kvinnerett.* Oslo: Universitetsforlaget, 1985. Print.

Dahle, Anne Berit and Hege Kitterød. *Time Use Studies in Evaluation of Household Work. The Norwegian Experience.* Oslo: Statistics Norway, 1992.

Devereux, John. and Luis Locay. "Specialization, Household Production and the Measurement of Economic Growth." *American Economic Review* 82 (1992): 399-403. Print.

Eisner, Robert. *The Total Incomes System of Accounts.* Chicago: University of Chicago Press, 1989. Print.

—–. "Black Holes in the Statistics." *Challenge.* January-February 1997: 6-16. Print.

Ferber, Marianne, and Julie Nelson. *Beyond Economic Man: Feminist Theory and Economics.* Chicago: University of Chicago Press, 1993. Print.

Folbre, Nancy. *Who Pays for the Kids?* New York and London: Routledge, 1994. Print.

Folbre, Nancy. "Holding Hands at Midnight: The Paradox of Caring Labor." *Feminist Economics* 1 (1995): 73-92. Print.

Fuess, Scott M. and Hendrik van den Berg. "Does GNP Exaggerate Growth in 'Actual' Output? The Case of the United States." *Review of Income and Wealth* 42 (1996): 35-48. Print.

Georgescu-Roegen Nichelas. *Analytical Economics.* Cambridge: Cambridge University Press, 1966. Print.

Gilman, Charlotte Perkins. *Women and Economics.* New York. 1966 by Harper & Row. (First edition 1898). Print.

Goldschmidt-Clermont, Luisella. "Monetary Valuation of Non-Market Productive Time. Methodological Considerations." *Review of Income and Wealth* 39 (1993): 419-33. Print.

Goldschmidt-Clermont, Luisella and Elisabetta Pagnossin-Aligisakis. "Measures of Unrecorded Economic Activities in Fourteen Countries." New York:United Nations Human Development Report Office, *Occasional Papers* 20. (1995) Print.

Haraldsen, Gustav and Hege Kitterød. Døgnet rundt. "Tidsbruk og tidsorganisering 1970-90." Tidsnyttingsundersøkelsene. (Around the clock. Time use and time organization 1970-90. Time budget surveys.) *Social and Economic Studies* 76 (1992). Oslo: Statistics Norway. Print.

Ironmonger, Duncan. "Counting Outputs, Capital Inputs and Caring Labour: Estimating Gross Household Product." *Feminist Economics* 2 (1996): 37-64. Print.

Ironmonger, Duncan. *Household Works.* London and Sydney: Allen and Unwin, 1989. Print.

Jorgenson, Dale W. and Barbara.M. Fraumeni. "The Accumulation of Human and Nonhuman Capital, 1948-1984." in: The Measurement of Saving, Investment and Wealth. Eds R.E. Lipsey and H.S. Tice. *Studies in Income and Wealth* 52. Chicago: Chicago University Press Vol. 52 (1989): 227-282. Print.

Kiær, Anders N. *Intægts- og formuesforhold i Norge.* Oslo: Statsøkonomisk Tidsskrift, 1892 and 1893. Print.

Kiær, Anders. N. *Norges nationalindtægt og nationalformue samt kapitalverdien av vort folks arbeidsevne.* Oslo: Statsøkonomisk tidsskrift, 1913. Print.

Koren, Charlotte. *Kvinnenes rolle i norsk økonomi.* Universitetsforlaget, 2012. Print.

Lindahl, Erik, Einar Dahlgren and Karin Kock. National Income of Sweden 1861-1930. University of Stockholm, 1937. Print.

Mitchell, Wesley Clair, Willford Isbell King, Frederick Robertson Macaulay and Oswald Whitman Knauth. *Income in the United States, Its Amount and Distribution.* National Bureau of Economic Research, New York, Harcourt, Brace & co, 1921. Print.

Nelson, Julie A. "Of markets and martyrs. Is it OK to pay well for care?" *Feminist Economics* 5.3 (1999): 43-59. Print.

Nelson, Julie A. "Gender, Metaphor, and the Definition of Economics." *Economics and Philosophy* 8 (1992): 103-125. Print.

Nordhaus, William D. and James Tobin. "Is Growth Obsolete?" *Economic Growth, Fiftieth Anniversary Colloquium* (1972): 509-32. New York: NBER. Print.

Ohlsson, Ingvar. *On National Accounting. National Institute of Economic Research.* Stockholm: Konjunkturinstituttet, 1961. Print.

Reiakvam, Janne and Tor Skoglund. "Ulønnet arbeid skaper store verdier." *Samfunnsspeilet* 2/2009: 7-11. Oslo: Statistics Norway. Print.

Reid, Margaret G. *Economics of Household Production.* New York: John Wiley and Sons, 1934. Print.

——"The Economic Contribution of Homemakers." *Annals of the American Academy of Political and Social Sciences.* May 1947, 61-69. Print.

Rosen, Sherwin. "Public Employment and the Welfare State in Sweden." *Journal of Economic Literature* 34 (1996): 729-740. Print.

Statistics Norway. *Nasjonalinntekten i Norge* 1935-1943. Realkapitalen

1939 og kapitalreduksjonen under krigen. Okkupasjonskostnadene. (National income in Norway 1935-1943. Real capital 1939 and capital depreciation during the war. Costs of German occupation.) Oslo: Statistics Norway. NOS X 102 (1946). Print.

Statistics Norway. *Døgnet rundt fra 1971 til 2010.* (Around the clock, 1971-2010.) Samfunnsspeilet 4/2012. Oslo: Statistics Norway. Print.

Statistics Norway. *Verdien av ulønnet husholdsarbeid.* (The value of unpaid household work.) Statistics Norway 2012, Web 30 June 2012.

United Nations. *A System of National Accounts and Supporting Tables.* Statistical Office of the United Nations. New York: Studies in Methods. Series F, no. 2 (1953). Print.

United Nations. *System of National Accounts* 1993. ST/ESA/STAT/SER. F/2/Rev.4. Prepared under the auspices of United Nations, 1993. Print.

United Nations. *Human Development Report* 1995. New York: United Nations Statistical Office, 1995. Print.

United Nations. *Updates and Amendments to the System of National Accounts* 1993. United Nations, Department of Economic and Social Affairs, Statistics Division, Series F (2004). New York. Print.

Wagman, Barnet and Nancy Folbre. "Household Services and Economic Growth in the United States 1870-1930." *Feminist Economics* 2 (1996): 43-66. Print.

Waring, Marilyn. *If Women Counted. A New Feminist Economics.* London: Macmillan, 1989. Print.

5.

Women's Unpaid Work Was Counted But...

JOHANNA VARJONEN & LEENA M. KIRJAVAINEN

INTRODUCTION

IN HER BOOK *If Women Counted*, Marilyn Waring demonstrated the illogical reasoning that caused unpaid work to be excluded from the production boundary of the System of National Accounts (SNA). The strong statements no doubt positively contributed to the later development of the statement at the Beijing Conference for Women that demanded making women's economic contribution visible in the statistics. Many points that she showed to be unfair, incorrect and illogical in national economic accounting were amended in the 1993 version of guidelines for the SNA. It introduced the concept of satellite accounts, the main purpose being to give an integrated picture of a given field of economic activities, flexibly expanding the analytical capacity of national accounting without overburdening or disrupting the central system (21.4). It further suggested that the production of domestic services by members of the household for their own final consumption may be brought within the production boundary (2.247) for which the satellite accounts could be compiled. Eurostat took the initiative to develop the methods for household satellite accounts for Europe, and the Committee on National Statistics contributed the method development in the USA (Abraham and Mackie).

However, things change slowly. Unpaid work is still largely unrecognized in economic analyses. People that do not participate in paid work are termed the "inactive population" in European Union (EU) statistics (Eurostat, *Active* 38). These poor people may be women or men. The SNA and the pervasiveness with which the system has been adopted in every country have cemented the importance of the monetary economy. In hard economic times such as those Europe is experiencing at present, it seems to be even more important to check and forecast the changes of Gross Domestic Product (GDP) than it does in better times. Research, however, claims that an increase in income does not increase the happiness of people after achieving a certain point of income level (Layard 30-32). The measurement of well-being also became an object for development in statistics after the Stiglitz Committee published its report (Stiglitz et al.). The measurement of unpaid work was given a new incentive after several quiet years. Experts in statistics have produced papers of experimental estimates of household production (OECD; Salamon et al.; Landefeld et al.; Kuwahara). However, methodological development work had been done in Europe before then. Discussion about women's work was boosted in Europe in the 1980s by nationally representative time use surveys that presented the difference between the time women and men spent on housework and childcare for the first time. The object of our paper is to describe the method and results of household satellite accounts compiled in Finland for 2006 (Varjonen and Aalto, *Kotitalouksien*). First, the history of value measurement of housework in Finland is described, as it explains why time use researchers and home economists have been active in developing valuation methods and producing satellite accounts. Second, the value of unpaid production by service type and its variation by family type is presented. Third, the magnitude of the value is compared to GDP. Fourth, how the results of the first satellite accounts were received by the economists and academics is pondered and reasons speculated. Finally, conclusions on the meaning and possible uses of the value of unpaid work calculations are discussed and put forward.

HISTORICAL CONTEXT

The value of women's work has been actively discussed in Finland for decades. Theoretical discussion by economist and teacher Laura Harmaja paved the way for the first survey on housework in rural households. The study was performed in the 1930s by Elli Saurio, who was the first professor of household economics in Finland. Both Harmaja and Saurio were women. The first estimates of the value of unpaid household work were made in 1943 by statistician Valter Lindberg. He presented estimates for the value of household work together with the national income for the period 1926-38. He pondered different aspects of the concept of housework and concluded that it is economic production but it should be kept separate from national accounts for practical reasons (113). Harmaja regarded the solution as patriarchal, as being from men's worldview, claiming that: "Men enjoy the services but do not have any experience of the work involved in producing them" (5). The next extensive development work was done in the 1980s when a large survey called "Housework Study" was carried out by the Ministry of Social Welfare and Health (Kilpiö). The study clarified the definitions and contents of unpaid work and collected data about time spent on unpaid work as well as the amount and quality of outputs, i.e. goods and services produced by the household for its own use. The value of housework was estimated using the replacement cost method. Several reports were published on food preparation, clothing care, child care, etc. (Säntti et al.; Suviranta and Mynttinen).

METHOD DEVELOPMENT IN EUROPE

The statistical office of the European Union, Eurostat, financed the development of European time use survey guidelines in the 1990s. This encouraged authorities to develop guidelines for the household satellite accounts so that requirements could be taken into account in activity classification of time use surveys. The methodology for the household satellite accounts was actively developed in the latter part of the 1990s, mainly sponsored by Eurostat. Two proposals were produced. The first one focused only on the *input approach* (Varjonen et al.), while the second considered both *input and output approaches* (task force report to Eurostat, *Household*). Representatives from seven countries and Eurostat worked in the task force. The proposal, published by the task force in 2003, was a stage report. Therefore, it included some discussion and left open many issues providing only alternative solutions. Unfortunately, the work has not proceeded any further. These proposals were unanimous on the scope of the household satellite accounts: they should include all household production, goods and services, whether included in the SNA or not. Thus, the accounts give a comprehensive picture of all unpaid productive activities carried out by households. The SNA production for households' own consumption includes two main categories: housing services of owner-occupiers and food items from agricultural production, and home gardens and various non-wood forest products such as berries, mushrooms and game from nature. The value of these products could be taken from the core national accounts. However, the reproductive activities of women did not feature in discussion. Only the activities filling the third party criterion were included.

The task force agreed that the accounts should consist of the production account. This means that in addition to the value of labor, capital consumption (or capital services) and intermediate consumption also need to be estimated. The whole sequence of accounts and the required modifications to the SNA household accounts would be easy to compile after the production account is completed. It means that the effects of unpaid production on actual individual consumption, disposable income, household investments and savings are reported in the accounts.

The Eurostat task force members were not as unanimous about how the household production should be described. The proposal put forward by Varjonen et al. applied a principal function concept to household production (17). The principal functions concept is comparable with the government sector description according to national accounts. The main functions of the production are: (1) providing housing, (2) providing meals and snacks, (3) providing clothing (including laundry and clothing care), (4) providing care (children, adults in need, elderly), and (5) volunteer work (informal and unpaid help to other households and organizations).

The principal functions are based on the basic tasks, also called "life care services," that have mostly been the responsibility of households themselves. Only when a household has not been able to provide these services has the community helped with it. All activities that contribute to housing, such as maintaining the dwelling/building, making repairs, taking care of the yard, mowing the lawn, etc., are included in the housing principal function.

Transporting children or driving to the store for grocery shopping is included in those functions which require transportation, such as child care, food, housing matters, etc. Similarly, shopping for clothing is included in the providing clothing function (Table 1).

The principal function approach has been used in unpaid work measurements for example in the United Kingdom, Finland, Australia, Spain and Hungary. It is very helpful if the output method is applied because then the outputs of household production need to be defined accurately. In addition, when applying the input method it is easier to separate interme-

	Housing	Nutrition	Clothing	Care	Volunteer Work
	Accommodation services, furnishing Cleaning, maintenance, gardening Renovation, repairs	Preparation of meals and snacks Baking, preserving Growing vegetables and fruits, picking berries, mushrooms	Producing garments Washing laundry, ironing Mending, care of shoes	Child care Adult care Care of pets	Informal help to other households Unpaid organizational work Renovation, repairs
Shopping	Shopping for dwelling: furnishing, maintenance, cleaning, etc.	Shopping for groceries, facilities for cooking etc.	Shopping for shoes and clothing material and facilities, etc.	Shopping for goods for children and adult care	
Transport/travel	Transport and travel related to renovation, maintenance, etc.	Transport and travel related to nutrition	Transport and travel related to clothing	Transport and travel related to child care and adult care	Transport and travel related to volunteer work
Planning and management	Related to all functions				

Table 1: Household production by principal function

diate consumption from the final consumption if the outputs are defined. It is also possible to compare the outsourcing of household production to a household's own production when this description is used in measuring. Households tend to decide separately on buying meal services (eating out, take-away, ready prepared meals from supermarkets), clothing services or care services. These services are purchased and classified as final consumption, not as household production. The grouping facilitates comparison between market and household production at a more detailed level than just as a total sum that is called "routine housework" in the OECD paper (13).

VALUE OF UNPAID SERVICES IN FINLAND

The Finnish household production accounts are based on the framework of national accounts consisting of the whole sequence of non-financial accounts with all transactions from output up to net lending. In the methodology, the total value of service output is targeted rather than only the value of labor input used in the work. In estimation of the value, the input method was applied. The analysis and description of household production followed the principal functions approach.

Unpaid production did not include reproductive aspects, no birth giving or immaterial aspects such as parental love and its implications. We believe that it is not possible to give them monetary measures, at least not in any direct way. Unpaid production included only those productive activities that can be outsourced to a third party. The value of labor was based on the replacement cost of a generalist housekeeper and other personal care workers such as caretakers. All work was valued by the same wage for women and men, young and old. No quality adjustments were made as the USA guidelines propose (without any research-based evidence). The assumption was that people are masters of their own life. They know what services are needed, what sort of unpaid work needs to be done and how routine tasks at home are carried out (see also Salamon et al. 229). The method and data are described in more detail in Varjonen and Aalto ("Household") and a short summary in Annex 1. The compilation of the satellite accounts was performed in cooperation with Statistics Finland.

VALUE OF SERVICES

Gross value added of household production in 2006 in Finland in relation to the GDP for the same year was 39 per cent. Another six per cent of the unpaid services, mainly related to owner-occupied housing, was included in the GDP. Recognizing the value of self-produced services would have increased actual individual consumption by 55 percent (Varjonen and Aalto, *Kotitalouksien* 11).

Output was organized by service type (principal function): providing housing, meals and snacks, clothing, care and volunteer work (Figure 1). Providing housing forms the largest part of household production. From the non-SNA production, it constitutes one-third. Providing meals is nearly as significant as housing services and the others together make up one-third of the value. The proportion of the value of capital consumption is fairly small, except in housing.

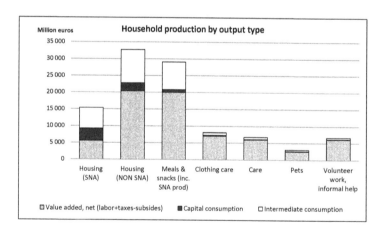

Figure 1: Value of services by services type, 2006

One may be surprised at the relatively low value of care services. There are two main reasons for this. First, only primary time for care was taken into account. Keeping an eye on children when doing something else at the same time was not included. Preparing meals or washing the laundry for children was allocated to meals and clothing care functions. Helping elderly parents who live in their own household was allocated to informal help/volunteer work. Second, less than one-quarter of the Finnish households had children. Furthermore, public day care is available to all children under school age. Parents who took care of their children at home were paid an allowance that is deducted from the value following the SNA counting rule.

Unpaid work was divided fairly traditionally between women and men (Table 2). Men do more maintenance and repairs on the house, as they do with vehicle maintenance, which is included in travel. Women make more meals, take care of clothing and perform childcare. Informal help to other households and shopping is evenly divided between men and women.

	Men	Women
Housing, excluded from the GDP	39	61
Housing, included in the GDP	80	20
Meals & snacks	27	73
Clothing	9	91
Care	32	68
Pets	35	65
Informal help and volunteer work	48	52
Shopping	45	55
Travel related to unpaid work	69	31
Total	38	62

Table 2: Unpaid work by men and women, % of the total

The value of household production varies between families in different stages of life. It increases with age and the number of household members (Figure 2). Economies of scale in production occur. A family of four does not prepare four meals separately but all in the same production process. This is not enough to cover all additional work in larger families. The value of household production seems to increase after retirement. A similar result was found in a German study by Melanie Lührmann (17). She proved that German retirees reduced household expenditure and substituted it through home production. The most obvious example of this was in cooking and gardening.

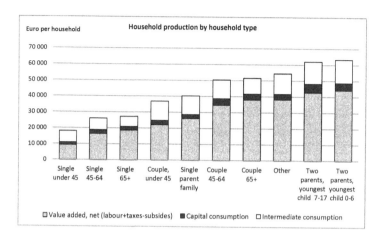

Figure 2: Value of household production by household type, 2006

HOUSEHOLDS' UNPAID PRODUCTION AND USE OF MARKET SERVICES

Replacing household production with purchased services is most frequent with respect to acquiring meals and snacks. Young single people and couples substitute most often eating out for home meals or snacks, for approximately one-third of all meals, while the retired population purchased only one-tenth of all meals. Purchasing care services from private businesses remained very marginal in 2006, with the exception of households in the oldest age groups. Clothes and textiles are cared for by households themselves, with the use of laundry services remaining very minor. The results also indicate that readiness to outsource domestic work is higher in households of the youngest age groups (under 45) than among older age groups. However, the total value of household production at the national level will probably increase in the short term. This is due to the growth in the number of pensioners and the fact that they carry out a significant amount of domestic and voluntary work. The high share of voluntary work, particularly in families with children and retired persons' households, also indicates its importance as a driver of social well-being.

HOUSEHOLD PRODUCTION IN LOW-INCOME AND HIGH-INCOME HOUSEHOLDS

Economic theory suggests that leisure time is preferred over housework. Many studies have examined the factors that influence the amount of outsourcing of unpaid work. We produced separate estimates for the value of production for different income quintiles. The quintiles were composed using the equivalent disposable income per household. Unpaid work was valued by the same wage for all income groups, which means that the amount of time was actually the determining factor for the value of work. Results indicate that there was very little difference in the value of unpaid work in different income groups. Instead, material elements (capital, intermediate consumption) increased the value of total output, i.e., the value of services, more in higher-income households (Figure 3). The lowest quintile included more single person households compared to other quintiles, which explains the lower value of production. It seems that the number and age of household members affect the value of household production more than income. However, high-income households spend more money on purchased services such as eating out or buying clothing than low-income households.

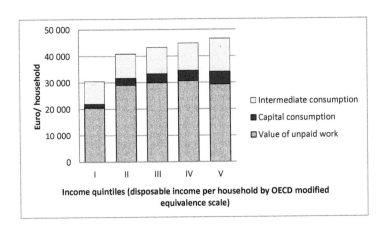

Figure 3: Values of unpaid work and other inputs of services produced by households, 2006

To conclude on the results of the calculations, we would like to emphasize that if we estimate the total value of unpaid services instead of mere unpaid work, we get a more complete picture of household production. We may compare the values of purchased market services to that of self-provided services and see how the household and the market economy interrelates. We also see how household production is tied to market goods and services, as unpaid work alone does not make meals or other services. It can be seen how income levels affect the value of services, whether it is produced at home or at the market.

FEEDBACK ON THE WORK AND RESULTS

The development of the method for satellite accounts was an inspiring and exciting task. It felt that finally we were doing something that might have a true meaning: the value of unpaid work would become visible and the value of unpaid production might be taken into account. It could be integrated into the core national accounts. The satellite account project had a steering group that included economists, statisticians, sociologists, etc. They were active in participating in the meetings, expressed opinions on the problems faced, and were positively interested in the results. A press conference was organized to publish the accounts. Several newspapers published articles on the value and the proportion compared to the GDP. Some journalists carried out interviews for periodicals. However, the study team experienced great difficulties in talking about the "self-evident" housework in statistical terms to people who were not familiar with household task classifications or valuation concepts. Most reporters were not familiar with the economic or "statistical language." A young female reporter came and requested more information and clarifications on the study outcomes, but when she reported the study in an article, the title read: "Is it right to pay children for taking the bin bag out or tidying their room?" which reflected a complete misunderstanding of the topic, figures and research results. The research team had believed that now the household production value figures were finally "properly" estimated according to the rules of the SNA, the value of household production would appear in economic calculations. This did not happen. Economists in their research institutions continued their work on time series and pondered the growth of GDP to the accuracy of one-tenth of a percentage points as they did before. The Statistical Yearbook mentioned neither the value of household production nor the increase it brought to the value of individual consumption, because the study did not belong to the official statistics. Only later, after the measurement of well-being became popular, the value of unpaid production was mentioned as one possible addition to the measures. Academic disciplines such as women studies did not express any interest. Perhaps estimating the monetary value for housework was regarded as a representation of the mainstream patriarchal economy because the macroeconomic concepts of production and methods were used. The same difficulty is expressed by Marilyn Waring when she ponders the possibilities and problems of imputing value to women's work:

> While I shall insist that we work to transform the system in this way, and use all its tools to do that, we must not rest there. With all its immediate relief and distinct policy possibilities, we would still be left with a system that reduced women's lives to statements of mathematical formula. (287)

Finnish feminist Aino Saarinen concludes that there should be economic research done by women and for women (245). Another academic discipline, home economics, which has traditionally been one of the advocates of the economic value of unpaid work, had developed a new body of knowledge that is based on a broad holistic approach. According to this approach, home economics can be seen as a combination of human development, healthy living, social responsibility, the sustainable use of resources, and cultural diversity (Vincenti and Turkki 47). Home economist Henna Heinilä ("Domestic"; "Writing") describes her research where the emphasis is placed on bringing up the non-economic or spiritual value, rather than on the economic value of production. Work at home, caring, preparing meals, etc. includes a dimension that produces human capital that carries on throughout one's whole life. Its most important function relates to quality of life even though it may contain economic value, too, by reducing the need for social or health services, be they public or private. This non-economic value is difficult or impossible to measure (email Feb 27, 2012).

DISCUSSION

This article reflects feelings of slight disappointment after developing the satellite account of household production. Has the need for making it visible passed? Who would be interested in it? Where could these estimates be used? Marilyn Waring said in one of her later interviews: "It is not that

I want to estimate its [women's unpaid work] monetary value. I want to make it visible for policy-making purposes, for fairness and equity." We claim that it may not be possible to make women's work recognized unless the economic value is estimated. However, it needs to be understood to be separate from the other important qualities and values of unpaid work. It is only one element and there are other important dimensions in unpaid work. To allow for unpaid work to be noticed and valued, joint action is needed from all researchers, educators, development practitioners and public media professionals, so that all possible ways and means are sought and used to make unpaid work recognizable, both nationally and globally. Economic equality between women and men is currently understood to mean equal opportunities to create a career. Equal pay, equal positions in companies and equal economic power are the aims of development. Talking about the value of unpaid work is easily interpreted to mean that women are drawn back home—because their work is so valuable. Therefore, it is better not to keep it up in public discussion. But one should not forget that men also do unpaid work. The value of household production has recently received a new meaning. In welfare states such as Finland, the government sector has provided most social services, including children's daycare, elderly care and help for families with multiple problems. This is why we pay relatively high taxes. In the worsening financial situation, the question is emerging: "Who will provide the services when the population ages?" Households become promising providers of care once more. As Table 2 indicates, informal help provided to other households is evenly divided between women and men. The question of unpaid work may not be an issue of gender equality as it used to be before. It is becoming more an issue of providing well-being. It is more about the division of work between generations: who are supporters of the welfare state and who are the receivers of care. By including unpaid production into the equation, the total picture becomes more balanced between the generations, as the calculations by Donehower and Guevara in their PAA conference paper suggest. Now, it is the statisticians that are interested in its value (e.g. OECD). It is where it should have been right from the beginning.

ANNEX

Method and data for satellite account for household production:
Accounting rule for the input method:
Value of labor (units of time valued at suitable wages/time)

+ other taxes on production
− other subsidies on production
+ consumption of capital
= gross value added
+ intermediate consumption
= value of total output (sum of costs)

Value of labor is estimated on the basis of the time spent in unpaid work and a certain wage to assign value to the work time. Time use surveys therefore provide an essential data source for the estimation of the value of labor. Taxes on production include the annual vehicle tax and real estate tax for households. Subsidies such as the child homecare allowance and family nursing support are paid to households that care for babies and small children at home. These subsidies are paid "as a consequence of engaging in production" (European System of Accounts, ESA 1995, 4.36). The subsidies were deducted for calculating the net value added. Consumption of goods and services, defined as final consumption in national accounts, were divided into three groups: 1) those that are used directly to final consumption; 2) those that are used as intermediate consumption goods in household production; and 3) those that are used as capital goods in household production (durable and semi-durable goods).

Capital goods/investment/durables were defined as goods whose service life is longer than three years. These consisted of all household durables as well as some semi-durable goods such as household textiles, kitchen appliances and cutlery, baby carriages and car seats. Estimates of service life are based on expert opinions (e.g. Work Efficiency Institute TTS, home appliance repair shops), estimates published in the Eurostat methods report (Varjonen et al.) as well as figures used in German and UK satellite accounts. The service life for cars is based on average scrap age according to Finnish Central Organisation for Motor Trades and Repairs statistics from 2006. The yearly consumption was estimated using the perpetual inventory method (PIM). Calculations for capital consumption were carried out by Statistics Finland and the data was drawn from national accounts database.

Data source: Statistics Finland

Data for unpaid time was drawn from the national time use survey 1999-2000. Data was modified according to the needs of satellite accounts by Statistics Finland. The time spent to unpaid work by detailed categories per whole household was calculated.

Data for hourly wages came from wage statistics. Hourly wage included holiday and sick leave but no bonuses.

Data for consumption per household was drawn from nationally representative household budget surveys and was divided by different household types.

Data for taxes and subsidies on production was given to us from Statistics Finland. They were drawn from different governmental registers.

WORKS CITED

Abraham, Katharine G., and Christopher C. Mackie, eds. *Beyond the Market: Designing Nonmarket Accounts for the United States.* Washington DC. The National Academies Press, 2005. Print.

Donehower, Gretchen and IVàn M. Guevara. *Everybody Works: Gender, Age and Economic Activity.* Extended abstract submitted for PAA 2012. Web. Mar 29, 2012.

Harmaja, Laura. *Kotitalous kansantalouden osana. Kansantaloudellinen yhdistys.* WSOY: Porvoo. 1946. Print.

Eurostat. *Active aging and solidarity between generations. A Statistical portrait of the European Union.* Eurostat: Statistical books. Web. Mar 29, 2012.

—. "Household production and consumption. Proposal for a Methodology of the Household Satellite Account." Task force report for Eurostat, Division E1. (2003) *Population and Social Condition, Working papers and studies.* Web. Feb 20, 2012.

Heinilä, Henna. "Domestic skills as the art of everyday life. An inquiry about domestic skills as a way of being in the world in the light of existentialist-hermeneutics phenomenology." (2007) (In Finnish, abstract in English). Dissertation. University of Helsinki. Finland. Web, Mar 15, 2012

—. "Writing new maps Considering the Phenomenological Attitude as a Theoretical Framework for the FutureOrientated Field of Home Economics." 101-110, *Creating Home Economics Futures. The Next 100 Years.* eds. Donna Pendergast, Sue LT McGregor and Kaija Turkki. (2012). Australian Academic Press: Australia. Web. Aug 18, 2013.

Kilpiö, Eila. "The Concept of Unpaid Housework and the Determination of its Value. Description of the Study and Sample." *Housework Study,* Parts 1-2. Ministry of Social Affairs and Health, Research Department. Finland. 1981. Print.

Kuwahara S. (2010) "A note on monetary valuation of unpaid work in Japan." *Working Party of National Accounts.* (2010) 9. Web. Mar 20, 2012.

Landefeld, J. Steven., Barbara M. Fraumeni, and Cindy M. Vojtech. "Accounting for Household Production: A Prototype Satellite Account using the American Time Use Survey." *Review of Income and Wealth* 55.2 (2009): 205-25. Print.

Layard, Richard. *Happiness. Lessons from a New Science.* Allen Lane: Penguin Books. 2005. Print.

Lindberg, Valter. *Suomen kansantulo vuosina 1926-1938.* Suomen Pankin suhdannetutkimusosaston julkaisuja sarja B:1. 1943. Print.

Lührmann, Melanie. *Consumer Expenditure and Home Production at Retirement – New Evidence from Germany.* Mannheim Research Institute for the Economics of Aging. 120 (2007). Web. Mar 20, 2012.

OECD. "Incorporating estimates of household production of non-market services into international comparisons of material well-being." *Working Party of National Accounts.* (2010) 9. Web. Mar 20, 2012.

Saarinen, Aino. "Missä viipyvät feministiset talousteoriat?" *Tieteen huolet arjen ihmeet.* ed. Päivi Korvajärvi, Ritva Nätkin and Antti Saloniemi. Vastapaino: Tampere.1993. 235-245. Print.

Salamon, Lester M., S. Wojciech Sokolowski, and Megan A. Haddock. "Measuring the economic value of volunteer work globally: concepts, estimates, and a roadmap to the future." *Annals of Public and Cooperative Economics* 82(3) 2011, 217-252. Print.

Saurio, Elli. *Maalaisemännän ajankäyttö suhteessa laatuun ja henkilörakenteeseen.* (Use of time of rural Finnish homemakers in relation to the character and composition of the household.) WSOY: Helsinki-Porvoo. 1947. Print.

SNA93. *System of National Accounts 1993.* United Nations, Inter-Secretariat Working Group on National Accounts. Brussels/Luxembourg, New York, Paris, Washington, DC: EU, IMF, OECD, UN, and WB.1993.

Suviranta, Annikki and Arto Mynttinen. "The Value of Unpaid Cooking Work in 1980." *Housework Study. VI.* Ministry of Social Affairs and Health. Research Department. Helsinki. 1981. Print.

Stiglitz, Joseph, Amartya Sen and Jean-Paul Fitoussi. *Report by the Commission on the Measurement of Economic Performance and Social Progress.* 2009, Web. Mar 22, 2012.

Säntti, Riitta, Ritva-Anneli Otva and Eila Kilpiö. "Unpaid Housework." *Housework Study VIII.* Ministry of Social Affairs and Health. Research Department. Helsinki. 1981. Print.

Varjonen, Johanna, Iiris Niemi, Eeva Hamunen, Taru Sandström, and Hannu Pääkkönen. "Proposal for a Satellite Account of Household Production." [Luxembourg]: Eurostat, 1999. Print. *Eurostat Working Papers*; 9/1999/A4/11. Print.

Varjonen, Johanna and Kristiina Aalto. "Household Production and Consumption in Finland 2001." *Household Satellite Account.* Statistics Finland and National Consumer Research Centre. 2006. Web. ncrc.fi. Mar 29, 2012.

—. "Kotitalouksien palkaton tuotanto ja ostopalvelujen käyttö. (Households' unpaid production and use of market services)". National Consumer Research Centre. Publications 2/2010. (Abstract in English) Web. Mar 29, 2012.

Vincenti, Virginia B., and Kaija Turkki. "Celebrating the Past" 33-54, *Creating the Past – Creating the Future.* ed. Donna Pendergast. IFHE proceedings. XXI World Congress. July 26-31, 2008. Luzern, Switzerland. Print.

Waring, Marilyn. *If Women Counted. A New Feminist Economics.* Harper & Row, Publishers: San Francisco. 1988. Print.

6.

Accounting For Death

Infant Mortality, the MDGs, and Women's (Dis)Empowerment

MONICA J. CASPER & WILLIAM PAUL SIMMONS

INTRODUCTION

IN 1906, British physician George Newman published *Infant Mortality: A Social Problem*, linking infant death to social, cultural, and economic conditions. There has since been abundant research on infant mortality (IM), typically defined as the number of babies per 1,000 to die before their first birthday. Garrett et al. write,

> The wealth of studies carried out on infant mortality testifies to its continuing fascination for the modern researcher. Infants are the most vulnerable members of society, they rely exclusively on others for their survival and hence the rate at which they perish is often taken to be a measure of that society's well-being. (5)

Demographers, epidemiologists, economists, anthropologists and sociologists seek both to measure infant mortality rates (IMRs) and associated phenomena (Williams and Rucker) and to provide textured cultural accounts of infant death in social context (Scheper-Hughes). The bulk of such research—especially measurement of contributions and causes—is quantitative, and thus embodies a collective "trust in numbers" (Porter). Accurate statistical methods are presumed to provide definitive answers to complex questions.

Casper and Moore demonstrated that in demographic and epidemiological studies, infant mortality is framed not in terms of grief and trauma associated with loss of a child, but rather as a socio-technical object. Casper defines the IMR as a "portable abacus," a mobile, standardized, shared technology that enables global assessments of risk. Governments, clinicians, and NGOs use the rate as an aggregate measure to link infant death to the health of nations. Wrapping human experiences of death, dying, and loss inside a numeric object facilitates rational, institutional responses. Yet the IMR is complicated by a multiplicity of bodies and lives across time and space; messy human stories are not easily containable.

We explore issues related to the IMR as an "objective" measurement, specifically its use as a "large number" (Desrosières) in governmental health practices. Analyzing the U.N. Millennium Development Goals (MDGs), we suggest that such a demographic register may not be optimal for assessing and responding to infant death. Like Waring, who showed that GNP and other metrics do not account for women's labor, environmental costs, or war and peace, we argue that the development field's current accounting system has mobilized mortality as statistical justification for expansion of neo-liberal policies. Just as GNP did not adequately capture a country's well-being, neither do the MDGs.

This project situates infant mortality within a progressive women's health paradigm (Clarke and Olesen). The domain of "maternal/child health" in which IM is located is a set of practices targeting women's bodies that may not, in fact, foreground women's needs and interests, raising urgent questions about how nations can reduce child death rates without defining and treating women as exclusively reproductive. We suggest that women's empowerment could readily be used in place of the IMR, leading to policies more favorable to women while also improving infant death rates. Our analysis owes much to Foucault's genealogies. Social practices and institutions established to regulate a population's quality (and quantity) of life are termed biopolitical, whereas biopower refers to disciplinary practices that operate on and through bodies to create subjects. Foucault identifies biopower as originating at the dawn of the nineteenth century, with the proliferation of medicine, demography, and psychiatry. These new regimes of knowledge and practice generated certain kinds of bodies and subjects, such as the prisoner, the insane, and the patient, while also cultivating and building on developing technologies.

With each regime have come new biopolitical objects, or socio-technical entities around which knowledge and practices congeal through the work of building institutional practices. In the late nineteenth-century U.S., when rates of child death were very high especially among immigrants, vital statistics allowed for measuring and aggregating patterns of human biological processes such as birth and death. The infant mortality rate emerged as a biopolitical object, and the infant-at-risk became a new subject of governance (Armstrong). This object—quantified, aggregated, and mobilizable—became the impetus for the U.S. Children's Bureau, immigration policies, and maternal education initiatives. As rates decreased these initiatives also declined, so much so that currently there is no federal program designed to ameliorate high infant death rates in the U.S.

We are interested in a uniquely twenty-first century form of transnational governance: the U.N. Millennium Development Goals. If at-risk-infants are the subjects in question, and the IMR the flexible object, then the MDGs must be considered part of a biopolitical apparatus designed to fix the problem of infant mortality. This apparatus—comprised of human, technical, and discursive elements—relies heavily on the "fact" of the infant mortality rate. Through the rate's distribution across various networks, the infant-at-risk is continually reproduced rhetorically. Yet rarely is its facticity challenged. Thus, we are not merely asking whether statistical measures need to address what is left out, but whether the register itself is fundamentally flawed (Waring).

FROM INFANT MORTALITY TO WOMEN'S EMPOWERMENT

Infant mortality is ever-present in international studies, frequently used as a proxy for poverty and social development and as a supplement to economic development indicators (Newland 5). Infant mortality is both an independent variable, for example proving to be a factor in predicting civil wars and regime changes (e.g. Goldstone et al.) and a dependent variable negatively related to democratization and GDP per capita (McGuire). It is principally a geopolitical marker: a key "indicator of the goodness of a society—its general welfare, the justness of its political system, the efficacy of its public works, the benevolence of its powerful; a high rate of death among the very young [is] an index of a community's shame" (Condran and Murphy 474).

Yet the rate's influential role as an indicator is seldom questioned; it is rarely examined as a biopolitical object. While it is integral to discourse around the MDGs, both as target and measurement tool, child survival is the Goal that has most escaped serious interrogation. While debates swirl around other MDGs such as women's empowerment and combating infectious diseases (e.g., Barton), it is assumed that infant mortality is uncontested. It is time to reflect on what this category means and what work it does in and for governmental practices.

The following quote from ethicist Peter Singer's essay "What should a Billionaire Give—and What Should You?" is representative of infant mortality being mobilized for an economic agenda:

> "How could I never have heard of something that kills half a million children every year?" [Bill Gates] asked himself. He then learned that in developing countries, millions of children die from diseases that have been eliminated, or virtually eliminated, in the United States.... As Gates told a meeting of the World Health Assembly in Geneva last year, he and his wife, Melinda, "couldn't escape the brutal conclusion that—in our world today—some lives are seen as worth saving and others are not." They said to themselves, "This can't be true." But they knew it was. (Singer 2006)

Singer relates the story of Bill and Melinda Gates stirred to action upon discovering that 500,000 children die from preventable deaths every year. They set up a foundation to rescue these children. By the essay's end, it is clear that billionaires and others in the top tax brackets in the U.S. should give, as should nation-states through foreign aid. Indeed, Singer—usually a philosopher of dilemmas—notes this ethical issue is clear-cut:

> How easy it would be for the world's rich to eliminate, or virtually eliminate, global poverty. (It has actually become much easier over the last 30 years, as the rich have grown significantly richer.) I found the result astonishing....Measured against our capacity, the Millennium Development Goals are indecently, shockingly modest. If we fail to achieve them— as on present indications we well might—we have no excuses (Singer 2006).

Infant mortality is similarly mobilized in William Easterly's *The Elusive Quest for Growth*, in a section titled "The Death of the Innocents." He primes us for his proposed economic solution by employing stark figures of the number of children who die from such preventable causes as diarrhea and pneumonia. By an aggregative sleight of hand in the next chapter, we learn that the problem of infant mortality, which has captured us emotionally, is transformed into one of economic growth: neo-liberal policies must target ever-elusive growth to save fragile babies. Easterly shows, through an alchemy of regression analyses and anecdotes, that such false elixirs as education, debt forgiveness, population control, and foreign aid will not save babies because they do not lead to economic growth.

Other popular book-length works on development (e.g., Collier; Sachs) follow a similar pattern: mobilizing dead babies as the problem and neo-liberal policies as the solution. These works suggest infant mortality can be conquered if only a few economic and political steps are taken. But is it as simple as securing sustained economic growth, which Easterly accurately compares to a quest for the Holy Grail? Economic growth of the magnitude desired by policymakers does not appear forthcoming. More alarming, the economist turned trickster has transformed infant mortality—a collective tragedy in which vulnerable babies die before they crawl—into cold, hard data of fiscal growth. The MDGs, too, posit economic growth or poverty alleviation from a neo-liberal model as the tonic for infant mortality. This neoliberal discourse has further transformed the profusion of dying and dead babies into a rational problem for economic development.

Globally, child mortality has in fact declined since 2000. But in hardest-hit Africa, it had only declined six per cent by 2006, and would need to drop by another sixty to seventy per cent to achieve MDG Four by 2015. Those who espouse an economic growth model for reducing infant death would be hard pressed to explain the meager declines in death rates, as most of Africa saw moderate to substantial growth during this time period. Substantial increases in foreign aid have also failed to reduce child mortality. Most studies show only a modest relationship between economic growth or foreign aid and infant mortality rates (e.g., McGuire). For example, in Uganda, which saw rapid economic growth and dramatic reductions in poverty over the past fifteen years, IMRs have remained static (Ssenwanya and Younger).

The infant mortality rate, then, appears to serve two major functions in international studies. First, it is a passive indicator that represents something else (e.g., a nation's health) or is used to predict something else (e.g., failed statehood). Second, the passive indicator can come to life as an intermittent rallying cry for mobilizing the public and policymakers, to grab their attention so they are more willing to buy the proffered panacea.[1] It is a compassion badge showing that the dry economic analysis to follow is informed by a heart, a desire to "save babies." Yet cultural meanings and political agendas lurk within this "neutral" statistic.

We begin to glimpse the beauty and utility of the IMR as a portable abacus, an indicator to be employed liberally by economists and others. It is not one that inherently mobilizes support; it is a number, after all, and not a picture of a tiny coffin. The pictures and anecdotes of infant death, when they do appear, can be ignored on the basis of compassion fatigue, or they are not shown out of respect. But the IMR is mobilizable: it can lay dormant as a static indicator, employed occasionally as a battle cry without necessarily calling into question the entire development enterprise. Of all the indicators, it also lacks a transnational advocacy network; the victims themselves cannot stand up. And because infant loss differentially impacts the most vulnerable populations, mothers will likely be unable to stand up for their dying and dead children.

Attentive to biopolitics, we query whether other indicators could be used in the IMR's place and the impact of such substitutions. Infant mortality rates are frequently highly correlated with a range of development indicators, but such correlations are seen as another "data point" to support the reliability of the other indicator. The Human Development Index is shown to be reliable, in part, because it is already highly correlated with infant mortality. Infant and maternal mortality are also found to be very highly correlated (McAlister and Baskett), as are infant mortality and life expectancy (Lee et al.). Surely, these measures could be used as substitutes for the IMR rather than co-indicators.

Gender empowerment is also shown to be highly correlated with infant mortality. One study (Varkey et al.) found that scores on national Gender Empowerment Measures (GEMs) were strongly correlated with variables that measure the health of communities, including low birth weight and fertility. But the strongest association was between gender empowerment and infant mortality. An Egyptian study found that key aspects of women's empowerment, including "lifetime exposure to employment" and "family structure amenable to empowerment" (positively) and "traditional marriage" (negatively), were strongly related to child survival (Kishor).

What if gender empowerment—seen as multi-dimensional, stratified, and highly variable over time—and not the IMR became the rallying cry in development literature? What if Singer began his essay with Bill Gates learning about women disempowered around the world? Would this have the same rhetorical effect? Easterly offers an account from a trip to poverty-stricken Lahore and surrounding regions in Pakistan. While meeting with the men of a household, he notices a woman looking out a window:

> I think again back to the woman I saw peering out at me from a house in a village in Pakistan. To that unknown woman I dedicate the elusive quest for growth as we economists, from rich countries and from poor countries, trek the tropics trying to make poor countries rich. (15)

Perhaps, instead of a dedication, Easterly could have sought to learn from that woman and so many others similarly situated, asking how they are dis-empowered and how they would address issues such as infant death. East-erly, like many, narrows his gaze to focus clinically on economic growth, in lieu of calling for greater empowerment for women as a means of improving national health.

We suggest rearranging the indicators and prioritizing women's em-powerment. Turning next to the Mexican experience, we discuss the com-plex relationship among development, infant mortality, and women's em-powerment. The Mexican case is ideal for understanding externalities not counted by neoliberal accounting systems (cf. Waring), including massive disruption of family structures and violence inflicted through migration spurred by NAFTA and other neoliberal economic "solutions."

CASE STUDY: MEXICO AND EPIDEMIOLOGICAL PARADOXES

Mexico is in the enviable position of already having achieved the specified target for MDG Four. By 2005, it had reduced by more than two-thirds the under-five mortality rate from 1990; most of the gain came during the 1990s. The infant mortality rate—deaths within the first year of life—saw similar declines by 2000. Aggregated statistics, however, veil wide dispar-ities among regions and populations. Geographically, the southern states of Oaxaca and Chiapas both experience IMRs of two to three times higher than wealthier states. Similarly, the rate for indigenous peoples can be up to three times the national average in some communities (Cf. Fuentes and Montes).

But the static and "objective" indicator of infant mortality is built on shifting sands, which obscure embodied human realities marked by neolib-eral policies. In the Mexican case, we must consider the lived experiences of millions of people on the move, literally and figuratively crossing borders.

Mexicans move internally from rural to urban areas, to the U.S.-Mexico border for work in maquiladoras and then back to hometowns, and to the United States and back again. Migration of Central Americans through Mexico further destabilizes the numeric register.

Nowhere is this instability more apparent than in the so-called epidemiological paradox of infant mortality rates among Mexican Americans in the U.S. Numerous studies have found that Mexican Americans, despite their generally poorer rankings on several key factors normally associated with IMRs—such as mothers' educational attainment, economic status, and access to health care—have significantly lower IMRs than other minority groups, and in some cases have lower rates than non-Hispanic white U.S.-born women (Hamilton et al., 125). Yet the longer Mexican-American immigrants stay in the U.S., *the infant mortality rates rise.*

The phenomenon is additionally puzzling when we consider the added stressors that confront migrants which logically should increase the infant mortality rate. Migrants, especially women and children, face harrowing paths in trying to enter the U.S. (Marrujo Ruiz; Simmons and Téllez). Their journeys have become more dangerous as the border has been militarized and as migration has become a big business increasingly dominated by organized syndicates and cartels. Each year, hundreds of migrants die and countless thousands of others become lost, disoriented, dehydrated, or suffer other traumas in the deserts and mountains of the Southwest. Recent studies have documented particular risks for migrant women, especially sexual violence both in Mexico and the U.S.[2]

Other studies have shown that stress, including stress resulting from racist attitudes, appears to increase infant mortality rates among minority groups (e.g. Williams et al.). With increased anti-immigrant fervor in the U.S., especially along the U.S./Mexico border, we would expect IMRs to be even higher. This would particularly affect undocumented families in places like Phoenix, Arizona, that have faced real risks of being rounded up and deported or being detained long-term.

Hummer et al. focus on two major theories to explain the epidemiological paradox: selective migration of healthier Mexican women or negative acculturation; that is, as Mexican immigrants arrive in the U.S. they embrace a generally healthier lifestyle, which slowly declines as they remain in the country (12).

The complexity of the story increases when we examine the other side of the epidemiological paradox (Frank and Hummer), that those families in Mexico experiencing disruption through out-migration frequently have more positive health outcomes. Most studies analyzing this paradox point to the important effects of financial remittances and return migration that bring both economic and social capital back to Mexico, and likely have the most impact in rural communities (Hamilton et al.). On closer inspection, out-migration has a mixed impact on health outcomes. Those households that receive remittances have lower infant mortality rates (López-Córdova), but those with recent out-migration experience higher IMRs likely due to disruption of the family (Kanaiaupuni and Donato). There is also evidence of a community-level effect over time. Those communities, especially in rural areas, that have experienced higher levels of out-migration have slightly lower IMRs (Hamilton et al.), and there is good evidence this is due to financial remittances.

Research has shown remittances to reduce IMRs substantially. These are used for a wide variety of purposes, but one study has shown that almost half of migrants sending remittances intend them to go directly for health issues (Amuedo-Dorantes, et al.); and a large portion of remittances are used for health care and other services (e.g., sanitation, education, and transportation) that improve health outcomes. It appears that health outcomes improve as migration and remittances become institutionalized over time and can be regularly expected by family members.

The story of migration, remittances, and family dynamics is complex, but it seems clear women's empowerment could play a role in lower IMRs. Men generally have decision-making power in the family as to who migrates and when, often without "discussing this decision with their wives" (King, 899). When women migrate, it is after much discussion within the family and often against the wishes of husbands. When husbands leave wives behind, women face the risk of "intermittent and inadequate financial support and sexual infidelity or even abandonment," which can lead to increased rates of depression (King 900). Nonetheless, when remittances are sent back to Mexico, they are almost always sent back by men (Sana and Massey), presumably with women in control of spending, and as the remittances increase and become institutionalized, women may have greater empowerment. One study showed that women who stayed in a village were able to use remittances to have new homes built and even participated in their design (Pauli). It would make sense, then, that remittances would lead to decreases in the IMR especially in comparison with targeted health aid (Cf. McGuire), which focuses little on women's empowerment.

These findings suggest that explaining the epidemiological paradox requires a closer look at women's empowerment. The self-selection process of healthier migrants postulated by Hummer, in conjunction with greater empowerment of women who decide, often on their own, to migrate, could offset risks and disruptions of the migrant experience. Women who have made the journey and are able to live in the U.S., despite obstacles, likely are more empowered than women who never make that journey. A similar dynamic could be at play in understanding the other side of the epidemiological paradox: those families in Mexico that have experienced household disruption through outmigration often have better health outcomes, including lower IMRs. Several studies have shown that remittances seem to be the most important factor behind this counter-intuitive finding (e.g., Frank and Hummer) and as discussed, financial remittances can enhance women's empowerment in addition to direct effects on health outcomes.

FROM NEOLIBERAL "SOLUTIONS" TO STRUCTURAL CHANGE

At the outset, we positioned infant mortality within biopolitics, noting that the IMR as a portable abacus has co-emerged with the infant-at-risk. It is often assumed that biopolitical problems framed in the aggregate predispose us to biopolitical solutions, also framed in the aggregate. The IMR is too high, ergo new forms of governance must be instituted to lower it—all in the name of national health, development, and transnational governance. But an aggregate solution is not always, or even often, the same as a structural solution, one attentive to the intricacies and obduracies of inequality and systemic vulnerability. We must ask, with Waring, on and in whose bodies are neoliberal solutions wrought?

We framed the MDGs as part of a global biopolitical apparatus engineered to respond to high IMRs, among other problems. We drew attention to ways in which the goals and rates "work," for example in the discourse of macro-development theories to reinforce the call for neoliberal solutions. As a portable abacus, the infant mortality rate is a useful and flexible tool, easily enrolled in the service of implementing preferred programs (e.g., pro-development agendas). In efforts to reduce rates, such as the MDGs or institutionalized preconception care (Casper and Moore), the IMR serves as both impetus and justification for neoliberal intervention. Yet closer analysis often reveals gaps in biopolitical solutions, such as lives negatively affected by neoliberal policies. Because neoliberalism creates conditions that foster ill health in the first place, neoliberal "solutions" are not likely to save lives.

In showcasing demographic shifts in Mexico, our account relied on certain established categories (e.g., migrants, victims of sexual assault) to identify spaces where "solutions" have not worked as planned. Nevertheless, the epidemiological paradox shows that the positive effects of neoliberal policies on the IMR are much more complex than they initially appear. We strongly suggest that women's empowerment—not as a result of intentional policies, but as a response of individuals coping with the effects of neo-liberal "solutions"—has helped to ameliorate the disruptive and nefarious effects of such policies. If instead of turning to neoliberal policies based on economic growth models, policymakers had turned first to women's empowerment to reduce infant mortality, we might have sidestepped the great upheavals to families and other added stressors.

We conclude that folding the messy layers of human life into numeric objects like so much excess skin may give us "efficient" biopolitical tools and neoliberal solutions. And these may or may not reduce death rates, depending on the geopolitical context. But privileging the numeric rather than lived realities creates actuarial categories that obscure real women and babies, and their ghostly presence may haunt the very solutions intended to help them.

[1] The IMR as a social indicator has a long history of mobilization: consider the success of the March of Dimes, which transformed from a polio eradication effort to one focused on infant health.

[2] A study from Nicaragua strongly suggests that sexual violence against women is a significant factor in high infant mortality rates (Asling-Monemi et al.)

WORKS CITED

Amuedo-Dorantes, Catalina, Tania Sainz, and Susan Pozo. "Remittances and Healthcare Expenditure Patterns of Populations in Origin Communities: Evidence from Mexico." INTAL Working Papers 1450, Inter-American Development Bank, 2007. Print.

Armstrong, David. "The Invention of Infant Mortality." *Sociology of Health and Illness* 8 (1986): 211-232. Print.

Asling-Monemi, Kajsa, Rodolfo Peña, Mary Carroll Ellsberg, and Lars Ake Persson. "Violence against Women Increases the Risk of Infant and Child

Mortality: A Case-Referent Study in Nicaragua." *Bulletin of the World Health Organization* 81.1 (2003): 10–16. Print.

Barton, Carol. "Where to for Women's Movements and the MDGs?" *Gender and Development* 13 (2005): 25-35. Print.

Casper, Monica J. "Phantom Babies and Spectral Women: Infant Mortality, Maternal/Child Health, and Women's Empowerment." *American Anthropological Association.* New Orleans, LA. 20 November 2010. Conference presentation.

Casper, Monica J., and Lisa Jean Moore. *Missing Bodies: The Politics of Visibility.* New York: NYU Press, 2009. Print.

Clarke, Adele E., and Virginia Olesen, eds. *Revisioning Women, Health, and Healing: Feminist, Cultural, and Technoscience Perspectives.* New York: Routledge, 1999. Print.

Collier, Paul. *The Bottom Billion: Why the Poorest Countries are Failing and What Can Be Done About It.* Oxford: Oxford University Press, 2007. Print.

Condran, Gretchen A., and Jennifer Murphy. "Defining and Managing Infant Mortality: A Case Study of Philadelphia, 1870-1920." *Social Science History* 32.4 (2008): 473-513.

Desrosières, Alain. *The Politics of Large Numbers: A History of Statistical Reasoning.* Cambridge: Harvard University Press, 2002. Print.

Easterly, William. *The Elusive Quest for Growth: Economists' Adventures and Misadventures in the Tropics.* Cambridge: MIT Press, 2001. Print.

Foucault, Michel. *The Birth of Biopolitics: Lectures at the College de France, 1978-1979.* New York: Picador, 2010 [1979]. Print.

Frank, Reanne, and Robert A. Hummer. "The Other Side of the Paradox: The Risk of Low Birth Weight among Infants of Migrant and Nonmigrant Households within Mexico." *International Migration Review* 36 (2002): 746–765. Print.

Fuentes R., and A. Montes. "Mexico and the Millennium Development Goals at the Subnational Level." *Journal of Human Development* 5.1 (2004): 97-120. Print.

Garrett, Eilidh, Chris Galley, Nicola Shelton, and Robert Woods. *Infant Mortality: A Continuing Social Problem.* Hampshire: Ashgate, 2006. Print.

Goldstone, Jack A., Robert H. Bates, David L. Epstein, Ted Robert Gurr, Michael B. Lustik, Monty G. Marshall, Jay Ulfelder, and Mark Woodward. "A Global Model for Forecasting Political Instability." *American Journal of Political Science* 54.1 (2010): 190–208. Print.

Greenhalgh, Susan, and Edwin Winckler. *Governing China's Population: From Leninist to Neoliberal Biopolitics.* Palo Alto: Stanford University Press, 2005. Print.

Hamilton, Erin R., Andrés Villarreal, and Robert A. Hummer. "Mothers', Household, and Community U.S. Migration Experience and Infant Mortality in Rural and Urban Mexico." *Population Research and Policy Review* 28 (2009): 123-42. Print.

Hummer, Robert A., Daniel A. Powers, Starling G. Pullum, Ginger L. Gossman, W. Parker Frisbie. "Paradox Found (Again): Infant Mortality among the Mexican-Origin Population in the United States." *Demography* 44 (2007): 441-57.

Kanaiaupuni, Shawn Malia, and Katharine Donato. "Migradollars and Mortality: The Effect of U.S. Migration on Infant Survival in Mexico." *Demography* 36.3 (1999): 339-353.

King, Mary C. "Even Gary Becker Wouldn't Call them Altruists! The Case of Mexican Migration: A Reply to Sana and Massey, SSQ June 2005." *Social Science Quarterly* 88 (2007): 898-907.

Kishor, Sunita. "Empowerment of Women in Egypt and Links to the Survival and Health of Their Infants." *Women's Empowerment and Demographic Processes: Moving Beyond Cairo.* Ed. Harriet B. Presser and Gita Sen. Oxford: Oxford University Press, 2000. Print.

Lee, Kwang-sun, Kwang-sun Lee, Sang-chul Park, Babak Khoshnood, Hal-Lung Hsieh, and Robert Mittendorf. "Human Development Index as a Predictor of Infant and Maternal Mortality Rates." *The Journal of Pediatrics* 131.3 (1997): 430-433. Print.

López-Córdova, Ernesto. "Globalization, Migration and Development: The Role of Mexican Migrant Remittances." IADB-INTAL-ITD Working Paper 20, 2006. Print.

Marrujo, Olivia. 2008. "The Gender of Risk: Sexual Violence against Undocumented Women." *A Promised Land, A Perilous Journey: Theological Perspectives on Migration.* Eds. Daniel G. Groody and Gioacchino Campese. Notre Dame: University of Notre Dame Press, 2008. 225-242. Print.

McAlister, Chryssa, and Thomas F. Baskett. "Female Education and Maternal Mortality: A Worldwide Survey." *Journal of Obstetrics and Gynaecol-*

ogy Canada 28.11 (2006): 983-90. Print.

McGuire, James W. *Wealth, Health, and Democracy in East Asia and Latin America.* New York: Cambridge University Press, 2010. Print.

Newland, K. "The Health of Societies: Infant Mortality Rate is a Good Measure of Country's Ills." Washington, D.C.: Worldwatch Institute, 1991. Web.

Newman, George. *Infant Mortality: A Social Problem.* London: Methuen, 1906. Print.

Pauli, Julia. "A House of One's Own: Gender, Migration, and Residence in Rural Mexico." *American Ethnologist* 35 (2008): 171–187. Print.

Porter, Theodore M. *Trust in Numbers: The Pursuit of Objectivity in Science and Public Life.* Princeton: Princeton University Press, 1996. Print.

Sachs, Jeffrey D. *The End of Poverty: Economic Possibilities for Our Time.* New York: Penguin, 2005. Print.

Sana, Mariano, and Douglas S. Massey. "Family and Migration in Comparative Perspective: Reply to King." *Social Science Quarterly* 88.3 (2007): 908-11. Print.

Scheper-Hughes, Nancy. *Death Without Weeping: The Violence of Everyday Life in Brazil.* Berkeley: University of California Press, 1993. Print.

Simmons, William Paul, and Michelle Téllez. "Sexual Violence against Migrant Women and Children in Arizona." *Localizing Human Rights Abuses: The U.S.-Mexico Experience.* Eds. William Paul Simmons and Carol E. Mueller. Forthcoming.

Singer, Peter. "What Should a Billionaire Give – and What Should You?" *New York Times Magazine* 17 December 2006. Web. 21 Aug 2013.

Ssenwanya, Sarah, and Stephen D. Younger. "Infant Mortality in Uganda: Determinants, Trends, and the Millennium Development Goals." *Journal of African Economies* 17 (2008): 34-61. Print.

Varkey, Prathibha, Sarah, Kureshi, and Timothy Lesnick. "Empowerment of Women and its Association with the Health of the Community." *Journal of Women's Health* 19 (2010): 71-6. Print.

Waring, Marilyn. *Counting for Nothing: What Men Value and What Women Are Worth.* Toronto: University of Toronto Press, 1999. Print.

Williams, D.R., and Rucker, T.D. "Understanding and Addressing Racial Disparities in Health Care." *Health Care Financing Review,* 21.4 (2000), 75-90. Print.

Williams, D. R., H.W. Neighbors, and J.S. Jackson. "Racial/ Ethnic Discrimination and Health: Findings from Community Studies." *American Journal of Public Health.* 93 (2003): 200–208. Print.

7.

Substantive Equality, Stockholm Syndrome and the Costs of Child Sexual Abuse

SHIRLEY JÜLICH

INTRODUCTION

I FIRST MET MARILYN WARING as a Masters student having just submitted a thesis proposal to her as an assignment for an advanced research methodology course. I wanted to ask adult survivors of child sexual abuse what their understandings of justice were. I wanted to know what would provide them with a sense of justice and how this could be best achieved. On the basis of this proposal, Marilyn invited me to transfer to the doctoral program and so began my journey of writing a doctoral thesis with Marilyn Waring as my supervisor.

In this chapter, I will focus on three elements of my work: equality, Stockholm syndrome and the costs of child sexual abuse. These elements might appear unrelated; however, they were central arguments throughout the thesis. The first argument was that victim-survivors seeking justice needed a process based on substantive equality so that they could experience a sense of justice. The conventional criminal justice system with its focus on meting out justice to offenders, does not meet the justice needs of victim-survivors. They do not experience a sense of justice in this system. Indeed, participant victim-survivors reported that they felt more trauma- tized as a result of engaging with the conventional criminal justice system. The second was that experiencing a sense of justice would enable a victim- survivor to progress his or her journey of recovery. My work with victim- survivors convinced me that recovery and justice were difficult to untangle, one depended on the other. The majority of victim-survivors do not report historical or current sexual abuse to any investigative authority. Those who do report to the police often seem ambivalent or contradictory when mak- ing statements, to the extent that they present as unreliable witnesses. Some might even withdraw charges. I used the Stockholm syndrome to explain this phenomenon. The third argument was that an alternative model for justice might encourage victim-survivors to engage and minimize the eco- nomic impacts of child sexual abuse. A cost benefit analysis would provide the necessary evidence that might influence policy makers, but this needed a costing analysis of child sexual abuse in New Zealand. As none were avail- able, I completed this work myself.

As a researcher, restorative justice appealed to me and I wondered if adult survivors of child sexual abuse would think the same. Restorative jus- tice is based on an old and simple concept: "crime is a violation of people and relationships, violations create obligations, the central obligation is to put right the wrongs" (Zehr *The Little Book of Restorative Justice* 19). It pro- vides an opportunity for all stakeholders to discuss the offending behavior and how this has impacted on them. Zehr found that for victims to progress their journeys of recovery they needed to ask questions:

> What happened? Why did it happen to me? Why did I act as I did at the time? Why have I acted as I have since that time? What if it happens again? What does this mean for me and for my outlook (my faith, my vision of the world, my future)? (*Changing Lenses* 26-27)

While many different models of restorative justice exist internationally, the model of choice in New Zealand is a conferencing model that brings to- gether the victim, the offender, and their communities of care or interest. The courts will only refer to restorative justice if a guilty plea has been en- tered. Participation for all is voluntary, and the process is facilitated by an impartial facilitator who is a member of community-based restorative jus- tice provider group. As yet there is no career path for restorative justice facil- itators. While the government funds facilitator training courses it does not directly contract facilitators, instead it contracts provider groups throughout the country to provide a finite number of conferences. Although facilitators receive some pay for their services this is insufficient to provide a living, and so many do their restorative justice work in addition to their regular employment.

I interviewed more than 20 adult victim-survivors of child sexual abuse. In each and every interview they asked questions similar to those outlined by Zehr above. They needed to know what had happened, why it had happened and why it had happened to them. I learned that they too were interested in restorative justice. When I asked, they described processes that would provide them with a sense of justice. These could only be identified as restorative justice, but when I told them about restorative justice they were excited such opportunities existed but one response in particular typified a reluctance to engage with restorative justice: "I can see how that could work in other families but it won't work in mine." I concluded that restorative justice would have to develop beyond the model I described above—a one size fits all model—if it were to provide a sense of justice to victim-survivors of sexual violence.

I continued reading, re-interviewing victim-survivors when they remembered something important they wanted to tell me. I interviewed community experts; I reflected and thought about what I had learned. I attended counseling with a victim-survivor for about a year and learned much about the victimization process. I convened focus groups for the purpose of writing a submission aimed at influencing legislation. I talked to anyone who was prepared to listen, but I did not write. I was disappointed that the participant survivors had not embraced restorative justice as I had anticipated. I felt paralyzed. Over time it had become much easier to research than make sense of the data I had gathered. Marilyn urged me to "just write, write anything; trust the writing process" and so I began by defining justice and equality. I hadn't thought previously about equality in any great depth, but this was an exercise that was to have a lasting impact on me, and on my work.

EQUALITY

The concept of equality is important to victim-survivors of sexual violence. Victim-survivors, who were sexually abused as children, have never experienced equality. Their powerless position in the family made them particularly vulnerable to sexual victimization and the victimization process reinforced the pre-existing power imbalance. Unless justice processes can accommodate inequality it is unlikely that a sense of justice could ever be experienced by victim-survivors of child sexual abuse. The challenge is to deliver justice across two groups with very different needs—victims and offenders.

There are a number of historical commitments to equality. An early example is the creation story in Genesis, "And God said Let us make Mankind in our image, after our likeness..." (Fletcher 122). Another is the Aristotelian approach to equality which was to treat like persons alike, and unlike persons unlike (Scales "The Emergence of Feminist Jurisprudence: An Essay"). It was taken for granted in the days of Aristotle that people in society were not equal, more specifically it was evident in his writing, that he believed women to be naturally inferior to men (Barnett 283). Assumed inequality was not widely challenged until the Age of Enlightenment, with the writing of philosophers such as Immanuel Kant, but notably, the different nature of men and women, common in the history of philosophy, continued throughout this period (Mendus 271). The first writer to show concern for the legal position of women was Mary Wollstonecraft with the publication of her essay "A Vindication of the Rights of Women" in 1792 (Barnett 60).

Equality is complex. There are two approaches which have been debated by theorists since the time of Wollstonecraft. Sometimes referred to as Wollstonecraft's dilemma, or the sameness versus difference debate, the first approach is to treat all people the same, the second is to accommodate the differences between people. Those supporting the equal or same treatment debate, formal or procedural equality, claim that emphasizing the difference between men and women infers that women are deviating from the "norm" (Holtmaat 491). On the other hand those who support the different or special treatment debate, equality of outcome, argue that true equality is based on the recognition of the differing needs of men and women that arise from their different experiences (Bender 206).

Gender-neutral treatment, or formal equality, has been adopted in law and the concept "equality of all before the law" is fundamental to western legal systems. Catherine MacKinnon observed that few women benefit from this gender-neutral approach (225). Martha Fineman argued that formal equality could not possibly address all inequalities existing within society (446). "True equality requires not just women in men's institutions, but also that those institutions be replaced by others broad enough to accommodate the full range of human activities" (Scales "Towards a Feminist Jurisprudence" 428). This definition of equality, substantive equality, not only requires an understanding of those discriminatory structures that foster inequality but also that they be eliminated (Waring *Three Masquerades* 138). Substantive equality recognizes the general social and economic position of women as a cause of their suppression, and the importance of biological and social differences between men and women. These differences negate women's abilities and capacities to make the same use of formal rights as men can (Mendus 271). The Convention on All forms of Discrimination Against Women (CEDAW) is a United Nations (UN) Convention to which many countries are signatories, including New Zealand. Adopted in 1979 by the UN, CEDAW recognizes that formal equality—equality of access—does not ensure substantive equality—equality of outcome. The convention provides a framework for "…realizing equality between women and men through ensuring women's equal access to, and equal opportunities in, political and public life … as well as education, health and employment" (OHCHR, Para. 4). It goes beyond formal equality, prescribing positive action to ensure equality of outcome. Despite this convention and the academic debate substantive equality remains elusive (Fineman 446).

While the equal or same treatment argument and the different or special treatment argument emphasizes gender difference, both arguments can be applied to differences between groups of people. Such groups include the differences between middle class, predominantly white groups and those with different racial or ethnic backgrounds; the differences between adults and children; or the differences between powerful groups and those who are powerless. This is not only very relevant for victim-survivors of child sexual abuse but also for victim-survivors of all forms of sexual violence. Further, it is an argument that is repeated in the work of Martha Fineman (Fineman 452). A framework for restorative justice must not only accommodate difference, but also it must move beyond an analysis based on gender to incorporate the complexities of human experiences. Conventional criminal justice systems do not recognize the complex relationships that exist between victims of child sexual abuse and those who have offended against them. However, restorative justice can and does.

On completion of the doctorate, armed with the findings of my research, a colleague and I called for a group to convene so that a program could be developed that would use restorative processes to address sexual violence. This resulted in the establishment of Project Restore, a specialist restorative justice provider group that now receives referrals from the New

Zealand District Court system and also from those in the community seeking to bypass formal police reporting¹. The processes provided are typical of restorative justice whereby the offender and the victim-survivor are brought together in an encounter meeting facilitated and supported by the Project Restore's clinical team: a restorative justice facilitator who has an in-depth understanding of the complexity of sexual violence, a survivor specialist and an offender specialist. The team prepares all intending participants—the survivor-victim, the offender and the people supporting them—in one-on-one sessions and small groups as appropriate. Each of the team meets with intending participants so that readiness to proceed with a restorative process can be assessed. Unique processes are developed for each case enabling victim-survivors to tell their stories in a safe forum witnessed by important people in their families and social networks.

Offenders and victim-survivors are treated differently as Aristotle advocated, but substantive equality is achieved by focusing on the needs of the victim-survivor, irrespective of gender. The process is not neutral but it is impartial. Rape myths, patriarchal explanations and any minimization of the sexual violence are challenged within the conference by Project Restore personnel. This program, funded by community and government agencies, attracts much international attention from academics and practitioners in the field of restorative justice, but more importantly an early analysis of Project Restore's practice indicated that victim-survivors of sexual violence can experience a sense of justice (Jülich, Buttle, et al.).

STOCKHOLM SYNDROME

Stockholm syndrome refers to a complex bond that exists between hostage and hostage taker, or as what others have previously identified as hostage identification syndrome (Turner 705) or traumatic bonding (Herman 384). Some have likened this bond to the complex relationships observed between abusers and battered women or abused children (Herman 379; Graham, Rawlings and Rigsby 31). Turner noted that the hostage identification syndrome became known as Stockholm syndrome to the general public following the events in a Stockholm bank. Popularized by the media, the term "Stockholm syndrome" was initially used in 1973 to describe the puzzling reactions of four bank employees, three women and one man, who had been held hostage by two ex-convicts during a bank raid in Stockholm, Sweden (Graham et al. 1).

During their six days of captivity, the hostages developed an emotional bond with the hostage-takers to the extent that they not only identified with the hostage-takers, but also came to view the police as the enemy and attempted to protect the hostage-takers from the police (Graham et al. 10-11; Goddard and Tucci 6). Their concern for the hostage-takers did not end with the siege. They did not stop viewing the police as the enemy but continued to see the hostage-takers as their protectors. This aspect was exemplified by an accusation made by a hostage, who claimed that a psychiatrist was attempting to brainwash her by turning her against the hostage-takers. The only male hostage reported how he had to force himself, after the event, to remember that the hostage-taker was not kind: "...[he] dared to take over our lives, ...[and he] could have killed us. I have to force myself to remember that" (Graham et al. 5). Although all four hostages testified against the hostage-takers six months later, the relationship persisted and they seemed unable to hate the hostage-takers. They demonstrated concern regarding the hostage-takers' prison conditions and at least one female hostage visited a hostage-taker in prison.

The contradictory nature of the bi-directional relationship emphasizes the differences between the feelings of hostages who have developed Stockholm syndrome and the perspective of outsiders—those unaffected by Stockholm syndrome (Graham et al. 12). Graham et al. queried whether the hostage's responses were idiosyncratic or if this syndrome could be generalized to other hostage situations, and if predictors could be identified to indicate who would or would not develop Stockholm syndrome. Graham et al. reviewed the literature related to nine victimized groups, to determine whether bonding occurred to an abuser, as it did in Stockholm syndrome. These groups, not usually thought of as hostages, were concentration camp prisoners, cult members, civilians in Chinese Communist prisons, pimp-procured prostitutes, incest victims, physically or emotionally abused children, battered women, prisoners of war, and hostages in general (Graham et al. 31). They found that in all nine groups of victims, bonding between an offender and a victim occurred when four conditions were co-existent. They argued that the following four conditions were precursors for the development of Stockholm syndrome.

> Perceived threat to survival and the belief that the abuser is willing to carry out that threat The victim's perception of some small kindness from the abuser within a context of terror Isolation from perspectives other than those of the abuser

Perceived inability to escape (Graham et al. 33)

Graham et al. also identified a range of cognitive distortions which according to them any victim-survivor of chronic interpersonal abuse could develop (43). Such as, self-blame, seeing the offender as a victim, and believing that if they only loved the offender enough the abuse would stop. They suggested there were at least two reasons why victims blame themselves for the sexual abuse (45). Firstly, as a survival technique, victims adopt the perspective of the offender who believes his or her actions are justified. Secondly, by self-blaming, victims believe they can stop the abuse, which encourages them to influence outcomes. These cognitive distortions enable victims to believe that they have some sort of control over their circumstances, which in turn reduces the terror and enables them to cope. Hence, to negate feelings of victimization, victims spend considerable effort determining how they are causing the abuse and attempting and concentrate their efforts on self-improvement (Graham et al. 46).

Cognitive distortions serve three functions (Graham et al. 46): they minimize the terror, facilitate bonding and instill hope in the victim. As terror is suppressed, the victim and abuser falsely attribute the victim's arousal and hypervigilance to love, as opposed to terror. This in turn facilitates bonding between the victim and the offender, which subsequently instills feelings of hope in the victim. This survival strategy, whereby the victim redefines the relationship as one of care, encourages the offender to do the same, and subsequently the chances of survival are increased. As Graham et al. emphasized, people who develop the syndrome do not do so because of a personality defect or because of previous socialization: it is a response to a threat to survival identifiable in human beings, irrespective of gender, culture or age.

In the interviews I conducted with survivors of child sexual abuse, I did not specifically ask questions related to Stockholm syndrome, neither did I describe it. It was not until I analyzed the interviews using the above precursors as a framework for analysis that I began to understand that the emotional bond to the offender was far more complex than I had initially realized. It appeared as though they had been exposed to the precursors as identified by Graham et al. Participant survivors perceived a real threat to their survival, they identified that they were isolated from other perspectives and they described their inability to escape. They did not explicitly identify that they had cognitive distortions regarding their relationship with the abuser, but I could identify these in their comments as they described their experiences.

I concluded that not all victims of child sexual abuse would be impacted by Stockholm syndrome, but it would seem that those who have been subjected to an on-going sexually abusive relationship within the context of their family or social networks could be particularly susceptible. The dependency of children on adults for nurture and protection promotes the development of an emotional bond in the first instance. The stronger the emotional bond and the closer the familial relationship between victim and offender, the more susceptible the victim-survivor of child sexual abuse could be to the effects of Stockholm syndrome. This syndrome could complicate the recovery process and might explain ambivalence about reporting sexual victimization to the police or using restorative justice to pursue justice.

There were other theories that explained the relationship between an abuser and the victim-survivor, such as Summit's child sexual abuse accommodation syndrome (181). Although this syndrome explained why participant survivors reacted as they had, it did not explain why these actions persisted into adulthood. Stockholm syndrome fitted almost perfectly and is an explanation that resonated for many of the survivor participants. Some expressed relief that they could now understand why they had acted the way they did. It was a common sense explanation that was readily accessible, not only to victim-survivors but also the public in general. These findings, published in the *Journal of Child Sexual Abuse*, continue to attract much international interest from victim-survivors, academics and others working in the field (Jülich *Stockholm Syndrome and Child Sexual Abuse*).

THE COSTS OF CHILD SEXUAL ABUSE

Many of the participant survivors I interviewed asked "Don't they realize how much it [the sexual abuse of children] costs"? I had to admit that at that time in the mid to late 1990s there were no studies estimating the costs of sexual violence to the New Zealand economy. This led me to undertake the first costing analysis of child sexual abuse in New Zealand that community groups continue to use to generate funding.

Victim-survivors of child sexual abuse live the on-going costs and consequences of child sexual abuse. Participant survivors of child sexual abuse had an understanding of what these costs and consequences meant and have continued to mean for them as individuals. They spoke of low self-esteem and low self-confidence and how these have impacted on their lives, and the lives of those dependent on them. They believed that avoiding the sexual abuse of one child was of paramount importance. This is not the language of policy makers. Feelings and beliefs must be translated into the language of funding authorities and people in positions of power, so that policy makers can be better informed of the nature and extent of the problem.

To explore the costs of child sexual abuse in New Zealand, I used Suzanne Snively's report *The New Zealand Economic Cost of Family Violence* as a starting point. I drew on the work of international researchers who had explored the economic consequences and subsequent costs of various forms of violence against women and children, and compared this to information provided by the participant survivors of child sexual abuse. This combination enabled the construction of a spreadsheet model that explored the costs of child sexual abuse in New Zealand. This required several steps. Snively's analysis was deconstructed to unit costs. Each cost was analyzed to determine its relevance to survivors of child sexual abuse. Relevant costs were extrapolated over the estimated numbers of child sexual abuse victims. Given the similarity between family violence and child sexual abuse, where possible, the percentages of victims determined by Snively were used, but the prevalence rate of child sexual abuse was applied, as opposed to the prevalence rate of family violence. Additional costs for adult survivors of child sexual abuse were identified and included. Wherever possible I used inputs relevant to the New Zealand context. A dollar figure for lost quality of life was determined and extrapolated over the estimated incidence rate of child sexual abuse.

It should be noted that the research did not set out to estimate the costs of child sexual abuse in New Zealand. However, in the interviews I had invited participant survivors to describe the impacts sexual victimization had on their lives. Most emphasized that the psychological impacts of child sexual abuse impacted negatively on their economic circumstances. Batya Hyman confirmed that the economic consequences of child sexual abuse were substantial but found some variations between the various categories of child sexual abuse: that is, intra-familial and extra-familial child sexual abuse both of which could be with or without force. My contact with survivors of child sexual abuse heightened my awareness of the difficulties of quantifying trauma. I concluded that it was not possible to categorize trauma according to the sexual violence participant survivors were subjected to as Hyman had. Perhaps, I did not know the right questions to ask. Or perhaps, it was because the methodology of Hyman's study varied from that of this research project. She analyzed a pre-existing data set; I listened to survivors of child sexual abuse and heard their trauma and pain. This might have accounted for the difference. This difference aside, other researchers estimated that the dollar costs of child sexual abuse for all victim-survivors and other forms of violence against women were significant, not only for victims and their families, but also for the broader society.

My costing analysis of child sexual abuse in New Zealand was soon superseded by a costing analysis of crime conducted for the New Zealand Treasury (Roper and Thompson). This study estimated that one incident of sexual violence cost NZ $72, 130, a finding that was close to mine. The community agencies I work with use spreadsheet calculators that I have designed. These calculators, using the most recent available data from a variety of sources, assist them to estimate the costs of sexual violence in their region, city or town as they apply for funding from both government and community agencies. Of course, any costing analysis can be critiqued. It quickly becomes out of date and meaningless, it might inadvertently double count costs, important categories might be overlooked, methodologies and methods differ, and so on. Clearly, the instinctive feelings of participant survivors were justified. The costs of child sexual abuse in New Zealand are substantial, and these costs contribute to gross domestic product (GDP) (Waring *Counting for Nothing: What Men Value and What Women Are Worth*).

CONCLUSION

Project Restore aims to deliver substantive equality to victim-survivors of sexual violence. As a concept substantive equality is intertwined throughout the entire program. Project Restore is not only empowering victim-survivors of sexual violence, but also it is inspiring others elsewhere to replicate the program and achieve similar outcomes. The Stockholm syndrome provides victim-survivors of child sexual abuse a "common sense" explanation for their actions as children and adults. Many have expressed relief that there was actually a theoretical explanation and said that it alleviated the guilt they had been feeling. For some this realization was sufficient to move them forward on their journeys of recovery. Finally, the costing analysis of child sexual abuse contributed to an emerging awareness regarding the economic impacts of child sexual abuse. Agencies traditionally focused on addressing the psychological impacts of child sexual abuse are now developing expertise in using costing analyses as they pursue funding. There can be no doubt that Marilyn Waring's influence has and is having positive outcomes for the sexual violence sector and victim-survivors of sexual violence.

[1]For an in-depth analysis of Project Restore and the processes it provides please refer to Jülich, McGregor et al.; Jülich and Buttle; Jülich, Buttle et al.

WORKS CITED

Barnett, Hilaire. *Sourcebook on Feminist Jurisprudence.* London: Cavendish Publishing Ltd, 1997. Print.

Bender, Leslie. "From Gender Difference to Feminist Solidarity: Using Carol Gilligan and an Ethic of Care in Law." *Source Book on Feminist Jurisprudence.* Ed. Barnett, Hilaire. London: Cavendish Publishing Ltd, 1997. 203-11. Print.

Fineman, Martha Albertson. "Evolving Images of Gender and Equality: A Feminist Journey." *New England Law Review* 43 (2009): 435-58. Print.

Fletcher, George P. *Basic Concepts of Legal Thought.* New York: Oxford University Press, 1996. Print.

Goddard, Chris, and Joe Tucci. "Child Protection and the Need for The Reappraisal of the Social Worker-Client Relationship." *Australian Social Work* 44.2 (1991): 3-10. Print.

Graham, Dee L. R, Edna I Rawlings, and Roberta K Rigsby. *Loving to Survive: Sexual Terror, Men's Violence and Women's Lives.* New York: New York University Press, 1994. Print.

Herman, Judith Lewis. "Complex Ptsd: A Syndrome in Survivors of Prolonged and Repeated Trauma." *Journal of Traumatic Stress* 5.3 (1992): 377-91. Print.

Holtmaat, Riki. "The Power of Legal Concepts: The Development of a Feminist Theory of Law." *International Journal of the Sociology of Law* 17 (1989): 481-502. Print.

Hyman, Batya. "The Economic Consequences of Child Sexual Abuse in Women." PhD. Brandeis University, 1993. Print.

Jülich, Shirley. "Stockholm Syndrome and Child Sexual Abuse." *Journal of Child Sexual Abuse* 14.3 (2005): 107-29. Print.

Jülich, Shirley, and John Buttle. "Beyond Conflict Resolution: Towards a Restorative Practice Process for Sexual Violence." *Te Awatea* 8.1&2

(2010): 21-25. Print.

Jülich, Shirley, John Buttle, Christine Cummins, and Erin Freeborn. *Project Restore: An Exploratory Study of Restorative Justice and Sexual Violence* Auckland: AUT University, 2010. Print.

Jülich, Shirley, Kim McGregor, Dorothy McCarrison, and Kathryn McPhillips. "Yes, There Is Another Way!" *Canterbury Law Review* 17 (2011): 222-28. Print.

MacKinnon, Catherine A. *Toward a Feminist Theory of the State.* Cambridge, Massachusetts: Harvard University Press, 1989. Print.

Mendus, Susan. "Feminism." *The Oxford Companion to Philosophy.* Ed. Honderich, Ted. Oxford: Oxford University Press, 1995. 270-72. Print.

OHCHR. "Convention on the Elimination of All Forms of Discrimination against Women." 2009. November 12 2012. <http://www.un.org/womenwatch/daw/cedaw/>.

Roper, T, and A. Thompson. *Estimating the Costs of Crime in New Zealand in 2003/2004.* Wellington: The Treasury, 2006. Print.

Scales, Ann C. "The Emergence of Feminist Jurisprudence: An Essay." *Lloyd's Introduction to Jurisprudence (6th Ed.).* Ed. Freeman, M.D.A. London: Sweet & Maxwell, 1994. 1048-62. Print.

Scales, Ann C. "Towards a Feminist Jurisprudence." *Indiana Law Journal* 56.3 (1980/81): 375-444. Print.

Snively, Suzanne. *The New Zealand Economic Cost of Family Violence.* Wellington: Family Violence Unit, Department of Social Welfare, 1994. Print.

Summit, Roland. "The Child Sexual Abuse Accommodation Syndrome." *Child Abuse and Neglect* 7 (1983): 177-93. Print.

Turner, James T. "Factors Influencing the Development of the Hostage Identification Syndrome." *Political Psychology* 6.4 (1985): 705-11. Print.

Waring, Marilyn. *Counting for Nothing: What Men Value and What Women Are Worth.* Wellington: Bridget Williams Books, 1989. Print.

Waring, Marilyn. *Three Masquerades.* Auckland: Auckland University Press, 1996. Print.

Zehr, Howard. *Changing Lenses: A New Focus for Crime and Justice.* Scottdale: Herald Press, 1995. Print.

Zehr, Howard. *The Little Book of Restorative Justice.* Intercourse. PA: Good Books, 2002. Print.

8.

A Pacific Way of Counting

TAGALOATELE PEGGY FAIRBAIRN-DUNLOP

INTRODUCTION

MARILYN'S CRITICAL PERSPECTIVE of the value of national accounting frameworks which take no account of the work women do was hugely welcomed by Pacific[1] women who have long argued against trying to classify the many activities carried out in Pacific family based and largely semi-subsistence communities within standard macroeconomic analysis. The publication of *Counting for Nothing* coincided with the beginnings of the regional Pacific women's movement and was a source of inspiration in a decade of pivotal action (1990-2000), which saw CEDAW being ratified by most Pacific governments and Pacific women writing their own Platform for Action for Women for Sustainable Development and thirteen critical areas of concern (SPC).

A number of points about how Marilyn and her writings have influenced Pacific women and concepts of counting and value are explored in this chapter. First, Pacific women learnt to question global models and not to try and fit their lives into the theoretical frameworks developed by others in other places. Second, that they were the authoritative voice on women's experiences—what women value and their vision of the future they want for their children and their children's children—and that was the data which must be counted and used in planning. Third, that women have a responsibility to work for change—not only to be bold and strong in their beliefs but to get to know and use the available processes to transform the existing systems.

This chapter also proposes that an additional step is needed to capture the values which are central to the Pacific worldview. This is supported by two givens. First, that Pacific values and beliefs are not solely motivated by economic (cash) returns but by a consideration for the spiritual, social, cultural and physical—the holistic view. Maintaining harmonious relationships between the creator God, people and the natural environment is the priority, with the spiritual acknowledged in every action. Second, the extended family is the main institution in Pacific communities and the source of identity and social and economic participation. The shared use of resources to ensure the family "good' is at odds with concepts of individual rights and economic growth models. Family is nurtured and reaffirmed in the many community (and now global) exchanges which represent vast networks of mutual recognition, reciprocity and care. Female and male roles are set within these family systems and comprise a division of roles by gender and a complementarity. Women's goods, such as the fine mat and tapa, play a central role in daily exchanges and bring the necessary sacredness to the ceremonials which mark life events, alongside the material goods contributed by males, such as cash and agricultural goods. In sum, production and use behaviours are based on a consideration for cultural values, social relations, politics and religion. What is not so well understood is that in the absence of robust government provisions, the family systems play a critical role in family and community security and development.

This chapter is in three parts. Part 1 reviews how Pacific women's work is being counted and ways women are using this data to argue for their concerns to be included in decision-making. Part 2 presents the views of a group of Pacific women regarding how they have been influenced by Marilyn's ideals and ideas. While these women met Marilyn in different forums, the words they use to describe her are remarkably similar: her gender expertise, her stand on equity and human rights and, her challenge to women to use the systems to affect change. To each, Marilyn has been an incredible role model, if impatient at times with our Pacific ways. In Part 3 two recently introduced strategies aimed at counting cultural ideals and practice are discussed. In the first, culture is framed as part of the global creative economy and in the second, within a well-being model.

COUNTING FOR SOMETHING

The journey to counting women's work has not been easy, given global assumptions of "productive"; the endurance of custom ways, such as resource sharing; the interplay of sacred—secular, as expressed in the Samoan concept of feagaiga (the sacred covenant which marks the brother-sister relationship). In addition are questions of how feelings of spiritual blessing can be counted or, for that matter, the feelings of "rightness" gained in forgoing individual interest to what is perceived to be a greater good, as evidenced in these comments by a woman graduate as she was declining the family request for her to be a matai (chief). She said, "I would rather my brother held the title. For him it is important. I am so proud to see my brother mixing with the other matai. And he is proud to be our matai" (Fairbairn-Dunlop, 89). Adding a further complexity, is that the use of goods in these predominantly semi-subsistence communities is determined by context, time and occasion (e.g. for the use of family, sale or exchange).

Counting women's work has become almost a routine matter, using parameters set in earlier studies. For example, time allocation studies in three Samoan villages (1989) identified three domains of women's work and that women spent almost a third of their time in each. While the three domains aligned with Moser's categories of reproductive, productive and community there were marked differences in the kinds of activities included in each, particularly in the production and community defined domains. For example, in addition to the small amount of waged employment (cash income) the decision was made to include time spent growing food crops and weaving fine mats and handcrafts in the "production" domain because while primarily for family use or exchange, these had cash earning potential. In the "community" domain, a highly significant finding was the amount and the absolutely essential nature of women's contribution. Women's committees were responsible for community education and village health (e.g. potable water, mosquito nets, nutrition and hygiene, food security) and the smooth running of church affairs. Women were also members of the school committees which financed the building and maintenance of schools and the small number of women who held chiefly titles sat on the Village Council of Chiefs, charged with village development, settling disputes and maintaining order and negotiating with national government. Each regarded their contribution as a service and obligation to the wider community, a duty (to God and the village) as necessary to ensuring quality village assets (so maintaining the village status) and also as their recreational time (Fairbairn-

Dunlop). This study confirmed the nature and extent of women's work and its value in reproduction, income generation and in reciprocal exchanges. While the place of the spiritual was not explored, this was affirmed in every interview and meeting.

Today, the counting of women's work had moved from small research studies into mainstream practice. Table 1 indicates how women's contribution was recognised and factored into this regional marine project (usually viewed as male work) from the project outset. The data collected showed that with the exception of Tonga, women in all Pacific Island Countries (PICs) participated in fin-fishing, and that there was a similar pattern of use by gender—women were more likely to use the catch for subsistence (food security) and gifting purposes (reciprocity) while males used the catch for sale and subsistence. In 11 of the 17 PICs women's subsistence use was over 50% with highs of over 80% in six of these.

Data such as this not only provides proof of women's contribution, it also indicates where services should be placed to support and grow this. For example, when data showed the extent of women's engagement in informal sector trading, business and small loans schemes for women were established such as VANWODS in Vanuatu and the Women and Business Foundation in Samoa.

Side by side with the growing recognition of the importance of data and numbers to inform planning, Pacific women began searching more acciduously for relationships between data sets and to use the language planners (and donors) understand. For example, when appeals to the "social" cost of violence against women (VAW) held little sway, an NGO worked out the annual cost of VAW to the Tongan economy to be $18.3 million TOP (Tonga paunga). Costs factored into this estimate included: production related costs (lost wages), consumption related costs, (replacement of damaged household items), second generation costs (counselling services, child protection) administrative, and other costs (legal services, temporary accommodation) and transfer costs (lost taxes, financial support by friends and family). This economic rationale was fiercely debated at the launching meeting, which I attended. Some welcomed the economic focus as strengthening the anti-domestic violence movement. Others regarded this as a "male focused" way of putting things and which took importance away from the social costs of VAW. Still others were vehement that human rights and equity must be the flagship for any VAW strategy (Fairbairn-Dunlop and Lievore). Arguments aside, this rationale was prepared in a way which would resonate with prevailing decision making practice.

Country/Territory	Fisherwomen (%)			Fishermen (%)		
	Gift	Sale	Subsistence	Gift	Sale	Subsistence
Cook Islands	42	9	49	33	22	45
Fiji Islands	4	14	82	9	55	36
French Polynesia	20	22	58	27	45	29
FSM	5	35	60	14	51	35
Kiribati	33	42	25	7	65	28
Nauru	15	6	78	19	12	69
New Caledonia	35	9	56	30	31	40
Niue	17	2	81	27	16	56
Palau	41	22	37	32	44	23
PNG	16	53	31	17	67	16
RMI	0	6	94	10	33	57
Samoa	11	12	77	11	44	45
Solomon Islands	12	6	82	10	37	52
Tonga	0	0	0	14	65	21
Tuvalu	12	0	88	11	27	62
Vanuatu	28	27	45	22	52	26
Wallis and Futuna	38	1	61	19	40	42

Table 1: Objective of finfishing for fisherwomen and fishermen, 2009

Presently, Marilyn is involved in a study on the economics of unpaid work, including the commitment by governments and the international community to the rights of women and children who are most likely to bear the brunt of unpaid care (Waring et al). Given the importance accorded to family and community in Pacific communities which has been described, and the feelings of love, duty and spiritual rightness this engenders, the attribution of a monetary cost to activities in the "caring" category will prove problematic for Pacific women.

Clearly a significant amount of the work women do is "productive" in the definitive sense of the word. At the same time and in spite of the growing data, women's contribution and the issues women hold important still remain invisible in the context of the global focus on commodifying, quantifying and accounting for all economic activities. Views are that little will change unless more women sit at the decision making tables. In trying to find a place at the table, Pacific women have been inspired and influenced by Marilyn to claim their voice.

PACIFIC WOMEN

This section presents the views expressed by seven Pacific women on how working with Marilyn and Marilyn's writings have impacted their thinking. It is organised according to the two inter-related themes which emerged in discussions, of "claiming our Pacific voice" and, using this strength to argue for women and families, in daily life, the workforce and especially for women's political participation. Overarching all, it can be seen that Marilyn's unwavering human rights stance has made these women reflect more on the influence of culture on women's experiences, traditionally and today. Comments made in each section are prefaced by a brief background of the speaker and how they met Marilyn.

CLAIMING OUR PACIFIC VOICE

Phylesha met Marilyn at the Outgames Conference where Marilyn had presented the opening keynote. Phylesha was a member of the Pacific delegation. Phylesha said:

> I was particularly taken by how Marilyn viewed the Lesbian Gay BTI community. She reminded us that utilising this umbrella term could be detrimental to other groups from the

Rainbow family. As a Pacific person hearing this and up until this time only ever identifying with my cultural identity I
found this totally challenging. I was empowered to further
my personal stance by reaffirming the importance and use of
Pacific cultural identity terms very strongly in my keynote. I
found people wanted to know more about our 22 Pacific cultural identity terms. For me, it was also reaffirming to know
that there was someone out there from the western world who
was in tune with the reality of my life and life in general. Her
views were from a place I had not heard of from any sector
I had crossed paths with - yet who make claims to support
my MVP FAFF communities[2]. Marilyn brought light to my
perspective as a Pacific person trying to make a difference for
my people with the work I do. Today, I echo Marilyn's voice
through my own with the hope that my Pacific MVP FAFF
people have the equal opportunity, funds and resources to
work through our own challenges and not survive on the band
wagon of others. If change is to take place, it is the time for the
Pacific to come together.

Both Ruth and Karanina said that working with Marilyn had challenged them to think about who they were, what they stood for and to listen
to the voices of "others" because, "people understand the complexity and
messiness of their everyday lives." Karanina said:

Marilyn is about leadership, courage, and clear messages. I
try to adapt my words, style of communication to max-
imise the chance that I will be understood, and to interpret things with more openness. I learnt that it was important to speak authentically, and not to be intimidated to
mimic/act/speak/be/write in ways that may dilute an important message, be it ours or of those we may be representing.
This practise has been liberating for me and always engages
responses.

Ruth likened Marilyn's mind to a knowledge highway, travelling at speeds
which made the most zealous of drivers hesitant. Ruth said:

As a learner driver, the defining moment for me was the realisation this was my highway. For the longest time, I had attempted to write or emulate the "established academics," who

fed my learning through my undergraduate years. The people they researched, spoke of and influenced public policy on behalf of, were people like my family and the communities I lived and worked in. They, however, were not like my family and nor were their words. Marilyn challenged the position of the voice, more specifically my voice. I learnt that by identifying my position within the research space, I could find freedom of thought and convey this in my writing. However, this came with a catch—to share and open my thinking to others was daunting. I also learnt the art of reciprocity in research and more importantly accountability. After 15 years of working as a social worker, I had seen the dis/connect between policy and practice, and the use of "tick box" processes to demonstrate "change". What I learnt from working with Marilyn, is that people understand the complexity and messiness of their everyday life. It is the folly of change agents to find easy, simple and "understandable" ways to convey these experiences into solutions. I wasn't the easiest of students, my fears of, not having the right voice, not being a valid "Pacific" or "Indian" voice, not being enough…. My highway wasn't a super highway, and there were plenty of off ramps, but Marilyn was always there.

Alice, was local counterpart to Marilyn when Marilyn was Gender Advisor to RAMSI[3] just before the launch of the Solomon Island "Women in Government Strategy" in 2007. Alice said:

Marilyn was effective and forthright in our RAMSI meetings. She could be relied on to support our women and the Women in Government Strategy activities. We learnt that "the government works this way—and if you want to be included…then you must work that way as well." She taught us how to make submissions, worked us through the process and, we made our first submission to a select committee. Then of course, there was the book *Being the First*, which we co-edited. This first book about women in the Solomon Islands records the stories of women who held senior positions in our government. Up until now, this has been absent from the literature. *Being the First* was well received. Both male and female acknowledged our effort in making sure women's contribution to this country was acknowledged. For me? Marilyn helped increase my confidence in the public arena.

Karanina and Mata raised questions about how and whether "caring" could be counted. Mata saw caring and relationships as central to the Pacific worldview and which could not (should not) be valued in financial terms. Mata said:

> It's all about alofa. That's part of being Pacific…that's what we do. Seven of my friends have just given up well paid government jobs to look after their parents…we can afford to pay for homes…but we don't put our loved ones there. That is our love to our parents, our joy, our knowing that we can repay even a little bit of the love and care they showed us. Our duty—as Samoans, and as Christians.

She recalled the many family members, friends and colleagues who had honoured her mother's passing and the exchanges of ie toga (fine mats) which had taken place on the day. She saw these actions as affirming family strength and as seamlessly binding together the past, the present (she and her brothers) to the future generations (their children). Whilst the shared grieving had signified love, respect and recognition of her mother's life, most of all, this had signified "family." Karanina said:

> the concept of unpaid work…by women in different contexts globally was very new to me. I hadn't recognised the economic value of these activities in homes and communities beyond those entities before. I have since utilised this learning to think much wider about what is 'value', 'work', women's contribution, and the need to make visible these contributions in the many strategic roles that I have occupied, and to create opportunities for underrepresented groups in areas that are counted as valuable in society.

RIGHTS AND POLITICAL PARTICIPATION

Fanaura and Roselyn are both experienced women's advocates. Fanaura viewed Women in Politics (WIP) as a direct equity and rights issue. She expressed disappointment that despite the many WIP programmes, "Pacific women's participation is poor!" Roselyn has begun researching the traditional ways to gain evidence which can be used as the platform for re-claiming ni-Vanuatu women's status roles.

Roselyn was formerly the CEO of the Women's Department. She read *Counting for Nothing* in 1991, when she was a student at the Australian National University. Roselyn said:

(At the time) Vanuatu had just celebrated 10 years of inde-pendence. But on looking at the public service staff, there were only three ladies holding any position of authority— I was head of the Government Training Centre, Touriman Haines was Manager of the Department of Health, Vila Cen-tral Hospital and Roslyne Vira was head of the Philatelic Bu-reau. Yet we all (men and women) had fought for indepen-dence. I understood that these were issues of gender equity that wouldn't just go away or readjust themselves but needed to be seriously addressed. So Marilyn's writings made a huge impression on me. On my return home from study I began to study the various cultures of our islands of Vanuatu and the issue of male and female roles. My personal opinion is that the issue of men and women's work needs to be viewed in the con-text of a particular country, or islands. For example, although there may be similarities, there are also vast differences within and between countries that are not often apparent or visible to outsiders. Vanuatu women are not treated as equal with men and, we have human rights people drilling it down our necks about our human rights.

I have found that in most Vanuatu islands there is no word for "rights" per se. What we have relates more to "position or place" in a particular occasion, a place, a ritual, death, birth and so forth for both male and female. Male and female have their own "vale" and duties that cannot be delegated to the other, but also some shared duties. Many of these responsibil-ities and duties were dismantled and relegated by missionar-ies and replaced by something different that elevated only the males but placed women solely in the domestic arena. Cur-rently, through the Kastom Governance Project we are do-ing more research into male female roles in the early days and through the Malvatumauri National Council of Chiefs...we are trying to rebuild some of those broken links.

Fanaura was a resource person with Marilyn in the WIP workshops run by CAPWIP[4] and UNIFEM (now UNWomen) in the 1990s. Fanaura was the first female Cabinet member in the Cook Islands Government. Fanaura said:

> I found Marilyn to be clear and forthright in her messages and pretty inspirational. She said things like: "You (Pacific women) have to be more pushy...for a good reason. Remember— you're not pushing for yourself... you're pushing for women and for gender equity and for better government.... Don't just sit around and talk about it...get it done" and then "Fana! you are too softy. But you are strong. Be more dogmatic...." I don't think she was trying to be domineering or, to make us more aggressive. She was pointing out that Pacific women were so quickly intimidated and we should learn to be more confident in ourselves. She would say things like: "Don't worry about how you stand, how you look...that's nothing. Just be confident! You can stand up in a crowd, you know what you're saying and how to go about it. Don't sit there saying "oh I've said something wrong, or, I shouldn't have done things." Make a mistake?...okay, but move on and go for your best. I know many Pacific women—and males—saw her to be a highly aggressive person, perhaps a know-all? Some said she should be more respectful, particularly to men. But you know, the same used to happen to me. When I worked in some places I know many women didn't like the things I was saying. They would say "Fana...that's not our culture." I can even remember a PM and some of the leaders in some countries saying to me "don't you come here and tell us what to do!"

Fanaura then asked "Did we make a difference?" Fanaura said:

> I've thought back a lot to those regional WIP meetings. Did we make a difference? Mostly the women attending these training were those who held high posts—because of their husbands. The rationale seemed to be that as wives, these women would influence the women of their families and villages...we should have been targeting village women and

young women who were not there to consolidate their own positions! The 1980s and 1990s were definitely the heady years of the Pacific women's movement. We did so much. Since then, traditional cultural perceptions of women's place seem to have become even more entrenched. I can't understand why…it may be that the church has become one of the most vicious in preventing women from being equal. On the other hand, our own women don't give the same support to a woman as they would to a male. Our women should focus on the message of equality and equity to our young ones today— male and female. Given the IT possibilities it should be much easier for women to encourage and reach out to each other.

A PACIFIC WAY OF COUNTING—COUNTING "CULTURE"

Marilyn has been a major role model and mentor as Pacific women have learnt to argue the value of the work they do and that these activities and issues be taken account of in national planning. The increased international recognition of "culture" and how culture can/ should be captured and incorporated into planning is seen in two recent interventions, which feature quite different perspectives. In the first, culture is classified as part of the "creative economy" and a key driver to economic social and sustainable development (UNCTAD). In the *Pacific Regional Cultural Policy and Strategic Plan* (2012) culture is incorporated into development thinking as institution, product and creative flexible resource. The focus on production for sale which underpins this model will: increase women's work (the major producers) and by lessening the time women have to contribute to family and community activities will weaken the traditional support systems so increasing women's (and family) vulnerability. In addition, the reliance on market forces renders this focus both unpredictable and unsustainable. Finally, the sacredness and family/community affirming values embedded in the production and use of cultural goods has no place in this commodification scenario.

In the second intervention, the *Alternative Indicators of Well-being for Melanesia* (VNSO), culture is framed within a well-being paradigm. The foreword to this ground breaking research notes the well-being approach fits the UN General Assembly Resolution 65/309 of "Happiness: towards a holistic approach to development" and states that this inclusive, equitable and balanced approach will promote sustainability, eradicate poverty and enhance well-being and happiness (VNSO). The three domains of wellbeing which set the basis for these indicators were: resource access (factors such as access to customary land), cultural practice (traditional knowledge, planting calendars, family history and wealth systems) and community vitality (knowing why community is important, trust and leadership, a chief's ability to settle disputes and manage community assets). These three domains were decided in national discussions on subjective well being. Almost half of the over 800 research participants were female. While this well-being paradigm goes some way to capturing the manifestations of Pacific culture, more research is needed to identity the values underpinning these documented actions and behaviours.

CONCLUSION

To conclude, Pacific women have learnt much from Marilyn. First, to stand tall and claim women's voice and to collect data to prove women's contribution to family community and nation. Challenging the prevailing concepts of work and value will be an ongoing factor here as will the influence of culture, place and changing contexts on women's experiences. Second, to use this data to make women's contribution visible—at family community, national and global level. Third, that there is likely to be little change until more Pacific women are sitting at more decision-making tables.

AUTHOR'S NOTES

Faafetai lava to contributors for being bold in sharing:

Phylesha Acton-Brown met Marilyn at the Outgames Conference run by the Human Rights Commission and Organised by the Lesbian Gay Bi-Sexual Transgender and Inter-sex community (LIBSIS).

Ruth Choudhary is of Cook Island—Indian ethnicity. She has extensive experience in the social services and after completing her M Phil at AUT, Ruth returned to work in that sector.

Fanaura Kingstone was the first woman Cabinet Minister in the Cook Islands Government and former teacher. As ESCAP Social Officer, Fanaura pioneered WIP and also disabilities education.

Mata is Samoan. She wanted to be known as "just Mata."

Dr. Alice Aruhe'eta Pollard is from the Solomon Islands and was local counterpart to Marilyn in the Regional Assistance Mission to Solomon Islands (RAMSI). She has a PhD in Education (VUW).

Karanina Sumeo is studying for her PhD at Auckland University of Technology. Karanina has extensive experience in social services and education especially but not only with Pacific peoples. She is Samoan.

Roselyn Tor is former CEO of the Vanuatu Women's Department and is now secretary to the Malvatumauri Council of Chiefs. She played a lead role in the preparation of the Pacific Platform of Action for Women (1996) and was a member of the Pacific delegation to the Beijing Women's Conference.

[1] The generic term Pacific is used in this paper. However, the Pacific comprises over 22 small nation states each with their own culture, language and history.

[2] MVP FAFF communities is the term framed by Phylesha to capture conceptual understandings of 'gay' in Pacific languages The acronym stands for: Mahu (Tahiti and Hawaii) Vaka sa lewa lewa (Fiji) Palopa (Papua New Guinea) Fa'afafine (Samoa and American Samoa) Akava'ine (Cook Islands) Fakaleiti/Leiti (Tonga) Fiafifine (Niue).

[3] RAMSI is the Regional Assistance Mission to Solomon Islands, a partnership between the people and Government of Solomon Islands and fifteen countries.

[4] The Centre for Asia-Pacific Women and Politics. This is based in Bangkok.

WORKS CITED

Fairbairn-Dunlop, Peggy. *E au le inailau a tamaitai: Women Education and Development Western Samoa.* Unpublished PhD thesis. Sydney: Macquarie University, 1991. Print.

Fairbairn-Dunlop, Peggy & Denise Lievore. *Tonga Report.* Pacific Police Domestic Violence Programme. Wellington: NZ Police, 2007. Print.

Moser Carol. *Gender Planning and Development: Theory, Practice, and Training.* London: Routledge, 1993. Print.

Pollard Aruhe'eta Pollard & Marilyn Waring. *Being the First.* Storis Blong Oloketa Mere Lo Solomon Aelan. RAMSI, Honiara, Institute of Public Policy and Pacific Media Centre, AUT. Auckland: 2009. Print.

South Pacific Commission (SPC). Pacific Platform for Action for Women for Sustainable Development, Pacific Women's Bureau. Noumea: SPC, 1996. Print.

Secretariat of the Pacific Community PROC *Fish Programme, Pacific Regional Oceanic and Coastal Fisheries Programme.* Noumea: SPC, 2009. Print.

Secretariat of the Pacific *A Pacific Toolkit,* Noumea: SPC, 2012. Print.

United Nations Conference on Trade and Development (UNCTAD). *Creative Economy Report* UNCTAD / DITC / 2008/2. Print.

UN General Assembly Resolution 65/309 . Web, 30 Aug 2013.

Vanuatu National Statistics Office (VNSO). *Alternative Indicators of Wellbeing for Melanesia,* Vanuatu Pilot Study Report. Vanuatu: Malvatumauri National Council of Chiefs, 2012. Print.

Waring, Marilyn. *Counting for Nothing: What Men Value and What Women are Worth.* Macmillan, Allen & Unwin. 1988. Print.

Waring M, R Carr, A Mukherjee & M Shivdos. *Who Cares? The Economics of Dignity.* London: Commonwealth Secretariat, 2012 . Print.

9.

Narrative Trumps Numbers

Marilyn Waring in the World

ROD DOBELL, WITH JODIE WALSH

The author (Dobell) wishes to recognize directly the invaluable comments and assistance of Jodie Walsh throughout the preparation of this paper.

INTRODUCTION

IN A 2011 VISIT to the University of Victoria, Canada, Marilyn Waring noted substantial progress in the measurement of economic activity and social well-being since her own early work on that subject. But, in retrospect, she questioned the wisdom of her related attempts to promote monetary estimates of the value of intangible social or environmental amenities and similar services or resources routinely ignored at the time in economic calculations and reports. She expressed concern that this is the path to the individualized and commodified free market society to which Margaret Thatcher famously argued that There Is No Alternative (TINA).

In this paper we take Waring to be arguing TIARA: There Is A Robust Alternative. In the search for that alternative, we note some current thinking about wrong turns many years ago, two fundamental errors steering us away from the better path not taken. That path leads us away from calculation and back to conversation, where narrative must trump numbers, deliberation and reason must set calculation in context, value must displace price, and there is no substitute for the stories of the folks in place. We conclude with brief speculation that perhaps the emergence of the social web makes pursuit of this goal possible in ways that previously could not have been considered.

PROGRESS IN MEASURING AND REPORTING SOCIAL PERFORMANCE

The original emphasis on the pursuit of human wellbeing as the purpose of economics slipped by the middle of the 20th century into a concern with growth in aggregate indicators of economic activity. By the end of the century, it seemed that an everlasting expansion of the monetary value of paper claims had become the overwhelming obsession for many people and in much public policy. Through the last quarter-century, however, growing misgivings led also to a wide range of critiques of this economistic fundamentalism as represented by the uses to which the ubiquitous UN System of National Accounts (SNA) was being put in guiding public policy.

Proposals for more comprehensive indices of economic wellbeing, appeal to broader measures of human development taking into account human and social capital, creation of the Genuine Progress Indicator taking into account natural capital, and similar initiatives, all gained increasing support among academics and civil society organizations. (The risks inherent in using words like "capital" in this context have been widely discussed, and are noted later in this paper. Here the intention is simply to capture in shorthand language the notion of diverse capacities or systems, tangible or intangible, that can be built up or run down and that can yield flows of services or benefits of value to humans or other species.) The critiques of the SNA became well-known, and the perverse consequences of its misinterpretation as offering social indicators much better understood.

Waring was a leader in this work, with her 1988 book *If Women Counted: A New Feminist Economics* bringing to public attention deep concerns that previously had been confined to arcane technical discussion.

Twenty-five years on, we have powerful support for these ideas. Beginning in 2008, renowned economists Joseph Stiglitz and Amartya Sen collaborated with Jean Paul Fitoussi, another leading development economist, on the Sarkozy Commission, established by Nicholas Sarkozy, then President of France. In 2009, the Commission released its report, *On the Measurement of Economic Performance and Social Progress*. The Report placed emphasis on indicators offering a better understanding of wellbeing and inequalities, with reduced emphasis on aggregate data masking the realities of people's situations. In 2010 it was translated into a book for a general audience, under the illuminating title, *Mis-measuring Our Lives.*

Much current work attempts to pursue this approach of improving the traditional GDP measure. Examples include the 2011 "Beyond GDP" Initiative that grew out of a 2007 high level conference involving the European Commission, European Parliament, Club of Rome, Organization for Economic Cooperation and Development (OECD) and World Wildlife Fund (WWF). This initiative is directed toward "developing indicators that are as clear and appealing as GDP, but more inclusive of environmental and social aspects of progress" (About Beyond GDP, para 1). Its website serves as a clearinghouse for work on many illustrative indicators.

Considerations of subjective well-being (happiness) entered public discourse in the early 1970s. In 1972, the King of Bhutan, upon taking the throne, declared his objective was to increase GNH, "gross national happiness," not GDP (Dickinson, para. 6). The first *World Happiness Report*, prepared for an April 2012 UN Conference (proposed by Bhutan), has now been released by the Earth Institute (Helliwell et al).

The literature critical of any of these aggregate measures is growing rapidly. The problems of course lie not in failures of the metrics in the purposes for which they were constructed, but rather in the goal displacement effects that arise from the decision ("in the absence of anything better") to use those metrics for purposes for which they were never designed or intended. Any translation of all this thinking into effective political support for the use of different metrics and subsequently the pursuit of different policies seems still to be lacking, however.

PROGRESS IN IMPUTATION OF MONETARY VALUES: ON TO FREE MARKET ENVIRONMENTALISM

One response to challenges to aggregate metrics has been to forego the convenience of a single aggregate indicator of progress or well-being and confront a quiver of different indicators coming closer to representing the significance of diverse services or resources. We all recognize the difficulty of representing incommensurable aspects of human welfare or ecological integrity. Yet, for many decisions in our existing market-based world, we have to weigh one against the other. We need to make things somehow commensurate in order to make inescapable trade-offs in the allocation of scarce resources.

The argument is summarized, for example, in Nancy Olewiler's 2012 report "Smart Environmental Policy with Full-Cost Pricing," which recommends full-cost pricing as an important approach to ensuring that ecosystem goods and services, and other intangible amenities, not be valued implicitly at zero and ignored altogether in the calculus of trading and resource allocation. Though the goal is obviously admirable, technically this task is very hard indeed, and inevitably quite subjective. Nevertheless, it is argued, some number is better than no number, though that claim remains hotly disputed.

There is a closely related question to be considered, namely the use of such market-like prices and economic instruments as information essential for permitting coordinated decentralized decisions on access to or allocation of resources, including those yielding ecosystem services, and ultimately determining claims of ownership or title to the returns from such assets or control over their disposition.

One entrenched approach to this problem of social organization is to assign property rights over all things—especially natural capital and corresponding ecological services—and thus create otherwise missing markets that will generate and be guided by otherwise absent price signals. Background available at the new Property and Environment Research Centre (PERC) website, among many others, illustrates the arguments of those dedicated to this cause of free market environmentalism (FME).

Thus, proceeding down this path, we might claim progress toward better aggregate metrics, progress toward sound imputation of economic values to social and environmental flows, and rapid progress in clarifying and extending private property rights. So we could argue for a triumph of Free Market Environmentalism in fully integrating social and environmental concerns into economic decisions.

But then we encounter some serious second thoughts. The depth and extent of the protracted (unresolvable?) debate calling this approach into question is well summarized in an excellent recent review, "Ecosystem Services: Tensions, Impurities, and Points of Engagement within Neoliberalism," by Jessica Dempsey and Morgan M. Robertson.

THE CHALLENGE: A FAILURE OF FRAMING

With the current global financial crisis it becomes increasingly obvious that some different societal mechanisms for allocation of access to services of global ecosystem resources are essential. Many would argue that speculative trade in paper title setting out claims of ownership to privatized portions of global ecosystems that form part of a common heritage of humankind, is not just unethical, but risks accelerating economic and social instability.

In the absence of such trade, however, we need to bring in something like the concept of strong sustainability as an alternative to tradeoffs based on monetary valuation. Proponents of this concept argue that some forms of natural capital or ecosystem services cannot be replaced. The economist's notion that one form of capital can be substituted for another may not apply to some features of ecosystems or ecosystem services on which we all depend. No amount of investment in physical or human capital, it is argued, can make up for loss of the ozone layer or compromise of the water cycle. In this case, there is no need to estimate any monetary values or equivalents: if the heirlooms are not to be traded, there is no need to ask their price. A case for this strong sustainability approach is set out in the New Zealand report, "Strong Sustainability for New Zealand: Principles and Scenarios."

Waring in her talk raised the more fundamental concern, "the rampant growth in the colonizing power of economics, a sort of contagious illusion that everything can be reduced to a price" (Waring "Is There Some Way" 3). If the value of social or ecological services or networks is successfully captured in monetary terms, reflecting utilitarian exchange value, will they then be seen only as commodities, failing to reflect values associated with the interests of future generations, other species, even those in other places or other classes? She questioned whether her own earlier strategy of promoting work on imputation of monetary values to such ecosystems services was not seriously misguided, the beginning of a slippery slope to commodification of unpriced ecological and cultural resources and ultimately to privatization of what should be recognized as a common heritage of humankind. In the context of existing distributions of income, wealth, political power and social influence, should attaching imputed (and disputed) market values to such resources as pure water or marine ecosystems not be seen as simply unethical?

With the growing recognition of the profoundly uncertain and possibly chaotic character of the complex social-ecological systems of which humanity is a part, we need to turn this FME vision inside out: rather than integrating environmental concerns within economic decisions, we need to set our view of economic mechanisms and institutions as social contrivances within their social context, and that in turn within the biosphere that sustains us all. Dobell's 1995 paper, "Environmental Degradation and the Religion of the Market" provides an early sketch of this idea.

Evidently we can and should use economic systems for social purposes. Markets and economic instruments offer the most effective signalling device and decentralization machinery imaginable—but without guidance they do not automatically pursue goals such as equality, social justice and community resilience that cannot be captured within the calculations of FME. We must be sure we have the overarching social controls and public regulation in place. Dobell develops this argument further in a 1996 chapter, "The Dance of the Deficit: Economic Management for Social Purpose."

The first step toward identifying an alternative approach might be to suggest that in the construction and evolution of economic institutions, humanity has made two fundamental errors. One is the creation of the corporate person, a legal fiction now endowed with almost all the fundamental rights of the person, but without moral responsibility (indeed with an over-riding fiduciary responsibility to an exclusive group of owners) and with only limited legal liability, in a unique position to take advantage of the second error.

The second error is the creation and now almost universal spread of a notion of property rights that defends the enclosure and privatization of the Earth itself—the resources and ecosystems that are the common heritage of humankind. From this error emerges the problem that paper claims to natural capital become the object of chaotic speculative trading that excludes the initial owners and fails to recognize the realities of the ecological systems within which all human activity is embedded. From the first comes the problem that the corporate persons that have become the major players, exercising overwhelming financial and political (and military) power, cannot effectively participate as moral persons in any alternative discourse around the community's management of rights of access to the adjacent resources and ecosystems within which they live.

MAYBE NARRATIVE CAN TRUMP NUMBERS?

The two errors just identified are rather fundamental—is there any hope they can be undone, that we can accomplish the figure-ground reversal that recognizes our economic institutions not as defining and dictating our world, but simply as social constructions within the overarching biosphere that gives us life? Given the degree to which present practices are entrenched in current institutional structures, and defended to the extreme by current power, is there any reason to believe that there could be any alternative? There is no space here to do more than note a few arguments that may suggest hope. It is not impossible to imagine action to regain some of the human rights and agency lost in the wake of the two errors mentioned. We do see growing reaction against privatization and enclosure of the common land, and increasing resistance to corporate action that compromises ecological integrity.

Any alternative to the FME approach must be careful about language. We can go back to the argument for sustainability, but cast more strongly now in terms of stories rather than calculations. In those constructions, we have to be aware that language can play a forceful role in excluding other perspectives:

> If you are not talking their language, if you are not talking their jargon, you are not part of the argument. There must be something wrong with you. You are not sensible or intelligent about your approach to this thing. So, the power of economics mirrors, to a certain extent, the political power rampant anywhere else. You operate with language as well as operating with mathematics. (*Who's Counting?* 79:20)

But, "Language is a tool available to all of us." (*Who's Counting?* 86:22). And in contesting the overarching hegemony of economistic fundamentalism, Canada's activist scholar Ursula Franklin reminds us, in *The Ursula Franklin Reader*, that people under occupation have refused to speak the language of the occupier. She advises that we too should avoid "the language of the market," which speaks of "service providers" and "clients," of "stakeholders" and of "the bottom line" and "customers" of the government rather than "citizens." Franklin notes that for us these individuals are our teachers and students, our friends, families and communities, not targets for commerce (125). When we allow the community conversation around forests and streams to be couched solely in terms of timber, fibre and return on investment, we have already lost the struggle.

We take from Waring the counsel that when it comes to the things that matter, narrative trumps numbers, cooperation outperforms competition, and the search for context is crucial. Margaret Visser, in her 2002 Massey Lectures, *Beyond Fate*, similarly urges attention to language and to context. (Iain McGilchrist's massive 2009 work, *The Master and His Emissary*, grounds that search for context in a fascinating link to fundamental brain function.)

With those reminders about language and context, we can look to some fragments that suggest the possibility of a robust alternative, despite the overwhelming power arrayed against any such effort. Possibilities are being clarified in many recent writings and developments contesting the primacy of rights of corporations and advancing the rights of current and future generations by promoting the inherent rights of Nature (as against corporate rights to Nature). Consider a few illustrative examples.

With effective nested institutions of the sort urged by Elinor Ostrom in her *Nobel Prize Lecture,* social consensus might be built on the pursuit of strong sustainability and on community norms or formal zoning governing access to those ecological resources and ecosystems. The power to allocate access to harvesting or withdrawal rights among competing purposes would rest with the community. Water rights, air rights, rights of way would all revert to that public owner when the rights of access or use are surrendered by those who currently hold them. Socially regulated creation of community quota for purposes of sustainable harvesting of renewable resources could be one component.

The extensive research program of Mathias Risse provides a strong philosophical rationale for such an approach (see, for example, "Original Ownership of the Earth: A Contemporary Approach"). That research program, and earlier reasoning of Henry George, who advocated ownership of land as common property with a public claim to the surplus arising from its rising scarcity value (George, *Progress* VI.II.3), provide a foundation for more comprehensive social regulation to constrain privatization of the common heritage of humankind.

In this spirit, we can also see the possibilities for a public trust doctrine that imposes on legislatures an obligation to stand against the claims of corporations when the interests of the public in ecological integrity seem threatened. One approach to such a public trust doctrine is outlined by Jackson et al. in the April 2012 issue of the *Journal of Environmental Law and Practice.*

The issue of civil and political rights of corporations more generally is illustrated by the Program on Corporations, Law and Democracy (POCLAD) in the United States. There seems to be growing attention paid to the perverse consequences of entrenched traditions of corporate rights flowing almost by accident from judicial observations from long ago; one important suggestion flowing from the POCLAD work is the need to reclaim the right to issue (or revoke) corporate charters to ensure that corporations are formed and function to serve some public interest.

With increasing support for the idea that corporations need what has been termed a "social license to operate" comes also the possibility that such a social license entails reciprocal obligations, and will be offered only with a contractual commitment to give up privileges such as corporate privacy rights in order to ensure full disclosure of information relevant to the community—for example, information on the chemical content of fluids used in "fracking" processes to produce natural gas.

The recent book by Anna Grear, *Redirecting Human Rights: Facing the Challenges of Corporate Legal Humanity*, addresses the crucial distinction between living human beings and disembodied legal subjects (corporations), and the need to privilege the former in human rights discourse. Pursuing a different path, a number of fragments suggest increasing attention to what might be considered the rights of Nature (as distinct from private rights to Nature). Examples include the April 2010 Cochabamba Universal Declaration of the Rights of Mother Earth (Proposal), recognized (in somewhat lukewarm fashion) in paragraph 39 of the document, *The Future We Want*, emerging from the 2012 UN Conference on Sustainable Development (Rio+20).

Anna Grear's later edited volume, *Should Trees Have Standing?: 40 Years On*, offers an academic update on the heels of Christopher Stone's own influential book, *Should Trees Have Standing?: Law, Morality and the Environment.* Action in line with the argument there can perhaps be seen in New Zealand, where a framework agreement signed in August 2012 between the Crown and the Whanganui River iwi (the local Māori people), provides that the river will be recognized as a person when it comes to the law, with guardians appointed to speak for it (Shuttleworth). Related developments in constitutional law or local action are described by Linda Sheehan at the website of the Earth Law Institute (www.earthlaw.org).

Of course, the idea of moving into the hands of the lawyers to drive a fundamentally new legal structure forward, in order to escape the clutches of the economist, may be seen as rather ambitious, if not foolish. Lee Godden, in an extensive review of the book *The Principle of Sustainability: Transforming Law and Governance*, by Klaus Bosselmann, captures this concern: "While the transcendental function of law should not be ignored, it is a large contention to construe sustainability as the foundation for reconstituting the liberal legal paradigms that currently govern a growth-oriented political economy and nation-state autonomy." (Godden 808). Perhaps there is hope to enlist both tribes of experts, however, along with other technical expertise in a broader initiative in which the web-enabled world supports co-creation of formal knowledge together with appeal to the "wisdom of crowds" in hybrid deliberative spaces (Dobell et al).

Thus we might deploy economic instruments and exploit economic institutions within a social frame that sees common resources used to serve social purposes, within an ethical frame that reflects the rights of those in other places and other times. We can have social regulation driven by ethical commitments, and still deploy all the magic of market mechanisms for purposes of efficient decentralization of resource allocation decisions and as a vehicle for effective realization of personal as well as societal goals. But this middle way hinges crucially on our ability to take back democratic control of political institutions, and to move away from a setting in which financial power dictates the composition and conclusions of those institutions.

So we can argue that there is indeed a robust alternative. It lies with the world of cooperative action and civil society institutionally, within a conceptual frame recognizing ecological integrity as the prerequisite to sustainability. The sustained reflections of James Tully (see, for a recent example, "A Dilemma of Democratic Citizenship",) outline more fully a possible path and perhaps reasons for hope. And perhaps, as just noted, one can see promise of tapping into the wisdom of crowds for governance reform through web-enabled platforms supporting deliberative democracy.

CONCLUSION: TIARA

We began with the argument that the global information apparatus built on the UN System of National Accounts represents a technical triumph, but is widely misunderstood and grossly misused as a measure of social performance or as a foundation for collective decisions. It is crucial that we see life more expansively, with attention to the people, communities and biosphere around us.

In the absence of actual market transactions signalling the value of these other features of life, we could imagine transactions in them, and impute corresponding prices as monetary values to ensure that these fundamental aspects of real life are not completely ignored in social reporting and decisions. But doing so creates two risks: first, using those imputed values leads to social decisions completely dominated by divisions of dollars; and, second, but worse, the argument becomes one for free market environmentalism urging the creation of private property rights to anything of value, privatizing what has been held in common (and should be held in trust), in order to create formal markets from which will flow observed, not imputed, prices on the basis of which all can be traded. Margaret Thatcher argued TINA: There Is No Alternative.

We have argued TIARA: There Is A Robust Alternative. But it entails that we change the discourse altogether, looking to narrative more than
numbers, watching our language carefully, restoring the relevance and persuasive power of the visual, the personal, the community stories, in shaping
the perceptions that go into community decisions around access to and use
of community resources, and especially into the integrity of community
norms, social capital and surrounding ecosystems on which all depends.

Such a transformation in narrative and discourse demands that we
move away from a society centered on paper claims to private ownership
of common resources. We must come to see it as a fundamental mistake to
transfer such ownership claims to a legal fiction, the corporation that has
become the overwhelmingly powerful political and social actor. These artificial persons offer no more moral responsibility than the decontextualized
machines and algorithms to which they (we) increasingly delegate responsibility for filtering content from chaos and signal from noise in the tor-
rents of text and firehoses of data that increasingly intrude on all attempts
to build a shared and reasoned foundation for social decisions. We have to
reject the temptation to duck all responsibility by throwing it all back on the
impersonal and inexorable "wisdom of the market," and instead must recognize the wisdom flowing from the lived experience of the more inclusive
crowd as more crucial. We need not—must not—subordinate our judgement, agency and moral compass to allegedly irresistible market forces.

Knowing we are facing an inescapable sustainability imperative, riding
what Ronald Wright, in the closing pages from his 2004 Massey Lectures,
An Illustrated Short History of Progress, characterized as a suicide machine
that must change direction, we have a choice.

We can follow an economic route to a globally consistent system relying
on full cost pricing, free market environmentalism and rational calculation
to generate a full system of impersonal price signals on which decentralized
decisions reflecting immediate self-interest can responsibly be based.

Or we can change the current discourse and move toward reliance on
contextualization, visualization and narrative within inclusive nested institutions to provide a foundation for deliberation and judgement leading to
responsible decisions at local scale based on norms of cooperation and con-
tinuity, recognizing inherent rights of Nature along with fundamental human rights, including rights to a healthy environment.

This paper stems from challenges posed by Marilyn Waring. It seems
unlikely that her work could have highlighted this search for context as it
has, had she been simply a gifted undergraduate going on to some demand-

ing scholarly discipline. Her grounding in the soil, on the farm with the goats, her embedding within neighbouring traditions (of teaching as well as governance), and experience of place, along with her extended field trip into formal parliamentary government, all had to go into the making of a teacher able to look with fresh eyes at entrenched conventional institutions. In doing so, she challenges us all to challenge them in order to do better ourselves.

WORKS CITED

"About Beyond GDP." European Commission, DG Environment and DG Eurostat, together with the Beyond GDP Partners. Web. May 31, 2012.

Dempsey, Jessica, and Morgan M. Robertson. "Ecosystem Services: Tensions, Impurities, and Points of Engagement within Neoliberalism." *Progress in Human Geography* (2012): 1-22. Web. October 31, 2012.

Dickinson, Elizabeth. "GDP: A Brief History." *FP: Foreign Policy.* January/February, 2011: April 30, 2012. Web. June 25, 2012.

Dobell, Rod. "The Dance of the Deficit and the Real World of Wealth: Rethinking Economic Management for Social Purpose." *Family Security in Insecure Times.* Ed. Heather Ebbs. II and III Vol. Ottawa, ON: Canadian Council on Social Development, Publications, 1996. 197-226. Print.

—. "Environmental Degradation and the Religion of the Market." *Population, Consumption, and the Environment : Religious and Secular Responses.* Ed. Harold G. Coward. Albany, NY: State University of New York Press, 1995. 229-250. Print.

Dobell, Rod, Michele-Lee Moore, and Martin Taylor. *Social Innovation and Civil Society: Might the Wisdom of the Crowd Improve the Metrics of the HERD?* Print.

Franklin, Ursula M. *The Ursula Franklin Reader: Pacifism as a Map.* Toronto: Between the Lines, 2006. Print.

"The Future We Want." *Rio+20.* June 20-22, 2012, Rio de Janeiro, Brazil. Web. October 31, 2012.

George, Henry. *Progress and Poverty.* Library of Economics and Liberty, 1912. Web. May 31, 2012.

Godden, Lee. "The Principle of Sustainability: Transforming Law and Governance." *Osgoode Hall Law Journal* 47 (2009): 807. Print.

Grear, Anna. *Redirecting Human Rights: Facing the Challenge of Corporate*

Legal Humanity. Palgrave Macmillan (2010). Print.

—. (Ed) *Should Trees Have Standing? 40 Years On* Edward Elgar, (2012). Print.

Helliwell, John, Richard Layard, and Jeffrey Sachs eds. *World Happiness Report.* The Earth Institute: Columbia University, 2012. Web. April 30, 2012.

Jackson, S., O.M. Brandes, and R. Christensen, 2012. "Lessons from an Ancient Concept: How the Public Trust Doctrine Will Meet Obligations to Protect the Environment and the Public Interest in Canadian Water Management and Governance in the 21st Century." *Journal of Environmental Law and Practice* 23(2), 175–199.

McGilchrist, Iain. *The Master and His Emissary: The Divided Brain and the Making of the Western World.* New Haven: Yale University Press, 2009. Print.

Olewiler, Nancy. "Smart Environmental Policy with Full-Cost Pricing." *SPP Research* 12.6 (2012) Web. May 3, 2012.

Ostrom, Elinor. "Prize Lecture: Beyond Markets and States: Polycentric Governance of Complex Economic Systems". Web. June 19, 2012.

PERC: Property and Environment Research Center. 2012.Web. October 31, 2012.

"Proposal Universal Declaration of the Rights of Mother Earth." *World People's Conference on Climate Change and the Rights of Mother Earth.* April 24, 2010. Web. October 31, 2012.

Risse, Mathias. "Original Ownership of the Earth: A Contemporary Approach." *HKS Faculty Research Working Paper series* RWP08-073 (2008) Print.

Sheehan, Linda. *Earth Law Centre.* 2012. Web. November 11, 2012.

Shuttleworth, Kate. "Agreement Entitles Whanganui River to Legal Entity." *New Zealand Herald* 2012. Web. October 31, 2012.

Stiglitz, Joseph E., Amartya Sen, and Jean-Paul Fitoussi. *Mismeasuring our Lives: Why GDP Doesn't Add Up.* New Press, 2010. Print.

—. *Report by the Commission on the Measurement of Economic Performance and Social Progress.*, 2009. Web. March 31, 2012.

Stone, Christopher D. *Should Trees Have Standing?: Law, Morality, and the Environment.* Oxford University Press, 2010. Print.

Sustainable aotearoa New Zealand incorporated (SaNZ). *Strong Sustain-*

ability for New Zealand: Principles and Scenarios. New Zealand: Nakedize, 2009. Web. June 19, 2012.

Tully, James. *A Dilemma of Democratic Citizenship. The Changing Face of Citizen Action Conference.* May 8, 2010, University of Victoria. 2010. Print.

Visser, Margaret. *Beyond Fate.* Toronto, ON: House of Anansi Press, 2002. Print.

Waring, Marilyn. *Counting for Nothing: What Men Value and What Women Are Worth.* 2nd ed. Toronto: University of Toronto Press, 1999. Print.

—. *If Women Counted: A New Feminist Economics.* San Francisco: Harper & Row, 1988. Print.

—. "Is There Some Way Out of Here? What's Next for Meaningful Environmental Goals?" *Centre for Co-operative and Community-Based Economy Distinguished Speaker Series: What Does Progress Mean for our Society and Communities?* April 4, 2011, University of Victoria. Print.

Who's Counting? Marilyn Waring on Sex, Lies and Global Economics. Dir. Terre Nash. 1995. National Film Board of Canada,. Web. June 12, 2012.

Wright, Ronald. *An Illustrated Short History of Progress.* Toronto: House of Anansi Press, 2006. Print.

10.

If Mothers Counted

Status Symbols for the Invisible Art of Mothering

HADARA SCHEFLAN KATZAV & SHIRA RICHTER

INTRODUCTION

IN TODAY'S ISRAEL, a democratic, western, capitalistic, family-oriented and militaristic society, there are several groups which are transparent from an economic point of view. This study focuses on one of the largest unacknowledged "non-profit organizations": mothers [1]. We offer a critical reading of the economic status of a mother's work in Israel, adopting Marilyn Waring's view of the value system of western capitalism according to which every item and activity exists solely through its monetary value.

One result of our joint research was the exhibition *Invisible Invaluables* (Tel Aviv Artist's House, March-April 2011; artist: Shira Richter; curator: Hadara Scheflan Katzav; assistant curator: Orly Roman), which transforms Waring's work into the language of art. The concept of "value" and its idiosyncratic construct in Israel is at the heart of this exhibition. We illustrate how it is loaded with double meaning and inner paradox. The Hebrew title of the exhibition, "Treasures of Status," reflects the ironic situation in which mothers have no economic status yet have significant symbolic status. Through visually enticing artistic language, illuminated photographs and the special design of the exhibition space, the exhibition conveys the tension between the sacred and invaluable status of motherhood in Israel on one hand, and its non-existent economic value on the other.

Throughout the world the Israeli woman is admired and respected. She is perceived as strong and independent, equal to men in shouldering the burden and in contributing to her country in social, political and military issues. Born of the womb of socialist Zionism, Israeli women too have been convinced they are counted (Friedman). However, there is a severe gap between ideology and reality. This gap is central to our research, and is found at the heart of every subject addressed in this paper.

The family, particularly the sanctity of motherhood, is a central value for broad sectors of Israeli society (Izraeli). The ideology of motherhood stems, in part, from the unique experiment of connecting Jewish law with a democratic state. This is well demonstrated in legislation regarding family issues, which is under religious law for all faiths. Due to this religious monopoly over marriage and divorce, Israeli society is imbued with the view that a woman's status and role is different from a man's (Raday).

One interesting implication of this connection between state and religion regarding the concept of "value" is the possessory attitude to the Jewish wife. Property relations in the family begin with the Hebrew meaning of the word "husband" ("Ba'al")—possessor. The marriage ceremony opens with an act of commerce: the husband signs the Jewish marriage contract ("ktuba") through which he purchases his wife for a specified sum of money. This refusal to see a woman as a subject in her own right is the basis of the perception of mothers as a commodity, or as the object of family needs.

It is well known that the best way to make a woman forget her inequality is to glorify her (unpaid) maternal roles. Judaism has perfected this method, even placing the injunction to "Be fruitful, and multiply" (*Sinai Publishing Jewish Bible*, Genesis 1.28) as the first commandment written in the Bible. Though this commandment is required only of the man (Mishnah, Tractate Yevamot 6:6) it is the Jewish woman who is designated to fulfill the sacred mission.

The Book of Proverbs describes the ideal wife as "eshet hayel" ("virtuous woman"), modest, pious, and the one who preserves the purity of the family—giving birth to, raising and educating children on Jewish values (Proverbs 31:10-31). Thus, her role becomes the most lauded of all—she is the keeper of the flame of the Jewish people and its legacy.

The idea of the "sanctity of motherhood" is reflected in our exhibition by a trio of photographs presented as a "holy glowing triptych" (Fig. 1). At first, the triptych seems to be an abstract work of unidentified forms in luminous yellow, but gradually the viewer discovers that the "holy triptych" is actually three simple pacifiers, not holy by any religion but certainly holy for the mother who depends on them during many hours of the day and night. In this way we replace the sacred motherhood myth with something mundane and simple—objects "transparent" to all but a mother's eye.

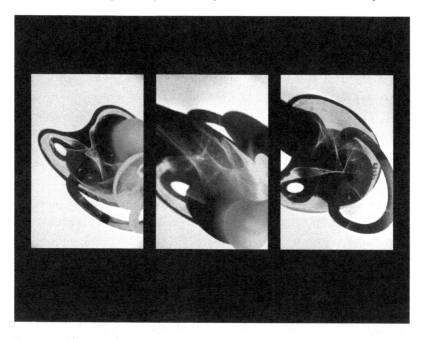

Figure 1: Shira Richter. 24-Karat Gold Triptich. Lightbox framed print. 129x87 cm. x 3. 2011.

It is interesting that even secular and civil law, ostensibly applied to all Israeli citizens without regard for religion, sex or race, is faithful to the religious commandment. According to Israel's Basic Laws, the right to parenthood is enshrined as a superior human right. However, though the state highly values procreation, this is not translated into real economic value for the procreators themselves.

To emphasize the way in which the myth of motherhood has become a mere glittering membrane covering the real status of the mother in Israel, we created a deceptive atmosphere for the exhibition, as misleading as the apparent status of mothers. Visitors encounter a well-orchestrated honey-trap which gradually exposes them to the conflicting, complex, intense emotions and unsolved issues of the subject.

HADARA SCHEFLAN KATZAV & SHIRA RICHTER

SINGLE-GENDERED ZIONISM

The pioneering work of psychologist and journalist Lesley Hazleton on Israeli-Jewish women traced three main factors influencing their status in Israeli society: the myth of equality and liberation, the religious tradition, and above all the ongoing threat of war. A country under siege, real or perceived, tends strongly towards traditional roles and social values. Finding refuge and security are a first priority. Personal aspirations or fulfillment take second place while self sacrifice for the good of the collective is the public expectation. However, at the same time, the myth of women's liberation, so embedded in Israel's short genealogy, persists. Hazleton asserts that this myth, adopted by Israeli women, especially by those from Europe, is a barrier on their path to achieving total liberation. In contrast, immigrant women from Arab countries and Palestinian women born and raised within traditional cultures did not expect the same equality (Mair-Glitzenstein 369).

We assert that the wider the gap between reality and the expectations derived from modern secular Enlightenment, the more intense the pain, inner conflict and disorientation. Therefore we concentrate on the conflicts of western Israeli women who felt and still feel betrayed and vulnerable. While these women were under the impression they were equal participants in Zionist ideology, they were constructed as consumers and not as producers of this ideology.

The Zionist revolution, aspiring to establish a state for the Jewish people, focused on masculinity in contrast to the feminine, weak image of the exiled Jew (Peled). In his text "Muscular Judaism," one of the founders of the Zionist movement, philosopher Max Nordau, seeks to depart from the stereotype of "the fearful blinking of the exiled Jew" and to renew the connection with the heroes of Jewish heritage: "Let's once again be deep-chested men, with alert limbs and a fierce gaze" (187). The encouragement of male solidarity was so widespread that historian David Biale declared that Zionism and masculinity are practically synonyms. Yet these ideas about masculinity and Zionism fail to accord with the general feeling in Israel and around the world that the new Israeli society enables equality for the feminine subject. This contradiction is the result of the frequent doublespeak used by Zionism since its foundation, beginning with the Zionist utopias which constituted the ideological basis for the establishment of the state.

Adopting a surprisingly similar approach to socialist feminist theories, all Zionist utopias agreed that in order to construct a new society, social institutions must be reorganized, primarily the family unit. In his article "Regulating elements of a workers community", A. D. Gordon wrote, "We have to release the woman from her subjugation to the house and allow her the possibility to participate in public life together with the man" (in Elboim-Dror 185).

Although for its time Zionism presented a revolutionary and modern standpoint, contemporary studies of the perception of womanhood in Zionist utopias expose how traditional they in fact were. All Zionist utopias were written by men. According to Rachel Elboim-Dror, in their approach to women there is little to distinguish between them; all reach a consensus based on the male fantasy regarding women, state and homeland. A "good woman" is first and foremost a mother of family and nation. This role naturally includes the production of children, but also childcare and education. Because Zionism values education highly, it might be expected that a mother's status as educator of the next generation is central. However, Elboim-Dror shows this as empty rhetoric since all Zionist utopias subscribe to the revolutionary idea that education be in the hands of the state.

In other words, a woman's ability to give birth does not grant her any political or economic power or facilitate any personal or professional development for her. Thus in most of the utopias women do not specialize professionally and those who do not marry and raise families are the exception.

In the application of Zionist utopian ideas in the developing country we see how women pioneers experienced a similar contradiction between the values of equality and femininity. Young Zionist immigrants of the Second Aliyah (second wave of immigration, 1904-14), who came to Palestine when it was part of the Ottoman Empire, were fired up with the idea of equality and believed in putting the needs of the collective over those of the individual. By cutting their hair and wearing pants, the women tried to resemble men. However, the developing female pioneer model was suitable only for the young single immigrants and the question of how a woman would combine work and family was not addressed. The birth of the first children seriously challenged the female pioneer's position and her equality within kibbutz society. They soon discovered that only women were designated to take care of the children.

The story of Golda Meir, who later became Israel's prime minister, illustrates how on one hand the kibbutz community raised the flag of equality while on the other hand the division of labor was based on sexual iden-

tity. Meir immigrated to Israel with her husband in 1921 and joined the Mer-
havia Kvuza². At first she worked with the men, digging, harvesting fruit
and laboring in the poultry industry. However, when her son was born,
the childcare of all five babies in the group was delegated to her. They were
housed in a two-bedroom apartment; the larger room was for the babies
of whom she took care 24 hours a day, while she was assigned the smaller
room (Erez 734-736). Meir's story shows to what extent the female members of the group internalized the division of the workforce and in most
cases even refrained from participating in the members' meetings in order
to avoid challenging the delicate status quo. The preference of the collective
over the individual was to their detriment; they renounced selfhood (Shilo).

Here we see how the global expectation of maternal altruism has a specific origin in Israel where the conflict between self-fulfillment and sacrifice
for the collective was at the heart of the pioneer existence. This conflict
would act as the central paradigm for many future conflicts of the mother
in Israel.

BALANCING DICHOTOMY: PORTFOLIO LIFE MOTHER

In Hebrew, only one letter differentiates between the word 'motherhood'
and the word 'art.' No wonder they both enjoy and suffer a similar fate.

It is interesting how the internal struggle between selfexpression and
taking care of others is reflected in the relationship between motherhood
and art. Many perceive art to be an egoistic pursuit while motherhood is
considered altruistic[3]. Thankfully, in recent years there has been an up-
surge of women artists who refuse this traditional dichotomy and create art
which connects their two subjective identities—mother and artist (Katzav;
Hadara; Scheflan).

A study of representations of mothers in twentieth-century Israeli art
reveals how the image of the mother was reduced to a political, national,
symbolic dimension. She was shaped as a category, as carrier of Jewish and
Zionist values; her own voice was never heard and she remained an object
of artwork. Only during the last two decades, much later than her sisters in
the west, have Israeli artists who are mothers managed to extract themselves
from the object trap and express their voices even if they do not accord with
the prevailing local ideologies of motherhood. At the same time, it must be
emphasized that this new kind of expression—voicing their own maternal
experience—is complex, and contains internal and external conflicts.

For example, at the entrance to *Invisible Invaluables*, visitors read Richter's poem "I'm Writing Now," in which she lists all the household and childcare chores she is expected to do but is not doing because she is writing. For instance: "I'm writing now instead of doing the dishes/...Instead of separating the summer clothes from winter/...Instead of sorting out my status at the National Insurance Institute..." This is an example of art created from within motherhood even as it announces its temporary refusal to obey motherhood's public dictates.

"None of that counts, she supposedly does all of this work for love. Now, that's not to say that people in the paid workforce don't work for love too, I love lots of my work. Love has nothing to do with it," says Waring, in the TV series *Woman, a True Story*, (1995). Sixteen years later we hear: "A mother's work comes from love. I don't think I should receive money for it. I get paid for my professional work." These are the words of one of the visitors at the exhibition *Invisible Invaluables*, a 65-year-old lawyer and single mother. The lawyer's comment reflects the family ideology and especially the motherhood myth which is deeply rooted in Israeli society; the reward for motherly care cannot be measured in money, its value is too sublime to enter the economic world. Her perspective, shared by many, also reflects the lack of serious local discourse regarding the economic value of mothering.

"No reader should refer to such workers as 'women who don't work' ever again," wrote Gloria Steinem in the preface to *Counting for Nothing* (Waring xii). The National Insurance Institute of Israel obviously didn't read the book because this institute formally defines the job of mothering as "not working" (using the feminine form of the verb). And to add insult to injury, the first months of taking care of a baby are called "birth vacation." According to the legislation of state institutions, it seems a mother is on perpetual vacation.

Waring's works have not yet been translated into Hebrew and their absence is felt especially in feminist discourse. For example, in April 2011, the NCJW's Women Studies Forum at Tel Aviv University held an event entitled "Gender aspects of economics." Even though the speakers, Palestinians and Israelis, discussed numerous topics, none of them mentioned housework, while the labor market, namely working outside the house, was a prominent issue.

Another example of local feminist failure to consider mothering as economic work is expressed in a recent campaign, "Who did you call housewife?" which protested the cuts to mothers' pension rights. The National

Insurance Institute cancels the pension rights of a working mother when she leaves the labor market and works in the house for four years or more even if she worked and paid national insurance fees all her life. The title of the campaign discloses the feminist aversion to the term "housewife" and shows how the working woman is demoted when she formally becomes a homemaker. Susan J. Douglas, author of "Confronting the Mommy Myth," sums it up by saying: "And remember Motherhood remains the unfinished business of the women's movement."

STATUS SYMBOLS FOR THE INVISIBLE ECONOMY OF MOTHERING

Our exhibition was conceived and created in light of this lack of discourse. Both personal and political, it declares the unacknowledged labor of mothering to be its central theme. During the washing of bottles, preparation of food and doing the laundry—in other words, during "sink work" or *sinking* [4],—while the children sleep and her hands are free, the artist photographs her political manifesto, a response to hundreds and thousands of invisible hours of work, devoid of political, economic or public value.

The spatial manifesto continues the political statement. Imagine entering a cathedral-like space, colorful "stained-glass windows" on black velvet walls, and at the east end, in the place of the apse, a shining yellow triptych. While walking along the "nave and aisles" we find ourselves in a prestigious "Tiffany display room" where we encounter illuminated-glass display tables. The murmuring sound of running water (of the kitchen sink) and angel voices (of children) [5] somewhere in the space create an almost magical and sacred atmosphere. It is in fact neither a cathedral nor a jewelry store, but it should be valued as if it were. Both the "stained-glass windows" and the "display tables" are actually illuminated photographs which, in stark contrast, are connected to the most routine work there is: boring, Sisyphean, unappreciated, yet so critical to life. Only when one reads the accompanying texts does one realize these forms are the most essential items: baby bottles, plastic nipples, pacifiers, and stale baby food ... which have become gemstones: 24-karat gold, white diamond, mystic topaz, amber, tiger eye ...

The photograph *Tiger Eye* (Fig. 2) demonstrates how these valuable treasures represent the care economy. This work captures the sunlight bursting in through the bars of the window shutters, glancing off a wet plate and scattering precious luminosity. The deceptive appearance of a valuable gemstone conceals the basic act of washing dishes. As in every ancient village, so too in our modern lives: at the source of water, the sink, life happens.

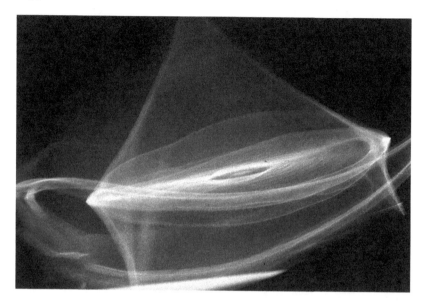

Figure 2: Shira Richter. Tiger Eye. Table Lightbox framed print. 46x56 cm. 2011.

This alchemy, this transformation of hardship into gold, has several meanings. Foremost among them is the idea that caring for another human should be worthy of the highest appreciation, not as a cliché but as a matter of life and death.

Black and white, cold and metallic, sexy and dripping with eroticism, *Iron Maiden* (Fig. 3) is unique, standing out from the other works in the exhibition. The seductive quality of the image allows the viewer to momentarily escape reality. The awakening is startling. One of the visitors, Ronit Avneyon-Fischer, clinical social worker, psychotherapist and mother of two, told us, "Unease welled up inside me when I realized that these sensual illuminated images were not jewelry, gold, or silver, but a mother's equipment! The last thing on earth I wanted to be reminded of on my night out!" Avneyon-Fischer voices a feeling many of us can identify with. Taking care of infants is a huge, non-stop responsibility. We are always just the blink of an eye away from some awful accident. A nipple hole of the wrong size may cause suffocation or malnutrition. A dirty pacifier can result in in-

Figure 3: Shira Richter. Iron Maiden. Lightbox framed print. 129x87 cm. 2011.

fection, disease, even hospitalization[6]. No wonder women are not keen to be reminded of it on their night out. Yet the virtue of art is its ability to present a grey reality in flamboyant colors.

This strategy of seducing the eye is inherent to every one of the works. Mystic Topaz (Fig. 4) is a stained-glass image of two colorful pacifiers. The captivating image does not allow us to forget the importance of these small "banal" objects, and reminds us how, for example, the daily task of driving with a screaming infant without a pacifier can end in an accident. "To pacify" also means "to make peace." There is value to the everyday peace-making efforts mothers make within their own families.

In our view, taking these objects for granted obscures the real price of life, making killing much easier, even cheaper. Those who treat life so cheaply—those who rush into military confrontation without exhausting every other option—must be unaware of the enormous achievement it is to make, create, and sustain a life. As mothers of children whose country conscripts at the age of 18, we turn our attention to and focus our camera on this.

Figure 4: Shira Richter. Mystic Topaz. Lightbox framed print. 129x87 cm. 2011.

SAFETY MEASURES

"While women, children and the environment are counted as nothing, the entire international economic system calls war productive and valuable." (Waring 135).

Israel is a leader in two industries: the arms industry and fertility treatments. Both are strongly connected to the deeply-rooted Jewish fear of annihilation. The decisive answer to this fear is primarily the size of the Defense Ministry's budget, which is the largest of all government ministries (Even 38).

Although Israel is the only country with compulsory conscription of women, its army is still a predominantly male organization, and provides special benefits for its warriors (Jerby). For example, Iris Jerby's research reveals some unique economic benefits of military service, operating in the psycho-social sphere. Military camaraderie creates a kind of brotherhood which continues in civilian professional life. Friends recommend or promote other army comrades, and military officers are easily appointed to key managerial positions (such as mayors, principles, managers of Health Ministry offices or CEOs). There is also a male sense of entitlement from having endangered their lives while fulfilling the mission of protecting the home front. This creates a new kind of class division which privileges military veterans with prestige and authority to voice their opinions, especially on security and military issues.

FEMINISTS CHALLENGE THE MALE HEGEMONY IN SECURITY AND MILITARY ISSUES

In line with UN Resolution 1325 (2000), which focuses attention on the impact of conflict on women and calls for women's engagement in conflict resolution and peacebuilding, two women's political organizations[7].wrote a report following the Second Lebanon War, named *Security and Resilience for Whom?* Jewish and Arab women presented the report in a feminist conference which was intended as an alternative to the prestigious Herzliya Conference of the governmental, military and business elite, held at the same time. The report revealed the extent to which the government's security concept is detached from the actual security needs of its people.

Resolution 1325 emphasizes the fact that during the last two decades the home front has become the front. Women and children are no longer distant from armed conflicts but are exposed to the violence. Houses are bombarded, missiles fall among civilians, and bombs explode in the streets. Schools and daycare centers are both targeted and closed. This causes grave economic insecurity, especially to mothers who have to be absent from their jobs in order to return to the domestic space to be with their children (Aharoni 2).

We expressed this spatial density by creating a narrow black-walled corridor at the entrance of the exhibition. Visitors walk along two parallel rows of images of windows and shutters which create a sense of imprisonment (Fig. 5). The need to physically demonstrate this feeling of suffocation and horror stemmed from our own experience. The works were created during a period in which Richter, a mother of baby twins, spent hours enclosed in her apartment because of the local violent conflict. The twins were born January 2002, at a time when the cycle of violence between Israel and the Palestinians was escalating following the start of the Second Intifada[8]. Both sides were dramatically affected. An unprecedented number of suicide bombings killed Israeli civilians, while the State of Israel launched Operation Defensive Shield which resulted in many Palestinian civilian casualties. Israel also began construction of the West Bank barrier (also called the "racial segregation wall," "separation fence" or "security fence").

Figure 5: Shira Richter. Joil Bars. Digital print. 130x90 cm. 2011.

CHILDREN AS DEMOGRAPHIC POINTS

Israel is a world-leader in IVF treatments. It has the largest number of fertilization units in relation to its population and subsidizes almost unlimited fertility treatments to women as part of their public health insurance, up to two children.

The state's investment in women's fertility reflects the local attitude that every woman is both entitled to be and should become a mother, to such an extent that in 2011 the preservation of fertility for women who are sick was added to the range of health services to which all citizens are entitled (the "health basket"). If a couple trying to have children do not achieve pregnancy within a few months, the situation is defined as a problem, and with the encouragement of gynecologists, they show up at one of the fertility units.

The fertility industry is one of the most profitable industries in Israel and is rooted in two ideas. One, based on religion, was noted above: "Be fruitful and multiply." The other is a product of nationalism: "The demographic danger." While a woman's right to procreate is passionately encouraged and maintained, her right to not procreate is systematically violated. Thus, the Israeli woman has become the national womb carrier and women who choose not to have children are considered deviant (Donath). There is a price to refusing to follow the accepted path: birth control pills have only recently (2005) been added to the "health basket," and are subsidized only till the age of 20. Abortion is dependent on regulatory approval and costs upwards of $425, regardless of the woman's income.

"IMPROPER" PROTESTS BRING HOPE

Invisible Invaluables was the opening and principal event of International Women's Month in Tel Aviv, and cooperated with feminist activist groups. In order to draw attention to local blindness to a mother's unpaid work, and hoping to create a wakeup call, we quoted Marilyn Waring's words about the way the UN's System of National Accounts regards this work as "of little or no importance" (from the documentary film *Who's Counting?*).

Three months later, in the summer of 2011, we witnessed a major public protest over the cost of living in Israel. This protest was unprecedented in its scope; moreover, Israelis had previously protested only over political issues, not over private issues, because they felt it was improper to protest such issues when the state was aflame with violent conflict.

It began with a consumer protest against the price of cottage cheese, continued with the famous "tent city" protests over the price of housing, was joined by doctors and teachers protesting their low salaries and employment terms, and finally included the "stroller protest" over the high cost of childcare. During a conversation with Richter in September 2011, Educational Director of the Adam Institute for Democracy and Peace Uki Maroshek-Klarman noted how all protests were linked by the motif of a house: "Even the logo of [Tnuva's] cottage cheese is a classic image of a house[9]." The house, as the private sphere, is becoming more political than ever.

Led by young women who spoke from their heart, the protests exposed the asymmetry between the cost of living and people's income. Nevertheless, a mother's work in the house was never mentioned.

The purpose of our exhibition, therefore, is to direct the attention of local feminist discourse to its own blind spot. This blind spot prevents us from seeing the obvious regarding the status of women in Israel. We use the language of art in order to aim directly at the invisible, because we believe art has the power, through the act of representation, to establish meaning in its own unique way.

In order to direct a spotlight on a mother's life-saving work, we expand our approach to the exhibition beyond its physical space or chronological time. The exhibition space has become a sphere of activity within a variety of partnerships with community organizations, gallery talks, seminars and more. During these meetings opinions are heard and various comments are made but one in particular still rings in our ears: "When we divorced and were dealing with the money issue, my husband said: You didn't work, or earn money, why should I give you anything?"

[1] The word "mother" in this chapter includes men who do mothering work as well

[2] "Kvuza" – collective farmstead, precursor of the kibbutz commune.

[3] The documentary *Who Does She Think She Is?* (2008), deals particularly with this tension between motherhood and being an artist. Artist Maye Torres, who appears in the documentary, says, "I had lots of people telling me that I was selfish. Is it selfish to do your own work when you're responsible for the care of others?"

[4] *Sinking Syncing* is a video-artwork (4 min.) featuring photographs and videos of "sink work."

[5] From the video-artwork *Sinking Syncing*

[6] Beterem Safe Kids Israel, an NPO which aims to promote child safety, states that "two thirds of child hospitalizations are due to home accidents... Most of these injuries are due to falls, burns, drowning, poisoning, choking, car accidents, and other 'every-day' causes" (Beterem annual report, 2010).

[7] Isha L'Isha Haifa Feminist Center and the Coalition of Women for Peace

[8] The Second Intifada (the Al-Aqsa uprising) broke out in 2000 and peaked between 2001 and 2003.

[9] In Hebrew the words for hospital and school include the word "house."

WORKS CITED

Aharoni, Sarai. The Effect of the War in the North on the Lives of Israeli Women and Girls. *Gender Analysis.* Haifa: Isha L'Isha – Haifa Feminist Center, 2006. Print. [Hebrew]

Beterem *Safe Kids Israel.* "Annual Report 2010." Beterem. Web. 2 Feb. 2012. [Hebrew]

Biale, David. *Eros and the Jews: From Biblical Israel to Contemporary America.* Tel Aviv: Am Oved, 1994. Print. [Hebrew]

Dayif, Amani, Dorit Abramovitch and Hedva Eyal, eds. *Security for Whom? Feminist Perspectives on Security.* Haifa: Pardes, 2007. Print. [Hebrew]

Donath, Orna. *Making a Choice: Being Childfree in Israel.* Tel Aviv: Miskal – Yedioth Ahronoth Books and Migdarim, Hakibbutz Hameuchad, 2011. Print. [Hebrew]

Douglas, Susan J. "Confronting the Mommy Myth." Article 723. *In These Times and the Institute for Public Affairs.* 19 April 2004. Web. 4 January 2012.

Elboim Dror, Rachel. *Yesterday's Tomorrow: The Zionist Utopia, Vol. 1.* Jerusalem: Yad Izhak Ben-Zvi, 1993. Print. [Hebrew]

Erez, Yehuda, ed. *The Book of the Third Aliyah.* Vol. 2. Tel Aviv: Am Oved, 1964. Print. [Hebrew]

Even, Shmuel. "Israel's Security Expenses: Data and Significance." Strategic Update. Vol. 12 no. 4. January 2010. Print. [Hebrew]

Friedman, Ariela, et al., eds. *The Double Bind, Women in Israel.* Tel Aviv: Hakibbutz Hameuchad, 1982. Print. [Hebrew]

Hazleton, Lesley. *Adam's Rib.* Jerusalem: Adanim, 1978. Print. [Hebrew]

Izraeli, Dafna N. "Culture, Policy, and Women in Dual-Earner Families in Israel." *Dual-Earner Families: International Perspectives.* Eds. Susan Lewis, Dafna N. Izraeli, Helen Hootsmans. London: Sage, 1992. Print.

Jerby, Iris. *The Double Price: Women Status and Military Service in Israel.* Tel Aviv: Ramot-Tel Aviv University, 1996. Print. [Hebrew]

Mair-Glitzenstein, Esther. "Jewish Cinderellas in Bagdad: the Struggle of Zionist Girls in Iraq for Equal Rights and Immigration to Israel." *Will You Listen to My Voice? Representations of Women in Israeli Culture.* Ed. Yael Atzmon. Jerusalem: The Van Leer Jerusalem Institute, 2001. Print. [Hebrew]

National Film Board of Canada. "The Second Shift," *Women, a True Story.* The National Film Board of Canada in Association with CTV Television Network Ltd, 1995. Television.

Nordau, Max. Zionist Writings: Speeches and Articles (1901-4). Vol. 2. *Jerusalem: Hasifria Hazionit,* 1948. Print. [Hebrew]

Peled, Rina. *The "New Man" of the Zionist Revolution.* Tel Aviv: Am

Oved, 2002. Print. [Hebrew]

Raday, Frances. "On Equality," *Mishpatim* 24, 1994:241-281. Print. [Hebrew]

Richter, Shira. "I'm Writing Now." *Being a Mother. Tamar Mor Sela.* Tel Aviv: Yediot Books, 2010. Print. [Hebrew]

Scheflan Katzav, Hadara. *The Encounter between the Maternal Subject and the Visual Signifier in Current Israeli Art.* Diss. Tel Aviv University, 2008. Print. [Hebrew]

Shilo, Margalit. "The New Hebrew Woman—The Hebrew Woman in Eretz Israel." *Blessed is He for Making Me a Woman?* Ed. David Ariel Joel et al. Tel Aviv: Yedioth Aharonoth, 1999. Print. [Hebrew]

Tamir, Tal. *Women in Israel 2006: Between Theory and Reality.* Ramat Gan: The Israel Women's Network, 2007. Print. [Hebrew]

United Nations Security Council. "Resolution 1325." *United Nations.* 31 October 2000. Web. 20 April 2012.

Waring, Marilyn. *Counting for Nothing: What Men Value and What Women Are Worth.* Toronto, Buffalo, London: University of Toronto Press Inc., 1999. Print.

Who Does She Think She Is? Dirs: Pamela Tanner Boll, Nancy Kennedy. Prod. Michelle Seligson. Mystic Artists Film Productions, 2008. Documentary. DVD.

Who's Counting? Marilyn Waring on Sex, Lies and Global Economics. Dir. Terre Nash, Prod. The National Film Board of Canada, 1995. Documentary. DVD.

11.

Whose Rights Count?

A Research Journey with Marilyn Waring on Unpaid HIV Care and the Economics of Dignity

MEENA SHIVDAS & ANIT N. MUKHERJEE

INTRODUCTION

O UR ASSOCIATION with Marilyn Waring began in Kampala, Uganda, in 2007 when Robert Carr presented an authoritative paper on financing gender equality in HIV interventions at a meeting of Commonwealth Ministers of Women's Affairs. His paper raised important issues on HIV care, challenging the existing paradigms on women and girls' roles and responsibilities and reflecting on their rights and donors' responses. Marilyn identified these as critical gaps in our conceptual understanding of the care economy in the context of HIV and AIDS and inspired a groundbreaking research project on women's unpaid work, human rights and social justice. Being with her and the late Robert Carr on this research journey has been a privilege and a learning experience which will always stay with us.

HIV AND UNPAID CARE

HIV is a crisis that hits hardest at the household level. Across the world unpaid, full time carers in HIV affected households form the backbone of care and treatment. By and large, it is the women of these households who subsidize HIV care because they assume the burden of looking after those who are affected. In concentrated epidemics, gay, bisexual and transgender people also care for their partners, something that is largely unnoticed by society and policy makers. To us, unpaid carers are the missing factor in the HIV treatment and care equation as their vital contribution goes unacknowledged and unvalued. In many cases, the carers were themselves HIV infected—the increasing feminization of the epidemic implies that women bear the double burden of the disease as well as full-time care.

The value of unpaid care-work is significant given the impact of the international public debt crisis on HIV interventions as governments and donors focus on efficient use of resources. As the epidemic matures in many parts of the world, significantly larger numbers of HIV positive people are being reached with anti-retroviral treatment (ART). While it is undeniable that treatment regimens have been effective in stemming HIV deaths, increasingly unpaid care-work is becoming essential to reaching or even maintaining treatment targets. Moreover, as HIV-positive people live longer and have more productive lives as a result of better treatment, there is a need to have structures which support their care needs. Yet, HIV programmes focus on a reduction of the national burden of HIV without necessarily acknowledging where that burden falls—in this case, almost exclusively on households, especially women.

The research journey charted here recounts how we went about the study to put the focus on the voices of unpaid carers across diverse settings around the world. In the following sections, we explain how starting from a traditional data gathering approach, Marilyn inspired the team to question the prevailing notions and come up with a new conceptual framework based on human rights and dignity for carers. We believe that this methodology holds the promise of providing a tool for future research on women's unpaid care in the context of social protection in general and disease burden in particular.

TRAVERSING THE HIV-CARE LANDSCAPE

In the initial research proposal, the focus was on working with time-use data to compute the direct and opportunity costs of care and demonstrate the need for rethinking care and support programmes. However, Marilyn was of the opinion that the bigger strategic question was to work out how to "compensate by policy inputs for the work that cannot be done, and not merely pay for it." This would lead us to think about the policy implication of the agency of the carer in the face of overwhelming stigma associated with

HIV and AIDS. We asked how the State could ensure the dignity and rights of the carer be it a child, spouse, partner, parent, grandparent or a paid carer in an institution.

Following this discussion, we conducted an extensive literature review to understand the situations that circumscribe unpaid HIV carers' daily lives. We recognized that the unpaid care experience would be exacerbated by factors such as disability and disadvantage stemming from unemployment, lack of education, social class, caste and age, culture and religion. In addition discrimination based on factors such as sex, colour and sexual orientation could make the unpaid care experience more onerous.

When we further developed the parameters for the study at the World AIDS Conference in Mexico City in 2008, we identified 11 countries on the basis of particular epidemic profiles and the fact that the unpaid care experiences and burden would resonate with the realities of HIV care elsewhere. We knew that interviews with carers would reveal important and textured aspects of the unpaid carers' work, life choices and perceptions of rights and responsibilities.

Based on the literature review, we moved from the traditional economic replacement value focus to a capability-based strategic policy intervention approach. A semi-structured interview format was drafted, piloted, reviewed and finalized for distribution through and with research partners in each country. Our research partners were engaged with communities and were able to identify unpaid HIV carers who were willing to share their stories as key informants. Due diligence was observed regarding the consent for using the life stories, including names, locations and events.

The interviewer recorded as much as possible about the carer before the beginning of the interview including name, age, education, distance from hospital or clinic or health centre, distance from closest basic shop for supplies, number in household, access to transport, access to drinking water, and type of fuel used for cooking. Questions were asked about their daily routine, "leisure" time and experiences of paid work and education.

Through carers' narratives we discerned notions of "rights", "responsibilities" and "duty of care." We found that the household experiences greater costs related to caring. Financial costs included increased costs of food, medications and commodities needed for caring. Opportunity costs were loss of income, loss of time, loss of subsistence production and loss of children's education. Invisible costs included the deteriorating physical and mental health of the carer, plummeting nutrition levels of the household, deteriorating living conditions and sometimes complete loss of shelter, loss of educational opportunities and loss of community participation and personal safety.

The research process advanced the analytical framework beyond the compilation and analysis of time-use surveys as it led to the examination of the concepts of dignity, time poverty and servitude in a new way. We explain it in detail below.

THE RESEARCH PROCESS: CONCEPTUAL FRAMEWORK AND WORKING WITH RESEARCH RESULTS

Review of the data gathered through the above process was instrumental in the rethinking of the prevailing paradigm of women's role in the care economy. The revised conceptual framework enabled us to place the unpaid care work performed by women and other carers at the centre of the discourse and privilege the dignity and rights of carers in HIV prevention and treatment strategies. Our intention was to provide an alternative to traditional economic methods of value judgement (economically understood) that are prevalent at the programmatic level.

By situating unpaid HIV care within the context of human rights and social justice, and by emphasising State obligation and responsibility via international human rights instruments, the study brought into sharp focus the responsibility of governments for the conditions of servitude under which carers often live their lives. This aspect of the conceptualisation was inspired by Marilyn's international advocacy for the recognition of women's unpaid care-work which compromises their capacity to take an equal part in civil and political life.

Amartya Sen's capability approach put forward in 1999 departs from other frameworks by providing direct support for a broad characterisation of fundamental freedoms and human rights that takes account of poverty, hunger and starvation, dignity and conditions of servitude. Individual substantive freedoms in the form of the capabilities and functionings that people can and do achieve can be included among the constituent elements of human freedom and incorporated into a framework of rights.

Capability freedoms focus on the set of valuable things that a person is able to do and be. For example, if a person has reasons to value a life without hunger and would choose such a life, then the capability of this person to achieve adequate nutrition is directly relevant to her/his real opportunity to promote her/his objectives and expand her/his freedom. Conversely, deprivation in the capability to achieve adequate nutrition restricts the person's real opportunity to promote her/his objectives and is admissible as a "freedom-restricting" condition. The classical case is that of servitude, which directly restricts the person's choice to do and be. Similarly, discrimination on the basis of creed, religion or state of health (as in the case of people living with HIV) also prevents a person from achieving a life that s/he values and prevents her/him from "taking part in the life of the community," which Amartya Sen regards as a basic functioning of human beings.

The central idea of "capability freedom" is then associated in Sen's conceptual framework with a set of "capability rights" and obligations that protect and promote valuable states of being and doing. The "capability approach" provides direct support for the characterisation of poverty, hunger and starvation, discrimination and servitude as "freedom-restricting" conditions. In this way: "Minimal demands of well-being (in the form of basic functioning, e.g. not to be hungry), and of well-being freedom (in the form of minimal capabilities, e.g. having the means of avoiding hunger)" can be conceptualized as rights that "command attention and call for support."

The "attention" is the catalyst for public action, including action on the part of the international community, and the "support" is from human rights instruments including the Universal Declaration of Human Rights (UDHR), the International Covenant on Civil and Political Rights (ICCPR), the International Covenant on Economic, Social and Cultural Rights (ICESCR), the Convention on the Rights of the Child (CRC) and the Convention on the Elimination of All Forms of Discrimination against Women (CEDAW)—which have been ratified by most countries—along with international human rights jurisprudence and case law.

In the context of HIV therefore, we associated the indignity of living with the disease with the idea of "freedom restricting" conditions in the capability approach. Our empirical evidence suggests that the feeling of living without dignity is part of the reality for both people struggling with HIV-related illnesses and their carers. The sense of living a life where they feel stigmatized and discriminated against flows directly from societal norms that disregard the ethical values of dignity and rights.

Social justice demands that those living with HIV and their carers be treated with equal respect and dignity to that afforded to each member of society. The absence of this means that most policies and programmes that seek to 'halt and reverse' the HIV epidemic in line with the Millennium Development Goals (MDGs), exacerbate rather than ameliorate the condition of HIV-positive persons and their carers. This is because programmes are generally designed and evaluated on the basis of efficient-resource use and achievement of target-oriented results rather than on advancing human rights and social justice.

In terms of the efficiency argument, the MDG targets are quantifiable measures to track the progress of countries over time. The critique of the efficiency argument on MDG targets is that they do not address the underlying process of removal of discrimination against women through protection and enjoyment of basic human rights as an instrument of achieving the goals.

Using the efficiency argument in the case of measuring indicators on health the standard framework that is applied in the health economics literature involves the evaluation of policies vis-à-vis their impact on disability-adjusted life years (DALY) or quality-adjusted life years (QALY) gained per dollar of expenditure. For example, if there are two treatment regimens, one is more efficient than the other if the same amount of DALYs or QALYs is enhanced for a lower unit cost.

Until now however, a critique of the efficiency argument has not been used to analyse women's unpaid work in HIV care. The extension is straightforward. First, by definition, as Marilyn has asserted the effort of women caregivers is not valued in economic terms since it falls outside the "boundary of production" defined by the UN System of National Accounts (UNSNA). In this case, evaluation of DALY or QALY is not possible since there is no monetary value attached to the "work." The fallacy, however, is that since unpaid work actually benefits the household economically, a situation where it does not exist would reduce the efficiency of the system from an economic perspective.

While there have been efforts to value the 'time cost' of unpaid work in household production, especially in recent developments in gender budgeting, this does not cover unpaid care work. In the case of unpaid care work, the concept of "choice" usually does not exist—the caregivers are not in a position to choose how much time they spend on market opportunities as the time expended for non-market transactions consumes the day. Any time that is left after the basic subsistence needs have been met is spent on providing care; the choice between "work" and "leisure" becomes non-existent. The efficiency argument therefore breaks down completely, becomes untenable and cannot be used as a tool to evaluate unpaid work in HIV care.

The lives of carers mirrored this disconnect between the realisation of human rights and the "efficiency" approach in HIV interventions. After the interviews were collated and transcribed, we employed a gender-responsive human rights lens to reconcile a cost benefit analysis of HIV with a political economy approach and assessed "dignity" and "human rights" in unpaid care-work.

Important aspects of the unpaid carer's work, life choices and perceptions of rights and responsibilities were examined against particular articles of international human rights instruments to identify how, when and why the unpaid carer's rights were compromised and their dignity eroded.

We were mindful about the ethics of further burdening unpaid carers through the gathering of information and ensured that they were compensated appropriately. We are still in touch with our network of interviewers/activists who have, in some instances, work-shopped our book with unpaid HIV carers to make them aware of their rights.

Given that we wanted to "action" the research findings for policy advocacy, we worked at different arenas to present the initial findings and receive feedback. In March 2009, we convened a side event in the wings of the annual session of the UN Commission on the Status of Women in New York. The presence of one of the carers, a gay man from Jamaica, with his full and informed consent, was powerful. He spoke his truth about his invisibility and discrimination. It brought home to us that, as researchers, we had kept to our ethics—to facilitate the telling of others' stories without taking it away from those who entrust us with their life-stories. Getting him to speak at the event was important for him, for us, as well as for those who heard him.

Another arena where we advocated for unpaid carers' rights was at a parliamentarians' workshop in the wings of a Commonwealth Ministers of Women's Affairs meeting in 2010 in Barbados. As a former parliamentarian well-versed in statecraft, Marilyn very ably got our message on the need for upholding the human rights of unpaid carers in national HIV policies to the legislators. In our framework, States have to take responsibility for violations of the norms of social justice when a community or an institution discriminates against those living with HIV and their carers.

THE ECONOMICS OF 'DIGNITY', 'RIGHTS' AND 'LOVE' AND 'FULFILMENT'

This section highlights the voices of unpaid carers within the analytical context of capability servitude in the household. "Capability servitude" describes a condition where a person's dignity and freedom are circumscribed by an inability to break away from a situation of constant work and no leisure, especially for unpaid women carers in HIV-affected households. Following from Sen's capability approach, this implies constrained access to and experience of basic freedoms and rights, and experiences and perceptions of stigma and discrimination to illustrate the approach of linking the lack of freedoms to human rights standards. The voices of the carers that follow are instrumental in providing the empirical backbone to our theoretical construct of a situation of capability servitude:

> He was in the same clothes in a corner bed [of the hospital], no sheets nothing. The food that they had taken for him was lying there. He was blind, crippled and not talking. (L, unpaid carer, Jamaica)

> When we started getting the [food] basket people use to laugh at us saying we are eating AIDS food. (Lillian, unpaid carer, Botswana)

> Right before she was brought to the hospital she was found lying in her own vomit with rotting food in her cell, cigarette butts everywhere and fruit flies all over. (Cynthia, unpaid carer, Canada)

> There is nobody on earth who can really stand beside me. Today I cannot do any work properly due to my HIV infection because people rebuke me or neglect me. (Hamida, unpaid carer, Bangladesh)

> The most difficult is that you have to stay indoors, you don't go out. Since she don't walk you have to stay indoors. She needs drinking water, she wants to go to the toilet, you have to carry her. (Amira, unpaid carer, Nigeria)

> My anger was with my own family because they would not come and visit us or bring food for her like what is normally done when someone is sick. It was like I had no family. (Ruth, unpaid carer, Papua New Guinea)

Our carers experienced acute time-poverty; the work was relentless with no help, free time or holiday. There was no respite and opportunities for education, training and employment were lost. They experienced stigma which often breaks down traditional and formal support systems. In one instance we found that a government programme providing a basket of food for the children of families with HIV positive members came to be known as "AIDS food" in the community. Because the stigma arising from the name "AIDS food" was so overwhelming, the family did not access it despite their need.

The carers faced discrimination in hospitals and clinics, calling into question the belief that care is available for households with HIV within the health system. We found that a significant burden of unpaid care work stemmed from the fact that the health system was the source of discrimination against HIV positive persons. Families preferred to care for their relatives and friends within the household rather than let them face stigma and remain neglected in health care institutions. Above all, the constant uncertainties were debilitating for our carers.

On choice:

> I have no choice about being the primary caregiver. There are four in the house who are HIV positive—myself, my husband, my brother, who also has cancer, and my 14-year-old daughter. My mother passed away, then, my son passed away. A few months after giving birth, the mother of my grandson just dropped her son off with his dad, my son, and ran away. I am taking care of my husband, my daughter and myself, we are all HIV positive. I am taking care of my brother who is HIV positive and suffering from cancer in his legs and feet. My 14-year-old daughter was not born with HIV—she was raped when she was 9 years old. (Sylvia, Namibia)

> I had no choice because there was no other person close to my mother to assist her when she fell sick or to look after my young brother and sister. (Jessy, Uganda)

> After the death of our own mother my aunt took care of us. Nobody else can do this. My grandmother is old now so I am the primary caregiver. (Geeta, India)

> I didn't have any choice about becoming a caregiver. It wasn't a choice, I would do anything for my brother. D lived with us for about 7 years, and he was diagnosed about 15 years ago.

There was certainly no choice about becoming a caregiver. We thought it was better for him to spend his time in Auckland with all his friends around him because that's where his support was. (Sharon, New Zealand)

The 16-year-old, I had no choice but to take him in at 4 months old when his mother, my daughter, died. In the case of the twins, she was my neighbour and we would share everything. The other girl is staying here to study. She is my granddaughter. Who would look after the children if I was not here? (Emily, Namibia)

I didn't have any choice, there is no one else to take care of my aunt. My aunt's first born is a boy so he cannot bathe his mother, and remember that my aunt took care of my mother too. (Lillian, Botswana)

My daughter, B, was living with me at home when she got sick. Whatever she wanted me to do, I would do for her if I could. At times people get sick of looking after sick people, but I wouldn't. This was my child. (Ruth, Papua New Guinea)

In the capability framework that we use, the presence or absence of choice is fundamental. None of those participating in our research felt that they had any choice. Article 6 of ICESCR "includes the right of everyone to the opportunity to gain his living by work, which he freely chooses and accepts."

But we can still discern a sense of love and fulfilment in the carer's voice from New Zealand as she describes how she cared for her brother. Care-work has its own rhythm and logic and provides a sense of fulfilment that is often not articulated. Often the carers would do anything for the loved one, but that did not negate their experience of lack of freedoms and choices. While the universally accepted definition of work does not encompass them, they cannot be seen to be at leisure. We therefore used the term servitude to describe their life-condition.

Our carers also encountered violence including rape and physical and emotional threats. Article 7 of ICESCR recognizes the right of everyone to the enjoyment of just and favourable conditions of work that ensure safe and healthy working conditions. This is mirrored in CEDAW Article 11 (1f). In this context, we asked carers to describe their work.

> I did household chores like washing dishes, washing clothes, cooking, weeding the garden, keeping the house tidy, fetching water. For water we would go to the centre of the village but if that water was not running we would walk to Doru, which is a fair distance. We would be fetching water all the time to wash them, to wash their clothes, which would be soiled. If we had food I would prepare a meal. If we did not have food we would spend all the time looking for means of getting food. K and her husband M's sores made life very hard for them. Their skin was always itchy. We would try to soothe it with warm water. Sometimes I was up all night. You know when people are sick you don't sleep in case they want something like water so we would light the fires to boil water for tea and to wash them. If they slept soundly then so did we, but if they had a restless night due to the itchiness then we would not sleep either. (Alice, Papua New Guinea)

> The hardest physical task for me was lifting. Near the end D was just a dead weight and it was very heavy to lift him. I had to build up momentum just to get him off the bed, change his bed sheets, things like that; getting him up and down the stairs, into the car. I am a pretty strong man but you know, sometimes I just thought wow—heavy....My toughest emotional task as a caregiver was watching him get sicker basically, that was quite tough watching him deteriorate. The meals I was preparing were nonstop and whatever he wanted, which got a bit extreme because he got really fussy. But then in the end he couldn't eat what we were cooking and I think that was the toughest thing. (Victor, New Zealand)

Emerging from the voices is the stark fact that unpaid carers do not have dignity or choice—freedoms and rights that are enshrined in international human rights instruments and which every human being has the right to enjoy.

In 1987, speaking at the 42nd session of the United Nations General Assembly, Jonathan Mann predicted three phases of the epidemic that was unfolding in the early 1990s: first the wave of HIV, then the second wave of AIDS, and third, the epidemic of stigma, discrimination and denial. Recent data from the Stigma Index confirm its persistence as do these testimonials from our carers:

> Initially he got along very well with individuals that live in the yard but as he got sick they started treating him badly not talking to him, scorning him, not hanging out with him as they usually did. There were times when he would try to make it to the bathroom to go use the toilet and was unable to make it because he was weak and as such he would sometimes filth on himself on his way, so there were times when I had to come home and get him from outside and take him in. He was scorn[ed] because people knew. People started talking how is it that he is losing weight, is the batty man [homosexual] etc. It was also the fact that it would be the gay disease and is because of our nastiness so. (L, Jamaica)

> We were in [the hospital] emergency [room] and she was very weak, she said she couldn't hold on anymore. She said "Look after my children." K died in the hospital. We brought her body back to the village. Only the immediate family went close to the body to mourn her but many didn't want to touch her. Only we touched her and cried over the body. Like with her husband, people were too scared to come close. They stood around but very few came close. Some came to pay respect while most came out of curiosity. (…) During the time of caring no one came to give me or the family a helping hand. We had no support. (Alice, Papua New Guinea)

> My daughter B was living at home with me when she got sick. I took her to the Barracks clinic which is about a mile from our house. They said she had malaria and pneumonia. It was only later I heard from others that she had HIV AIDS. I took her to the AIDS clinic. I was not scared, my heart did not fear, nor did I turn away from her. I would take her where she needed to go. Whatever she wanted me to do I would do for her if I could. Many times she would get angry and cry and feel sad and depressed that people were talking about her, the

gossip really affected her. She would cry and tell me that she didn't have this sickness and wonder why people were saying she had. She was scared and angry. She felt that people were just labelling her for nothing....No one helped me through this difficult time. I did it alone. Our traditional ways are that we help each other out during times of sickness but for some reason this time no one came, maybe they were scared. (Ruth, Papua New Guinea)

Despite the extensive analysis of stigma—and the arguably less extensive programming that has tried to address it, it remains a starkly defining feature of living with HIV and caring for people living with HIV. The contours of stigma remain the same as they have been for a decade or more: the association of HIV with contagion and contamination that is both physical and moral in its association and identification with groups already outcast or considered second class by dominant social norms.

The preambles of the UDHR and ICCPR each remind States that recognition of the inherent dignity and of the equal and inalienable rights of all members of the human family form the foundation of freedom, justice and peace in the world. But just as the texts of the international human rights instruments make clear State obligations, the caregivers' testimonies too attest to the omnipresent and debilitating experience of coping with a diagnosis of HIV in the absence of State protections.

Given the forgoing, the research lays the groundwork for a comprehensive framework bringing together economic, social, political and human rights strands in examining the impact HIV has on unpaid care-givers. We have used the findings to articulate a feminist approach to the design of social protection for unpaid carers entitled "anticipatory social protection framework."

CONCLUSION

The main question we asked was whether unpaid HIV carers were getting the dignity they deserve which is their human right? We pursued a qualitative enquiry—drawing on a human rights framework and the concept of capability to understand the situations of unpaid HIV carers who are overwhelmingly women. The research focused on carers' daily lives and struggles and which have implications for dignity and the realisation of human rights. As Marilyn emphasized at a panel on the AIDS care economy at the

XVII World AIDS conference in Mexico City, "...just what is the context in which these women can be seen as having no human rights because their situation in the current policies constitutes a justified limitation on the right to be free from discrimination ...".

Our research shows that carers, most often women and girls, believe they have no choice but to provide for their dying loved one; it is in this feeling of no choice that rights and dignity are breached, invisibly, and replaced by capability servitude. The carers' voices revealed how capability rights are violated for both the person living with HIV and also the carer. The carer does not have the freedom to choose those functionings that are valuable to her/him—for example, rest from work and participating in the life of the society. This condition is therefore termed capability servitude, where the carer's dignity and freedom is circumscribed by her/his inability to break away from the situation of constant work and no leisure. The violation of capability rights comes from the fact that, in most countries, policies and programmes do not exist that unshackle caregivers from the situation of capability servitude.

The research findings questioned States' obligation and donors' commitment to the standards agreed in key human rights conventions. We therefore call for a broad policy approach that understands the role of carers as well as the specific needs of households struggling with loved ones who are dying, mindful of the need for policy and practice to ensure that human capabilities 'command attention and call for support' qua Sen. This will ensure that a care and support policy predicated on rights is part of a national response to HIV. This means respect for the economics of dignity and what it takes to fulfil state and community obligations to ensure the dignity and rights of people living with HIV and their unpaid carers.

WORKS CITED

Jaising, Indra. "CEDAW and the realisation of rights: reflections on standard settings and culture." *Without Prejudice*. Eds. Meena Shivdas and S Coleman. London, Commonwealth Secretariat, 2010. Print.

Sen, Amartya. *Development As Freedom*. London: Oxford University Press, 1999. Print.

Waring, Marilyn. *If Women Counted*. New York: Harper Collins, 1988. Print.

Waring, Marilyn. 'The Economic Crisis, Informal Work and Social Protection', presentation at the 9th Commonwealth Women's Affairs Ministers' Meeting, Barbados, 8 June 2011. Web. 10 February. 2013.

Waring, Marilyn, R. Carr, A. Mukherjee and M. Shivdas. *Who Cares? Economics of Dignity*. London: Commonwealth Secretariat, 2011. Print.

AUTHORS' NOTE

We owe much to Marilyn Waring who guided the research and steered the work in the direction of a human rights analysis urging us to look out for the silences and listen to what was not being said. We learnt a lot. The work and life of Robert Carr was also particularly significant to the work. We would like to acknowledge Robert's fine mind which speaks through the analysis. We are also thankful to Elizabeth Reid who took the time to read the paper and provided insightful comments. The research would not have been possible without the participation of the unpaid HIV carers who gave up much of their valuable time to share their experiences of caring for loved ones. We are indebted to them.

12.

Rural, Northern Canadian Women's Caregiving Experiences in the Context of Economic Values

HEATHER I. PETERS, DAWN HEMINGWAY, ANITA
VAILLANCOURT & JO-ANNE FISKE

INTRODUCTION

THE CHAPTER EXPLORES THE experiences of women caregivers in four small, rural communities in northern British Columbia (BC), Canada. Research findings demonstrate that the devaluing of women's work is exacerbated by a number of factors including northern isolation, rural lack of services, economic decline, restructuring, and the downloading of previous governmental services to unpaid, female caregivers. The importance of relationships to caregiving activities further complicates the economic valuing of work.

THE BACKDROP TO NORTHERN AND RURAL WOMEN'S CAREGIVING

Waring's analysis of the economic market in connection to women's work identified that women's activities around the world are routinely excluded from discussions and calculations of economic value and growth. "'Growth' figures register 'market' activities, i.e. cash-generating activities, whatever the nature of that activity and regardless of its legal status" (Waring *Three Masquerades* 47). All of women's unpaid labour, from subsistence agriculture in developing countries to women's household activities such as taking children to appointments and soccer games in developed nations, is missing from economic calculations. Thus economic theory knowingly constructs a system that awards value to some work while rendering the rest invisible, and without value (Waring *Three Masquerades*; Waring *Counting for Nothing*).

Caregiving is strongly linked to gender in both unpaid and paid contexts. Women are more likely than men to engage in unpaid care for children and other family members, and this continues to be true even for women who are engaged in full time paid work (Hanlon et al.). Unpaid caregiving also takes place outside of the home and is typically referred to as informal or voluntary care work. In Canada, 75% of volunteers in the health care sector are women (Armstrong and Armstrong *Wasting Away*; Romanow). Women remain overrepresented in paid caregiving work including government health and social service positions as well as in the lowest paid occupations, many of which are also caregiving positions (Armstrong and Armstrong *Double Ghetto*). Consistent with Waring's analysis, women's caregiving work, whether paid or unpaid, is economically valued as being worth less than other types of work and, in particular, less than work more often performed by men (Aronson and Neysmith).

In order to understand women's caregiving in this research it is important to situate their experiences in the context of place. Canada is a vast country, second in size only to Russia. With most of the population stretching along the southern border with the US, this leaves extensive tracts of unpopulated or sparsely populated land stretching across the majority of the country (Schmidt). For the 20% of the population living in these areas life is very different than it is in an urban centre, or even than it is in a small southern community within an easy drive of the populated southern strip.

While small northern and rural communities are not homogeneous they do share some common characteristics which influence experiences of caregiving and other aspects of life (Peters et al.; Schmidt). Small northern communities are often separated from other communities by large distances resulting in social and physical isolation. These communities typically have limited infrastructure, a lack of services, poor transportation including limited or non-existent public transportation, and high travel costs

(Schmidt). Northern winter climates are harsh, making travel difficult and dangerous for half of the year (Schmidt). Many services are concentrated in only a few larger communities in the north; this combined with dangerous winter travel for up to five months every year make service access problematic much of the time.

These conditions existed for the women caregivers who participated in our study. They lived in four communities in northern BC which consists of two thirds of the province of BC stretching over approximately 1,000 kilometres west to east, and the same distance north to south. The region's population is about 300,000 (Northern Health). The urban centre of this area is Prince George, population of 76,000, located about 800 kilometres north of Vancouver, BC's largest city. The other three, rural, research communities lay between 125 and 700 kilometres from Prince George in different directions.

Economic analyses, gendered caregiving and rural geographies combine with neo-liberal ideology to collectively complete the backdrop to the research. Canadian society is founded on a premise of liberal ideology that perceives markets as being central to societal functioning (Hankivsky). The last 30 years has seen a move to the right with a focus on neo-liberal values of cost-effectiveness and cost-benefit analyses which emphasize the retrenchment of government services (Hankivsky; Smith). Neo-liberal ideology values individual freedom and personal choice, and argues that government services are an unwelcome intrusion into this freedom which only serves to limit choices (Harvey). With the neo-liberal focus on retrenchment of services, funding cuts and centralizing services in urban centres, the already under-serviced small and rural communities in northern Canada have been cut back even further in recent years (Hanlon and Halseth). "Increasingly, urban-based models of efficiencies and market parameters have been applied to welfare service evaluation, funding and provision. …A repeated result has been the closure of rural and small town services" (Hanlon and Halseth 7). Cuts included social and health services, as well as government agencies and the like.

Small rural and northern communities are also, for the most part, resource-dependent, often relying on a single primary industry to power the economy and are then subject to the boom and bust cycles of single-industry economies (Collier). During economic decline people in these communities suffer from high unemployment, decrease in personal wealth, increases in stress and poor health, and dislocation of families (Hanlon et al.). During the time of the research, the four communities were simultaneously undergoing economic decline, neo-liberal government cuts to services (Lee, Murray and Parfitt; Wallace, Klein and Reitsma-Street), and faced growing care needs, including the fastest growing rate of seniors in the province of BC (Northern Health Authority). Cuts to government care-giving services result in the downloading of care services to women with expectation that they will take on the work on a voluntary, unpaid basis (Hanlon et al.; Hemingway and MacLeod; Leipert and Reutter). This has had a profoundly negative effect on women's paid and unpaid caregiving, demonstrated by the participants in our study.

EXPERIENCES OF NORTHERN, RURAL WOMEN CAREGIVERS DURING ECONOMIC DECLINE

The research explored three types of caregiving: paid care work; informal unpaid caring for family or friends; and volunteer or community-based caregiving usually through an organization. Eight community meetings were held across the four communities and a total of 58 women were in-terviewed with approximately 15 from each community. Thematic and content analyses were conducted on the data and preliminary results were shared in each community with opportunity for the women to respond. Analyses were informed by critical discourse analysis, structural social work theory, political economy and socialist feminist theories, and critical theory. It is the contrasting but interwoven themes of economics and relationships that are the focus here. Additional findings have been reported elsewhere (Fiske et al.; Peters et al.).

NEO-LIBERAL SERVICE RETRENCHMENT AND PRIVATIZATION

Consistent with the literature, the women in this research talked extensively about the ways in which cuts to health and social services affected them. Women who were paid caregivers described the lack of services available for their clients, many of whom were also women. One woman talked about the government organization she worked for facing cuts that resulted in "very, very limited services." Another suggested that "what they [clients] re-ally need is things that aren't really offered in our system." In talking about the cuts to health care and the lack of access to services in northern and rural communities, one person said: "We're really proud of our universal health care. But it's not universal."

Participants described ways in which they took on more voluntary caregiving work to meet the needs of their family members and friends, often due directly to government cuts to services. One woman, Jean, described caring for her husband who was released early from hospital. She stated, it's "good to be at home and not in hospital …but responsibility falls on family." Another woman talked about providing care to her family member even in the hospital due to a lack of staff:

> Participant YB: And I stayed there, like you know, and I ate at the hospital. I had my breakfast with her and I feed her and …Interviewer: Where were the staff at the hospital? YB: Well there wasn't too many staff then. So I wanted to give her the care that she really needed. …And I learned how to run that tub, put her in the tub and bath her, take her out, put her in a wheelchair and put her back into bed. Let her sit up until the nurse come to put her to bed. Interviewer: Wow. And you did this every day? YB: Every day. Interviewer: For how long? YB: Every day for about maybe two months.

While feeling the stress of the extra caregiving load, women also were able to empathize with workers in agencies that were short-staffed due to job cuts. One woman stated: "It would be helpful if we got more support from them [paid staff]. But, but knowing their situation, there's one person doing one job there that should've been done by three or four people. Knowing that …they don't have the manpower either."

The centralization of services, particularly specialist services, in urban centres was a product of the cuts to social and health services and programs. This was problematic for rural participants. Travel and accommodation costs in order to access services were an added burden in the north. In talking about her client's health issues, Cassie said "she has to go to Vancouver [about 800 kilometres away] for eye surgery. Luckily she has a sister there, so that works out financially." Without her sister's place to stay the client may not have been able to afford to go for surgery.

Along with doing unpaid care work, women in volunteer positions also absorbed other costs. Gerda spoke of the more than 10 years' worth of volunteer hours she put into a community organization. When it came time to get more volunteer training, she was asked to go to Vancouver for the weekend, hundreds of kilometers away, which was difficult when she had an ill husband.

Neo-liberal ideology also espouses the privatization of government programs and services. Participants identified the ways in which these measures negatively affected them, including reduced wages. One participant
provided long term care and respite in her own home due to privatization
measures. She was paid a set fee, determined by the health care system. She
described how she was the only person in her home caring for up to two people at a time, 24 hours a day, seven days a week. Unlike long term or respite
care in a facility, she said, "We're there for stat holidays and everything, we
don't get double time and a half!" At one point in time she worked out
her hourly wage based on her set fee and her 24 hours a day of work; she
said she was essentially working for two dollars an hour. Yet she needed the
money and there were few alternatives for work. Another woman described
for-profit care work this way:

> [The for-profit agency] has some really excellent workers, but
> they don't get paid very much. They get paid eight-fifty an
> hour. [It] collects double that plus more. So ...the agency
> makes more money than the actual caregiver who's doing the
> lifting and the cleaning.

Participants were concerned with the move to privatization of public services and the resulting lower wages for women in paid caregiving work.

CONNECTING CUTS TO SOCIAL AND POLITICAL
STRUCTURES

Participants understood that the retrenchment of services and cuts to programs and jobs were not just happening in a vacuum; they connected them
to societal structures. One woman providing care to her ill husband at home
also talked about the need to restructure paid work in order to support unpaid caregiving downloaded to family members. In talking about caring
for her ill husband at home Jean said, "If we have the expectation that we
will provide care [to family members] ...I think our workplaces need to
support that." While her workplace did allow her the flexibility to do this
caring work, other women's workplaces did not. Another woman summed
up the ways in which cuts to supports had long term costs: "I just don't understand society's um, you know money-saving measures when we look at
the long terms costs...They've burnt out family members so there's nobody
left." She understood that these cuts were ideological rather than grounded

in what was best for families and communities. Another woman also connected the cuts to political ideologies and how those affected women in particular.

> There was always cutbacks to, you know, government supports under an NDP government as well, but, um, since 2001 with the BC Liberals it's even worse, you know. So there's even fewer supports for women to, to strike out on their own. And I think that that's also hugely emotionally taxing on women. So it really undermines, you know, their strength and their ability to be organized and to have the opportunities and to, you know, to, to do what they have to do every day.

CAREGIVING IS ABOUT RELATIONSHIPS

The participants were clear that their caregiving activities were about relationships. They often rejected the notion of caring as work and instead identified it as being about relationships with others. Three senior-aged women in one community described their care of a homebound neighbour whose family had moved away as an act of "friendship", not as work. Another woman said of paying clients that lived in her home for long-term care support, "They become a member of your family." Women feel that they have a responsibility to give back through their volunteer work: "I've always been raised with that kind of social conscience …I absolutely feel, um, a moral obligation to be giving back."

When women were not able to do all the care activities they felt they had to do, there was sometimes a sense of guilt: "I haven't been able to do that caregiving and the guilt that, you know, comes with it." In spite of understanding that services were taking advantage of them as women and as caregivers, they also knew that if they did not do it, someone could suffer. Cutting program funding and downloading services to women takes advantage of these notions of caring as relationships, the sense of obligation to give back, and the guilt when they cannot offer care that is needed. Not only is women's unpaid caregiving not valued, as explained by Waring, but it is also exploited by societies who use unpaid, gendered labour to perform work that they then do not have to pay for.

Job losses due to economic decline and government cuts also affect relationships in other ways. A "lot of our friends had to move away because …they didn't have a job anymore." Dislocation disrupts families as well as friendships when one spouse has to leave the community to find work or has to take on a position where they are required to be in a fly-in or other work community for a week or more at a time. Informal and familial support networks are vital to caregiving, both as supports to the caregivers, but also because people in need of care rely on family and friends. When communities and families are dislocated due to job losses and the need to move, these support networks are disrupted and people in need of care can lose their caregivers. Thus as the need for unpaid caregiving increases due to cuts, the disruption to support networks means that people may not have the informal care they need. The loss of familial or volunteer caregivers in turn can put more strain on the paid care systems; in spite of this, unpaid caregiving is still not recognized as having value.

IMPORTANCE AND INVISIBILITY OF UNPAID CARE WORK

As described by Waring, women's unpaid care work is vital to their families and communities, while also often being invisible. One woman said: "A lot of volunteer work happens in this town that no one knows about." Someone else said of her volunteer palliative care work that it: "flies under the community radar." Fiske et al. describe the taken for granted nature of women's unpaid care work:

> Community leaders had come to rely on volunteers as 'business as usual', as the norm. They felt community leaders perceived this to be either routine women's work or as an accepted way to rationalize and not pay for expensive services. Another woman told us: "personal caregiving that we were giving ... don't begrudge. But I am still very, very angry about the lack of help, the lack of response from public health, the lack of help from the medical world." (600)

The economic invisibility Waring described, translates into invisibility at the community level as well. While women will continue to do caregiving activities, they also want society to recognize and value their work. Once care is downloaded to unpaid women there is no longer a record of it happening or even being needed. Yet participants understood how important this work is: "...If women stopped volunteering, the world would fall apart, literally."

MULTIPLE CAREGIVING ROLES AND TENSIONS

With the loss of jobs and the downloading of care services to women, many women were pressured into taking on multiple caregiving roles simultaneously. Some women felt forced to take on paid care work, even if the wages were low, because they needed the money: "We've had to do it." Loss of jobs and economic decline means these women and their families struggled to get by. "Really the only time people...say, 'Oh well money isn't everything,' is if you've got enough to live on...I mean money...unfortunately it can buy you better health." As with caregiving in general, women felt that taking on multiple care roles was simply expected, even ingrained in them. Jean said "Women are socialized to do this double juggling."

Yet the multiple care work roles took their toll. Some women described being unable to do care work that they knew was important and they felt guilty about not being able to do it all. Others talked about turning to their female friends or relatives to ask for help. Young teen women assisted at home with caring for children, cleaning, cooking, etc. because their mothers were so overwhelmed. Some working women talked about hiring another woman to clean their home or bring in meals because they could not keep up with their job and their household duties. When women could not keep up with their multiple caregiving roles they frequently turned to other, often unpaid or poorly paid, women to help them.

HIERARCHY OF WOMEN'S CAREGIVING

The pressures women faced to take on more and more caregiving activities and roles meant that eventually women could not do it all. The prioritizing of caregiving roles happened in several ways. The first is one of pure pragmatism. When people are busy they have to make decisions about what they do, and do not, have time for. Predictably when people needed to work, paid caregiving took precedence over other caregiving activities. Caring for family and friends came next, with volunteer community-based caregiving coming in last.

Having to prioritize care roles was not easy and was often distressing for women. This was particularly true when women had to place their paid work in front of time with their families. One woman described being drained trying to balance her paid care work with having to take on the care of her grandchildren. After trying for months to make it work she was so exhausted and ill that she finally had to turn the children over to the care of the state. She could not work and care for her grandkids at the same time, but without a job she would not be able to keep the kids anyway. Another woman put it bluntly: "You go to work instead of care for your kids. You love your work and not your kids."

Hierarchies of caregiving were not only pragmatic, however. They were also embedded with notions of status and power, and these were connected to economic contexts. Waring demonstrated that economic systems value paid work and do not value unpaid work. Women in the research talked about how various types of caregiving work had status and value, while other types did not. In a type of pecking order the women could identify ways in which higher status caring roles had power over others. It is as if the economic system's valuing of some kinds of work, and not others, was translated into the reality of caregiving, but in a hierarchy more complex than just paid versus unpaid.

In one community meeting a participant described how women in government, or well-paid, care work had the most status. Women working for non-profit organizations, in lesser paying positions were in the middle, and women who were clients of care providers had little to no status or power. This participant described working in a community-based non-profit organization with a client who was also a client of government-based child protection services. She felt that she was being used by the government care worker to put pressure on the client, a mother, to follow certain directions or "orders" even though as a community-based worker she was not comfortable with the process. Given that government offices are often the funders of community-based organizations and services, (which was true in this example) this has an added component of an unspoken threat hanging over the heads of people working for the non-profit organization. If the woman working in the non-profit organization had not "obeyed" the instructions of a supposed colleague at the government organization, which funded the non-profit, then the non-profit's funding may have been at risk in the long term.

In small, rural communities these power dynamics are often played out not only at work but also in people's personal lives as workers often see each other and clients outside work settings, such as when buying groceries or attending a community event. Thus the power and status in different caregiving roles would have a profound effect on all aspects of a caregiver's life. For example, a mother, who was a client, would need to be careful about where she was seen in the community, as being seen in an undesirable place, whatever the reason, could be used against her the next time she tried to access services. This dynamic would also be true for the woman working at the non-profit when meeting the government colleague outside of work. This can increase the stress in caregivers' lives as power imbalances between caregivers play out in both work and personal spheres.

CONCLUSION

Although there has been progress, Waring's analysis of the economic de-valuing of women's work is still relevant today, and this understanding provides an important starting point in examining caregiving by women in northern and rural communities. The caregiving experiences of women in our research indicate that there are problematic personal, community and societal level implications of this economic devaluing. Women in our study appeared to implicitly understand, and sometimes explicitly articulate, the value of their caregiving work both in the economic realm and on the level of relationships. Whether paid or unpaid, there was a clear sense of the critical role their care provision played in the lives of those receiving care. Although seemingly contradictory perspectives, these women viewed caring work as embedded in and intimately tied to relationships, while at the same time acknowledging its economic role in the context of both identifying and opposing neo-liberal devaluing and downloading of care provision. Neo-liberal cuts to services increased the reliance on unpaid women caregivers, while economic decline meant people had to move for work resulting in the separation of family members and the loss of unpaid caregivers for some.

Particularly disturbing are the ramifications of the devaluing of care activities by the creation of a hierarchy of caregiving. One of the benefits of the development of the welfare state is that women's caregiving work has increasingly been incorporated into paid positions. Although this puts the work in the realm of now having economic value, according to Waring's, one of the paradoxical effects is that differing wage levels applied to different types of caregiving increases the alienation between women, and the oppression of some women by other women. The disparity of wages by types of caregiving has been exacerbated by neo-liberal actions to reduce welfare state costs by cutting funding and services, while increasingly privatizing services. This has led to a decrease in women's wages, and more so in some caregiving positions than others. In small, rural communities in northern Canada with its pre-existing lack of access to services, these disparities are felt even more keenly. The alienation and oppression between women based on status and power issues embedded in caregiving roles means that women are even less likely to come together to challenge the status quo because they are now divided.

In Waring's introduction to her second edition she writes of her internal conflict of wanting to include women in economic valuing while also seeing the economic system as flawed and wanting to "bring this system to its knees" (xxi *Counting for Nothing*). There is a similar conflict in this research. On one hand is the need to respect the role of relationships in caregiving, while simultaneously there is a need to value the work at an economic level. Yet the hierarchy of caregiving suggests that valuing also places caregiving in competition for status depending on the economic value of the work. All caregiving needs to be valued equally, while supporting women in their relationships and activities.

While there is no easy answer, there are options to begin the process. Caregiving downloaded to women in times of cutbacks needs to be restored to, at the least, previous levels of funding or better. Unequal pay between genders needs to be redressed so that caregiving work is not undervalued compared to traditional male roles. It is important to offer respite for caregivers. A universal guaranteed income minimum that provides a realistic living wage is an important part of recognizing the work of unwaged caregivers and addressing poverty in general. Most importantly, caregiving in government, non-profit, and unpaid sectors needs to be valued equally in terms of income for caregivers. And we need to find a way to realize that value means more than economic value.

WORKS CITED

Armstrong, Pat, and Hugh Armstrong. *The Double Ghetto*. Third ed. Don Mills, ON: Oxford University Press, 2010. Print.

—. *Wasting Away*. Second ed. New York: Oxford University Press, 2003. Print.

Aronson, Jane, and Sheila M. Neysmith. "Manufacturing Social Exclusion in the Home Care Market." *Canadian Public Policy* 27.2 (2001): 151-65. Print.

Collier, Ken. *Social Work with Rural Peoples*, Second Edition. Vancouver: New Star Books, 2006. Print.

Fiske, Jo-Anne, Dawn Hemingway, Anita Vaillancourt, Heather I. Peters, Christina McLennan, Barb Keith & Anne Burrill. "Health policy & the politics of citizenship: Northern women's care giving in rural B.C." *Rural Women's Health in Canada*. Eds. Leipert, Beverly D., Belinda Leach and Wilfreda Thurston. Toronto: University of Toronto Press, 2012. 589-612. Print.

Hankivsky, Olena. *Social Policy and the Ethic of Care*. Vancouver: UBC Press, 2004. Print.

Hanlon, Neil and Greg Halseth. "The Greying of Resource Communities in Northern British Columbia." *The Canadian Geographer* 49.1 (2005): 1-24. Print.

Hanlon, Neil, Greg Halseth, Rachael Clasby and Virginia Pow. "The place embeddedness of social care: Restructuring work and welfare in Mackenzie, BC." *Health & Place* 13.2 (2007): 466-81. Print.

Harvey, D. *A Brief History of Neo-Liberalism*. Oxford: Oxford University Press, 2005. Print.

Hemingway, Dawn, and T. MacLeod. "Living north of 65: A community process to hear the voices of the northern seniors." *Rural Social Work* 9 (2004): 137-46. Print.

Lee, Marc, Stuart Murray, and Ben Parfitt. *BC's Regional Divide*. Vancouver: Canadian Centre for Policy Alternatives, 2005. Print.

Leipert, Beverly D., and L. Reutter. "Women's health in northern British Columbia: The role of geography and gender." *Canadian Journal of Rural Medicine* 10.4 (2005): 241-53. Print.

Northern Health. "Quick facts about Northern Health". n.d.: Northern Health. May 2 2012.
<http://www.northernhealth.ca/AboutUs/QuickFacts.aspx>.

Peters, Heather I., Jo-Anne Fiske, Dawn Hemingway, Anita Vaillancourt, Christina McLennan, Barb Keith, & Anne Burrill. "Interweaving caring and economics in the context of place: Experiences of northern and rural women caregivers." *Ethics and Social Welfare* 4.2 (2010): 172-87. Print.

Romanow, R. J. *Building on values: The future of health care in Canada*. Final Report. 2002.
<http://publications.gc.ca/pub?id=237274\&sl=0>.

Schmidt, Glen. "What is northern social work?" *Northern & Rural Social Work Practice: A Canadian perspective*. Eds. Delaney, Roger and Keith Brownlee. Thunder Bay, ON: Centre for Northern Studies, Lakehead University, 2009. 1-17. Print.

Smith, Susan J. "States, markets and an ethic of care." *Political Geography*

24 (2005): 1-20. Print.

Statistics Canada. "Portrait of the Canadian population in 2006, 2006 census (Catalogue No. 97-550-XIE)." Ottawa, ON: Statistics Canada, 2006. Vol. 2012. April 26 2012. <http://www12.statcan.ca/census-recensement/2006/as-sa/97-551/index-eng.cfm>.

Wallace, Bruce, Seth Klein, and Marge Reitsma-Street. *Denied Assistance: Closing the front door on welfare in BC.* Vancouver: Vancouver Island Public Interest Research Group and Canadian Centre for Policy Alternatives, 2006. Print.

Waring, Marilyn. *Counting for Nothing.* Second ed. Toronto: University of Toronto Press Inc., 1999. Print.

—. *Three Masquerades.* Toronto: University of Toronto Press Inc., 1996. Print.

AUTHORS' NOTE

The authors wish to thank the Social Sciences and Humanities Research Council for funding this research (Grant # 410-2004-1646). Thanks are also due to the women participants for the time and knowledge they graciously shared, and to the communities including many organizations which assisted with the facilitation of the research process.

13.

Creating Conceptual Tools for Change

Marilyn Waring's Influence in Australia

MARTY GRACE & LYN CRAIG

INTRODUCTION

MARILYN WARING'S WORK has had far-reaching impacts in Australia. Her 1988 book was first published in New Zealand and Australia with the title of *Counting for Nothing: What Men Value and What Women are Worth*. Her work challenged conventional ways of seeing (or not seeing) women's unpaid work, and questioned mainstream economic concepts such as the production boundary. She wrote about how the conventions utilised in calculating the Gross Domestic Product (GDP) and Gross National Product (GNP) rendered women's unpaid work invisible, using the United States as an example:

> The GNP of the United States, as reported by the US Department of Commerce, includes only "final products". This means that the value of a product is counted only once, even when the product is found at intermediate stages in the production process within a short time span. Wheat is a good example: produced first by the farmer, it is then transported, processed, and milled into flour. The flour producer then sells the product to the baker, who processes it into a final product

for sale and consumption. The correct procedure is to count the wheat at point of first sale, then to include only the "value added" by labour at each point in the further production process. If a woman does all this herself it is neither production nor consumption. It is economic inactivity. It lies outside the production boundary. (Waring, *Counting for Nothing* 53)

In case women might agree that their unpaid work is too difficult to account for, and that their exclusion does not matter anyway, Waring explained how other apparently "difficult" activities, those carried out in government departments, are included in calculating the GDP and GNP:

If the market price valuation were used for general government activity in the same way as for business activity, the product (that is, the value added in the general government sector) would be a substantial negative amount. The government's purchases of intermediate goods and services from other sectors would exceed its sales to other sectors. The measure of the services that government provides is thus taken to be the cost of producing them. Despite the lack of a market price, a value of production attaches. The measure of the same services provided within a household apparently costs nothing to produce and is valued at nothing or assumed to be household consumption, if any expenditure is involved. (Waring, *Counting for Nothing* 53)

Waring argued that the location of so much of women's traditional work on the "no value" side of the production boundary reflected the ideologies and interests of those involved in its formulation, rather than a realistic assessment of the contribution of this work. This invisibility of unpaid work led to distortion in policy-making:

Like the GNP, the GDP is used to monitor rates and patterns of growth, to set priorities in policy making, to measure the success of policies, and to measure "economic welfare". Activities that lie outside the production boundary—that is, in every nation, the great bulk of labour performed by women in an unpaid capacity,—are left out of the GDP, as they are left out of the GNP. It is not a large step from that point to leaving them out of policy considerations altogether. (Waring, *Counting for Nothing* 53)

We characterise Waring's work as creating conceptual tools for change because her timely and meaningful ideas became shared concepts in the minds and conversations of the people influenced by her work. These shared understandings became incorporated into the Australian social policy discourse. Many academics, policy makers, politicians and ordinary Australians read and understood Waring's work, and used her concepts in talking to each other and developing understandings and proposals that have eventually led to change. The language, concepts and understandings introduced by Waring effectively became the conceptual tools we used to think about and discuss women's unpaid work, and to develop proposals for change.

International recognition of Marilyn Waring's work gave encouragement to like-minded Australians to make use of these new conceptual tools, and change the discourse in relation to women's unpaid work, freeing the imagination to work towards change at intellectual, everyday cultural, and social policy levels. Waring explained the value of the resources that go into unpaid work, and the benefit that women's unpaid work creates for the community at large. These ideas were taken up by authors such as Michael Bittman and Jocelyn Pixley in relation to the public benefit of the unpaid work of caring for young children, and the notion that the rest of the community are "free riders" on the work of mothers. These ideas, along with Lois Bryson's question "Who benefits?" and Carol Bacchi's question "What is the problem represented to be?" have influenced generations of social policy students, activists and academic researchers. Considerable research and advocacy work has explored the cross-over between economics and time use, including the idea that people's time has a value, and that caring work has tangible, as well as intangible, costs and benefits.

This chapter examines the influence of Waring's work within the Australian context. This influence can be seen as both a conceptual/theoretical contribution to discussions of "counting" the invisible work of women, and also as an explicit contribution to social policy development. We give two brief examples in relation to paid maternity leave and fair wages for people in the industries of care. We present a longer discussion of Waring's relationship with the development of time use surveys, a critical source of data that make it possible to count women's unpaid work. We discuss recent developments in this area of research, including the particularly Australian emphasis on the value of the intangible aspects of care work.

Waring ventured into economics, and articulated the issues in a way that made it possible to be optimistic about what might be the outcome. She influenced politicians and policy makers as well as scholars, whose efforts have seen many changes over the past two decades, including quite recent social policy changes such as the introduction of paid maternity leave and wage increases for care workers. In the following sections, we provide a brief discussion of these two recent changes, followed by a more extensive and detailed discussion of Australian time use scholarship and research.

PAID MATERNITY LEAVE

Feminist activists had been agitating for paid maternity leave for many years. However, it was Pru Goward, Australia's Sex Discrimination Commissioner, who championed the cause in a way that eventually brought about a national paid maternity leave scheme in this country. Waring's work had made it possible to think differently about the circumstances of mothers and carers, and a number of submissions that contributed to the eventual outcome (for example Submission 151 by Marty Grace) were explicitly influenced by Waring's ideas. The Human Rights and Equal Opportunities Commission (HREOC) 2002 proposal for a paid maternity leave scheme, a version of which was introduced in 2010, was influenced by Waring's ideas. The proposal appealed to particularly Australian worldviews because, as well as tangible economic and social outcomes, it emphasised the value of the intangibles—baby welfare and maternal well-being, and to a lesser extent gender equity. Scholars including Marian Baird and Gillian Whitehouse were also influential proponents of paid maternity leave (see for example Baird; Baird, Brennan and Cutcher; Whitehouse et al.).

FAIR WAGES FOR CARE WORKERS

Recent Australian increases in wages for care workers are the result of the advocacy of scholars including Barbara Pocock, who cites Marilyn Waring in her work on work/life conflict. Pocock draws on the idea of the invisibility of unpaid care work, referring to the 'shadowy ghost' of carers, who prop up the "productive" economy. HREOC's submission to the Senate Inquiry on Sex Discrimination also cited Waring in arguing the way in which unpaid work is essential to Australia's "economic prosperity" (HREOC:

254). This work highlights how care work in the market—childcare, aged care, healthcare—is persistently underpaid because it remains undervalued (Bretherton; Charlesworth and Marshall; Pocock). The ongoing relevance of Waring's work is evident in a continued push towards achieving appropriate levels of remuneration for paid care work. The nexus between the economic and human value of caring (Reiger, Garvan and Temel) as suggested through Waring's ideas, remains embedded in all aspects of social policy which concern women's paid and unpaid labour.

MARILYN WARING'S INFLUENCE ON TIME USE SCHOLARSHIP AND RESEARCH

Since 1988, a distinctively Australian scholarship has emerged, influenced by Marilyn Waring's work. This scholarship includes a strong emphasis on valuing the intangible, the love and care, as well as the tangible, the time, but with the focus on the number of hours spent, rather than replacement value (for example Grace "A 21st Century Feminist Agenda"). The *Counting for Nothing* title of Waring's work encapsulates the two meanings of "counting". One, referring to tangibles, is the idea that it is possible (or not) to count, add up, and document the hours that women spend in unpaid work. The other meaning refers to intangibles, whether something counts (or not), whether it is generally seen to be of value.

Internationally and in Australia, both tangible and intangible aspects of unpaid work have been explored in scholarly research and literature. The literal counting, as in valuing the tangible work, has been explored in two major ways—by counting the hours spent, and by attributing a replacement value to the activities undertaken. In Australia, more attention has been given to time use than to replacement value. Counting time as time, rather than ascribing it a monetary value, reflects the view that unpaid work activities are valuable in and of themselves. Quantifying the monetary value of unpaid work may be a powerful rhetorical tool in arguing for its worth, but it does not solve the problem of how to recognise and reward those who do it, or how to redress gender inequalities in the distribution of paid and unpaid work. In many respects the bottom line is not money but how we are to live. Care work, particularly, is socially necessary; it needs to be done for society to function. The following paragraphs trace the development of Australian scholarship in relation to time use and women's unpaid work.

Duncan Ironmonger ("Counting Outputs", "Bringing up Bobby and Betty") is a particularly important Australian scholar in the time use field.

Ironmonger and Waring influenced each other's thinking on the economic value of unpaid work. Ironmonger organised the Australian launch of Waring's book, and was an examiner of her PhD thesis ("Personal Communication"), and Waring paid particular tribute to Ironmonger in a 2005 book chapter "Changes in Household Make-up and Implications for Economic Policy: A Conversation to Honour Duncan Ironmonger." Both Ironmonger and Waring challenged dominant views and definitions of what constitutes economic activity, and advocated that unpaid work should be valued and added to national accounts. Accounting for the unpaid economy as part of the Gross Domestic Product (GDP) in "Satellite Accounts" would give visibility to unpaid work in official figures, formally recognise its value and thereby the economic contribution of women. Ironmonger ("Counting Outputs") was an early proponent of this endeavour, which now has the support of the United Nations. It is regarded as extremely important to acknowledge the extent of, and to show cross-national differences in, women's unpaid work (United Nations).

One of Ironmonger's central contributions was in developing and promoting Time Use Surveys (TUS) in Australia. To calculate the unpaid economy requires good information on how people spend their time. Dollar values are available for the visible economy, but the only way to quantify unpaid work is to ask how people spend their time. TUS give an otherwise unavailable picture of unpaid work. They collect data on all the things that people do over a 24 or 48 hour period, and thereby allow direct investigation of the amount and distribution of non-market work. They are a vital information source, providing the most accurate current estimates of all the unpaid work that takes place in society (Gershuny). They are necessary to the operationalisation of Waring's argument that unpaid work should be counted.

Active in promoting time use surveys worldwide, Ironmonger was also instrumental in the establishment of Australian Bureau of Statistics (ABS) TUS. Following a pilot survey in 1987, ABS TUS were conducted in 1992, 1997 and 2006. The next is planned for 2013. These data allow the estimation of the magnitude and worth of unpaid work to the Australian economy. This work is very important, since as Waring would argue, counting as productive only activities that are paid for in money has far-reaching social consequences and government and workplace policies are developed on the basis of incomplete information. The usual valuation method is to add up the time inputs, and calculate how much it would cost to replace that labour. Valuing the unpaid domestic work economy at the rate it would cost to hire per hour workers such as cooks, child carers, gardeners, laundry hands, or cleaners, the contribution to the country's national product in 1992 was $341 billion, compared with the standard market calculation in the dollar economy, a GDP of $395 billion (Ironmonger "Counting Outputs"). Ironmonger undertook substantial work on the monetary value of the household most prominently through his work which considered Gross Household Product (GHP). Ironmonger developed an analytic framework of Australian time use data (considering output as well as input) which undertook a far more comprehensive approach to counting domestic inputs than most comparable international studies of unpaid work (Ironmonger "Bringing up Bobby and Betty"; Ironmonger and Soupourmas). The subsequent comparison between GHP and Gross Market Product (showing the former to be greater than the latter) illustrated the very high dollar value of the household economy in Australia. Waring ("Changes in Household Make-up") applauded Ironmonger's efforts, and argued that if his approach had been more widely followed, and greater attention paid to economic aspects, rather than to social aspects, there could have been greater social policy impact of the work on time use. However, most time use studies in Australia that built on Waring's insights did not take the step of attributing a dollar value to the unpaid work of women. Rather, they counted the time itself.

In 1987, Ironmonger organised a workshop on the theme 'The Future of the Household Economy and the Role of Women' at the University of Melbourne. Michael Bittman, subsequently a prominent Australian time use scholar, attended that workshop. There he made contact with the Australian Government Office of the Status of Women (OSW), which later supported his research, leading to the landmark publication *Juggling Time* (Ironmonger "Personal Communication"; Bittman *Juggling Time*). This report analysed the gender division of labour in Australia using the 1992 Time Use Survey. No monetary value was ascribed—rather, Bittman added up and compared the time men and women spent in various tasks, including paid and unpaid work. Bittman's time use analyses and his commentary on gender disparities (Bittman and Pixley) had considerable public impact. He built a substantial research program, looking at many aspects of unpaid work, including the ways that family responsibilities have changed over time (Bittman "Changing Family Responsibilities"; Bittman "Now That the Future Has Arrived"; Bittman and Matheson), differences between men's and women's leisure (Bittman and Wajcman), trends in outsourcing domestic labour (Bittman, Meagher and Matheson), the effects of domestic technology (Bittman, Rice and Wajcman), and the effects of policy, non-parental childcare use, and relative income on the gender distribution of unpaid work and care (Bittman "Parenthood without Penalty"; Bittman, Craig and Folbre; Bittman, England, Sayer, Folbre and Matheson). Underpinning Bittman's work is the concern to make the invisible visible (Bittman, Fast, Fisher and Thomson), but not, as Waring and Ironmonger would advocate, by ascribing it a monetary value.

Prominent US feminist economist Nancy Folbre has also been influential in Australia. She is considered a pioneering thinker about the value of unpaid work. Folbre has written extensively on the worth of unpaid work and childcare. She began a fruitful collaboration with Bittman during a five year period during which she was a frequent visiting scholar at the Australian National University. Although her work also engages with valuing care in monetary terms, in these collaborations the emphasis was on accounting for the time inputs (Folbre and Bittman). Folbre is acutely aware that family care is a vital and valuable good in itself, and is concerned that current social organisation threatens its supply (Folbre *Who Pays for the Kids?*; Folbre *Valuing Children*; Folbre *The Invisible Heart*).

The time-focused approach was taken by subsequent Australian researchers, to whom the sustainability of social care, as well as gender equality in its distribution and costs, was important (Grace "Motherhood"; Grace "A 21st Century Feminist Agenda"). For example, Lyn Craig began a research program investigating the gender distribution of the time costs of children. In addition to quantifying the magnitude of parental time children absorb (Craig and Bittman), the program investigated differences in how women and men parent (Craig "Does Father Care Mean Fathers Share?"), multitasking (Craig "Children and the Revolution"; Craig "Is There Really a 'Second Shift'?"), and the associations between education, gender equity and time with children (Craig "Parental Education, Time in Work and Time with Children"). Craig was supported in her early research by a year long Time Use Fellowship awarded by the Office for the Status of Women (OSW), to promote analysis of the ABS TUS. Another OSW Fellowship recipient was Trish Hill, who did place a dollar value on unpaid work, to compare household incomes using conventional and 'full income' measures (Hill).

The predominant research emphasis on time rather than money reflects Australian attitudes towards care, particularly of children. In world terms, parental care time is high, and many Australians view it as important that children receive most of their care from their own parents (Gray, Baxter and

Alexander).

Internationally, concern for care sustainability with gender equity has generated calls that it be distributed more equally between men and women, and/or between families, employers and the state (see for example Lewis; Crompton, Lewis and Lyonette; Gornick and Meyers). This puts the activity itself, rather than the economic value of it, front and centre. Placing a monetary value on unpaid work, as argued by Waring, has given way to a focus on how to share the work itself more equitably. Current Australian research has taken up this challenge, looking at the effects of workplace characteristics (Pocock, Skinner and Ichii; Charlesworth et al.), work conditions (Craig and Powell; Craig, Powell and Cortis) and social policies (Craig, Mullan and Blaxland), on women's and men's work-family balance. There is an increasing focus on men, in addition to women, with researchers seeking to identify approaches that might encourage greater male involvement in unpaid work and care e.g. (Baxter et al.; Baxter and Smart; Craig and Mullan; Grace "The Unpaid Work of Caring for Young Children: Ideas for Long-Term and Short-Term Change"). Other commentators have argued for an inclusion of the right to receive care and the right to time for care into the definition of social citizenship (Knijn and Kremer; Lister; Hobson, Lewis and Siim). Some go further, and argue that participation in care should be regarded as a civic duty, perhaps linked to public pension entitlement, making 'explicit that informal care provision is a social responsibility just as much as paid work' (Kershaw:343; see also Craig "Valuing by Doing: Policy Options to Promote Sharing the Care"; Pascall and Lewis). New Australian research argues that care is fundamental to our humanity and that ensuring it is a social obligation for all is a prerequisite to achieving social justice (Leahy).

CONCLUSION

Marilyn Waring's early work captured the imagination of scholars, policy makers and ordinary Australians, connecting with a common disquiet, and articulating it in a way that was novel, but nevertheless made sense to people. Her ability to articulate burning issues within an economic context inspired others to believe that things could change. In Australia, she is seen as a close neighbour who has had international impact with her groundbreaking work. She influenced a generation of students, scholars, policy makers and politicians, who in their turn influenced, and continue to influence, scholarship and social policy change.

WORKS CITED

Baird, Marian. "Paid Maternity Leave in Australia: HREOC's Valuing Parenthood." *Australian Review of Public Affairs* (2002). Print.

Baird, Marian, Deborah Brennan, and Leanne Cutcher. "A Pregnant Pause in the Provision of Paid Maternity Leave in Australia." *Labour and Industry* 12.4. (2002). Print.

Baxter, Jennifer, Matthew Gray and Michael Alexander. *Mothers and Fathers with Young Children: Paid Employment, Caring and Wellbeing Canberra: Department of Families, Community Services and Indigenous Affairs.* 2007. Print.

Baxter, Jennifer, and Diana Smart. *Fathering in Australia among Couple Families with Young Children.* Canberra: Department of Families, Housing, Community Services and Indigenous Affairs (FaHCSIA), 2011. Print.

Bittman, Michael. "Changing Family Responsibilities: The Role of Social Attitudes, Markets and the State." *Family Matters* 50 (1998): 31-37. Print.

—. *Juggling Time.* Canberra: Australian Government Publishing Service, 1992. Print.

—. "Now That the Future Has Arrived: A Retrospective of Gershuny's Theory of Social Innovation." Social Policy Research Centre, Discussion Paper, No.110 (1999). Print.

—. "Parenthood without Penalty: Time Use and Public Policy in Australia and Finland." *Feminist Economics* 5.3 (1999): 27-42. Print.

Bittman, Michael, Janet E. Fast, Kimberly Fisher and Cathy Thomson. "Making the Invisible Visible: The Life and Time(s) of Informal Caregivers." *Family Time: The Social Organisation of Care.* Eds. Folbre, Nancy and Michael Bittman. London: Routledge, 2004. 69-89. Print.

Bittman, Michael, James Rice, and Judy Wajcman. "Appliances and Their Impact: The Ownership of Domestic Technology and Time Spent on Household Work." *British Journal of Sociology* 55 3 (2004): 401-23. Print.

Bittman, Michael, Lyn Craig, and Nancy Folbre. "Packaging Care: What Happens When Parents Utilize NonParental Child Care." *Family Time: The Social Organization of Care.* Eds. Folbre, Nancy and Michael Bittman. London: Routledge, 2004. 133-51. Print.

Bittman, Michael, Paula England, Liana Sayer, Nancy Folbre and George Matheson. "When Does Gender Trump Money? Bargaining and Time in Household Work." *American Journal of Sociology* 109.1 (2003): 186-214. Print.

Bittman, Michael, and George Matheson. "All Else Confusion: What Time Use Surveys Show About Changes in Gender Equity." SPRC Discussion Paper No.72. Sydney: Social Policy Research Centre, UNSW, 1996. Print.

Bittman, Michael, Gabrielle Meagher, and George Matheson. *The Changing Boundary between Home and Market. Australian Trends in Outsourcing Domestic Labour.* Sydney: Social Policy Research Centre, 1998. Print.

Bittman, Michael, and Jocelyn Pixley. *The Double Life of the Family.* St. Leonards: Allen and Unwin, 1997. Print.

Bittman, Michael, and Judy Wajcman. "The Rush Hour: The Character of Leisure Time and Gender Equity." *Social Forces* 79.1 (2000): 165-89. Print.

Bretherton, Tanya. *Developing the Child Care Workforce: Understanding 'Fight' or 'Flight' Amongst Workers Sydney: Department of Education, Employment and Workplace Relations*, 2010. Print.

Charlesworth, Sara, Lyndall Strazdins, Lean O'Brien, and Sharryn Sims. "Parents' Jobs in Australia: Work Hours Polarisation and the Consequences for Job Quality and Gender Equality." *Australian Journal of Labour Economics* 14 1 (2011): 35-57. Print.

Charlesworth, Sara, and Helen Marshall. *Chosen Sacrifices? Some Paradoxical Effects of Strategies to Attract and Retain Care Workers.* Melbourne: Centre for Applied Social Research, RMIT, 2010. Print.

Craig, Lyn. "Children and the Revolution: A Time-Diary Analysis of the Impact of Motherhood on Daily Workload." *Journal of Sociology* 42.2 (2006): 125-43. Print.

—. "Does Father Care Mean Fathers Share? A Comparison of How Mothers and Fathers in Intact Families Spend Time with Children." *Gender & Society* 20.2 (2006): 259-81. Print.

—. "Is There Really a 'Second Shift', and If So, Who Does It? A Time-Diary Investigation." *Feminist Review* 86.1 (2007): 149-70. Print.

—. "Parental Education, Time in Work and Time with Children: An Australian Time-Diary Analysis." *British Journal of Sociology* 57.4 (2006): 553-75. Print.

—. "Valuing by Doing: Policy Options to Promote Sharing the Care." *Journal of the Association of Research on Mothering.* Special Issue on 'Caregiving and care-work: theory and practice 10.1 (2008): 45-56. Print.

Craig, Lyn, and Michael Bittman. "The Effect of Children on Adults' Time-Use: An Analysis of the Incremental Time Costs of Children in Australia." *Feminist Economics* 14.2 (2008): 57-85. Print.

Craig, Lyn, and Killian Mullan. "How Fathers and Mothers Share Childcare: A Cross-National Time-Diary Comparison." *American Sociological Review* 76.6 (2011): 834-61. Print.

Craig, Lyn, Killian Mullan, and Megan Blaxland. "Parenthood, Policy and Work-Family Time in Australia 1992-2006." *Work, Employment and Society* 24.1 (2010): 1-19. Print.

Craig, Lyn, and Abigail Powell. "Nonstandard Work Schedules, Work-Family Balance and the Gendered Division of Childcare." *Work, Employment and Society* 25.2 (2011): 274-91. Print.

Craig, Lyn, Abigail Powell, and Natasha Cortis. "Self Employment, Work-Family Time and the Gender Division of Labour." *Work, Employment and Society* 26.5 (2012): 716. Print.

Crompton, Rosemary , Susan Lewis, and Clare Lyonette, eds. *Women, Men, Work and Family in Europe.* Basingstoke, England: Palgrave Macmillan, 2007. Print.

Folbre, Nancy. *The Invisible Heart: Economics and Family Values.* New York: The New Press, 2001. Print.

—. *Valuing Children: Rethinking the Economics of the Family.* Boston: Harvard University Press, 2007. Print.

—. *Who Pays for the Kids? Gender and the Structures of Constraint.* London and New York: Routledge, 1994. Print.

Folbre, Nancy, and Michael Bittman. *Family Time: The Social Organisation of Care.* New York: Routledge, 2004. Print.

Gershuny, Jonathan. *Changing Times: Work and Leisure in Post-Industrial Societies.* Oxford: Oxford University Press, 2000. Print.

Gornick, Janet, and Marcia Meyers, eds. *Gender Equality: Transforming Family Divisions of Labor* (Vol. Iv Real Utopias Project) London: Verso, 2009. Print.

Grace, Marty. "A 21st Century Feminist Agenda for Valuing Care-Work." *Journal of the Association for Research on Mothering* 8 1/2 (2006). Print.

—. "Submission to the Human Rights and Equal Opportunity Commission in response to the interim paper 'Valuing Parenthood: Options for Paid Maternity Leave', 11-7-2002, Submission 151." Electronic copy available from the author on request.

—. "Motherhood: Economic Exploitation in Disguise." *Just Policy* 21.March (2001). Print.

—. "The Unpaid Work of Caring for Young Children: Ideas for Long-Term and Short-Term Change." *Just Policy* 34 (2004): 23-31. Print.

Gray, Matthew, Jennifer Baxter, and Michael Alexander. "ParentOnly Care: A Child Care Choice for Working Couple Families?" *Family Matters*. 79 (2008): 42-49. Print.

Hill, Trish. "Time Use, Gender and Disadvantage in Australia: Conventional Income and 'Full Income' Approaches to Estimation." *The Economic and Labour Relations Review* 20.1 (2009): 13-34. Print.

Hobson, Barbara, Jane Lewis, and Birte Siim. *Contested Concepts in Gender and Social Politics.* Cheltenham: Edward Elgar Publishing Ltd, 2002. Print.

HREOC. "Submission of the Human Rights and Equal Opportunity Commission to the Senate Legal and Constitutional Affairs Committee on the Inquiry into the Effectiveness of the Sex Discrimination Act 1984 (Cth) in Eliminating Discrimination and Promoting Gender Equality." Available at <http://www.hreoc.gov.au/legal/submissions/2008/20080901/SDA.pdf> (2008). Print.

Ironmonger, Duncan. "Bringing up Betty and Bobby: The Macro Time Dimensions of Investment in the Care and Nurture of Children." *Family Time: The Social Organisation of Care.* Eds. Folbre, Nancy and Michael Bittman. London: Routledge, 2004. Print.

—. "Counting Outputs, Capital Input and Caring Labour: Estimating Gross Household Product." *Feminist Economics* 2.3 (1996): 37-64. Print.

—. "Personal Communication." To Marty Grace, 2012.

Ironmonger, Duncan, and Faye Soupourmas. "Estimating Household Production Outputs with Time Use Episode Data." electronic *International Journal of Time Use Research* 6.2 (2009): 240-68. Print.

Kershaw, Paul. "Carefair: Choice, Duty and the Distribution of Care." *Social Politics: International Studies in Gender State and Society* 13.3 (2006): 341-71. Print.

Knijn, Trudie, and Monique Kremer. "Gender and the Caring Dimension of Welfare States: Toward Inclusive Citizenship." *Social Politics. International Studies in Gender, State and Society* 4.3 (1997): 328-61. Print.

Leahy, Mary. "Care: A Matter of Choice or Responsibility?" *Human Development and Capabilities Association Conference: Innovation, Development and Human Capabilities.* 2011. Print.

Lewis, Jane. *Work-Family Balance, Gender and Policy.* Cheltenham, UK, Northampton, MA, USA: Edward Elgar, 2009. Print.

Lister, Ruth. Citizenship. Feminist Perspectives. London: MacMillan Press Ltd., 1997. Print.

Pascall, Gillian, and Jane Lewis. "Emerging Gender Regimes and Policies for Gender Equality in a Wider Europe." *Journal of Social Policy* 33 (2004): 373-94. Print.

Pocock, Barbara. *The Work/Life Collision.* Sydney: Federation Press, 2003. Print.

Pocock, Barbara, Natalie Skinner, and Reina Ichii. *Work, Life and Workplace Flexibility: The Australian Work and Life Index* Adelaide: Centre for Work and Life, Adelaide University, 2009. Print.

Reiger, Kerreen, Joan Garvan, and Sinem Temel. "Rethinking Care: A Critical Analysis of Family Policies, Caring and Women's Negotiation of Dependency." *Just Policy* 50 (2009): 16-22. Print.

United Nations, *Statistics Division The World's Women: Trends and Statistics.* New York: United Nations, 2010. Print.

Waring, Marilyn. "Changes in Household Make-up and Implications for Economic Policy: A Conversation to Honour Duncan Ironmonger." *Advances in Household Economics, Consumer Behaviour and Economic Policy.* Ed. Hoa, Tran Van. Aldershot: Ashgate Publishing, 2005. Print.

—. *Counting for Nothing: What Men Value and Women Are Worth.* Wellington: Bridget Williams Books, 1988. Print.

Whitehouse, Gillian, et al. "Parental Leave in Australia: Beyond the Statistical Gap." *Journal of Industrial Relations* 49.1 (2007): 103-12. Print.

AUTHORS' NOTE

The authors acknowledge the assistance of Duncan Ironmonger in commenting on a draft of this chapter. Any errors or omissions remain the responsibility of the authors.

14.

Making Mothers' Milk Count

JULIE P. SMITH

INTRODUCTION

IN HER 1988 CLASSIC *Counting for Nothing*, Marilyn Waring observed that although "men who win Nobel prizes are generally considered more observant than the rest of us," Sir Richard Stone had invented a system of measuring economic activity in which "reproduction is invisible" (Waring, 181).

The example of breastfeeding was used to scathingly critique the United Nations System of National Accounts (SNA)—Sir Richard Stone's "baby." Waring argued forcefully that these accounts perpetuated the invisibility and devaluation of women's contribution as infant food and health care producers. Breasts were only counted by the SNA when exploited in advertising, in pornography, in the lingerie industry, and cosmetic surgery.

Breastfeeding was not counted when applied to breasts' primary function—nourishing human infants. Meanwhile, breastfeeding was declining worldwide, due partly to a worldwide lack of consideration by employers—women who breastfed in accordance with best practice for mother and child health were "simply expected to get on with it, in their own time" (Waring, 171).

This vigorous feminist critique of the SNA inspired considerable feminist scholarship and activism on valuing women's work in economic statistics, and was an important contribution to the "accounting for women's work project" (Benaria 131). This aimed for all women's work to be counted in statistics, accounted for in the representations of how economies work, and taken into account when policy is made (Elson *Progress of the World's Women* 2000).

It is also important for economic advancement that public policy is informed by statistics which more accurately portray the economy and women's contribution to it. Nevertheless, some ask whether this accounting focus distracted from achieving greater economic justice for women. As Valeria Esquival observes, "producing household sector satellite accounts does not by itself change macroeconomic policy" (219). More recently, UN discourse has shifted in focus from "measuring" and "possibly compensating" unpaid work, to counting as "essential to well-being" but "costly" for those who provide it, and justifying claims for strategic policy interventions to reduce unpaid work and redistribute its burden within and between households. This is known as the "three R's of unpaid work: recognition, reduction and redistribution" (Elson *The Three R's of Unpaid Work*).

This chapter reviews the intellectual contributions stemming from *Counting for Nothing* in the area of women's breastfeeding work, and illustrates from an Australian perspective how this has been used in public policy advocacy. I explore how the feminist critique of the national accounts system influenced research on the economic value of breastfeeding since 1988, how it inspired women's breastfeeding advocacy and helped shape Australian health and employment policy. I also consider the barriers and possibilities for valuing breastfeeding in the SNA, and the important implications of doing so.

COUNTING FOR SOMETHING—VALUING MOTHERS' MILK

Counting for Nothing was not the first call to acknowledge the economic value of mother's milk and breastfeeding, though it was the first to demand its proper valuation and to insist that the costs of breastfeeding to women be accounted for.

Until the 1990s, assessments of the economic significance of breastfeeding valued breast milk as if it were cows' milk or commercial infant formula. This fails to count the economic value of breastfeeding for the health and development of infants. These studies were motivated to protect and promote breastfeeding but understated its economic value by equating human milk with bovine animal milk products (Berg; Almroth, Greiner and Latham). Importantly, these studies viewed women's time as "free," thus understating the economic cost of breastfeeding. In 1979, nutritionists noted the time spent breastfeeding as a cost (Almroth, Greiner and Latham). Such costs are especially important for resource poor mothers and may influence them to wean their children from breastfeeding prematurely (Sellen).

The "mothers' milk equals cows' milk" approach to valuing breastfeeding was challenged from the 1990s. Mother's milk production was counted in Norway's food production statistics from the early 1990s, and was valued in a 1994 study using the market price of donated breast milk traded between Norwegian hospitals (Oshaug and Botten). Using the same valuation approach, the economic value and strategic importance of breastfeeding in Sub-Saharan Africa was estimated at half the annual output of cows' milk (Hatloy and Oshaug). Conservatively valued at US$1 per litre, this added between two and five percent to GNP.

In the mid 1990s, Oshaug and Botten's insights on valuation were used to estimate the economic value of breastfeeding in Australia, within a national accounting framework. This research showed that the price of commercially modified bovine milk massively underestimated the economic value of mothers' milk and it was more appropriate to use the market price of expressed breast milk to value the supply of human milk (Smith, Ingham and Dunstone; Smith "Human Milk Supply").

Many people are surprised that markets in mothers' milk exist. Hospitals and milk banks exchange and sell donated breast milk, human milk is traded through the Internet, and breastfeeding services are sold by wet nurses. In the past five years, the "market" for human milk has expanded considerably. In 2009, ten North American milk banks distributed 1.5 million ounces of human milk for US$3 an ounce or $127 ($A153) a litre. In Europe it sold for €130 (A$222) per litre; a price reflecting costs of processing and storing donated milk.

Usually milk banking is conducted on a not for profit basis, but a for-profit company now sells donated and highly processed human milk for use in neonatal intensive care units at a price of around US$1183 (A$1429) a litre.

Individual women have also responded to demand for breast milk by expanding informal systems for milk exchange, facilitated by the Internet. Websites such as "Eats On Feet" help mothers share their milk with other mothers—recipients pay shipping costs only. Other sites such as "Only The Breast" operate systems for trading milk, its philosophy being to recompense mothers for costs including their time. Breast milk is bought and sold on this site for about US$2 an ounce, or US$131 a litre.

There is also a market for wet nurses. Wet nurses advertise with "Only The Breast" at around US$50 per day ranging up to $150-200 per day where childcare or housework is also offered. U.S. employment agencies quote wages of around US$1,000 a week for wet nurses while a recent media report cited wages in China of US$10,000-25,000 per year.

HEALTH CARE AND HUMAN CAPITAL BUILDING

As pointed out in 1988 "an inadequately fed infant is a cost to the health system, ...to the education system (because of brain development), and to society generally" (Waring, 207). National accounting experts now acknowledge the crucial, unpaid role of families in building human capital (Abraham and Mackie).

Breastfeeding contributes uniquely to human development through providing uniquely species-appropriate nutrition and care for infants and young children. Lack of breastfeeding is now a recognized risk factor for chronic disease in adulthood, as well as for acute infectious illness during infancy and childhood. Mothers' health is adversely affected by premature weaning, through higher incidence of depression and mental illness, and increased rates of breast cancer and other disorders among women with short breastfeeding duration (American Academy of Pediatrics et al.). Over a million infants a year die needlessly from lack of breastfeeding; improving breastfeeding practices is the most effective and cost effective intervention to improve mother and child health globally (Bhutta et al. 417-40; Black et al.).

Breastfeeding minimises health care costs. Several studies have estimated health care system costs attributable to formula feeding. The cost of pediatric health care and premature death attributable to formula feeding in the United States is around US$13 billion annually (Bartick and Reinhold e1048); it is also a significant proportion of acute and chronic disease costs in Australia (Smith, Thompson and Ellwood; Smith and Harvey).

Well conducted cohort and experimental studies in several countries now provide strong evidence that those deprived of human milk or breastfeeding in infancy have poorer cognitive and academic achievement in later life (Kramer et al.; Sacker, Quigley and Kelly; Oddy et al.). Ending exclusive breastfeeding before 4 months is estimated to reduce IQ by 3-7 percentage points, with larger impacts for premature or smallforgestationalage infants. This is comparable with the effects on child cognitive development of prenatal lead exposure (Walker et al., Table 4). Lifetime costs of special education for preterm infants in Australia would be $32 million lower if 20 per cent more were fed breast milk rather than exclusively formula fed (Drane).

Nobel Laureate James Heckman and colleagues (Heckman, Masterov and National Bureau of Economic Research; Doyle et al.) have shown the economic importance of early investments in children. They quantify how early childhood experiences influence the development of cognitive skills, socio-emotional functioning and health, and culminate in a way that measurably affects later life earnings and productivity.

ACCOUNTING FOR THE TIME COSTS OF BREASTFEEDING

Revealing women's time costs of breastfeeding can help redistribute the costs of care more widely in society; it is mainly others who benefit from women's time investment in breastfeeding (Smith "Mothers' Milk"). Failing to count women's time distorts public policies and results in long term economic loss as market work is favoured over economically valuable but unpaid care and nourishment of infants.

Some consider loss of employment opportunities as a cost of breastfeeding. However, the true picture is more complex (Van Esterik and Greiner). Rather than employment per se, factors such as travel time and distance to work, employment conditions, and workplace arrangements may be the critical determinants of breastfeeding continuation among employed mothers. Whether employed women have any real decision-making power over infant feeding methods is determined by structural and economic factors and is not simply a matter of personal choice or biology (Quandt; Galtry).

Our Australian Time Use Survey of New Mothers (TUSNM) found that having an infant added 44 hours a week to a woman's unpaid workload (Smith and Ellwood), and revealed the high time cost of breastfeeding in a developed country setting. It also showed that exclusive breastfeeding of infants for 6 months took around 17-20 hours a week of mothers' time, much less than formula fed or partially weaned infants.

Time is also important to understanding which mothers cannot afford to breastfeed, or "rationally" decide not to. For mothers without adequate family support, early weaning from breastfeeding gives them more time, whether for leisure, housework, personal care or employment. This may more than compensate for extra costs of commercial baby food and health care. A recent US study showed breastfeeding mothers suffered greater earning losses than other mothers due to longer labour force withdrawal (Rippeyoung and Noonan). Empirical research in Canada (Baker and Milligan), the U.S. (Mandal, Roe and Fein) and the U.K. (Hawkins, Griffiths and Dezateux), shows that breastfeeding is increased if mothers get more time such as through extended paid maternity leave. On the other hand, breastfeeding in the US was reduced by welfare reforms encouraging return to work by 12 weeks (Chatterji and Frick). Promotion of breastfeeding as free or costless has been "a convenient tool used by states to avoid responsibility for taking on more costly solutions to children's and women's health" (Rippeyoung, 36). How making visible these economic aspects of breastfeeding links to pursuing economic justice for women is discussed below.

COUNTING THE COST OF INVISIBILITY; INSPIRING AND STRENGTHENING WOMEN'S ADVOCACY

A focus on the economic value of breastfeeding and breast milk has made women's lactation work more visible and assisted women's advocacy on breastfeeding and maternity care. Influenced by *Counting for Nothing* and research on the economics of breastfeeding, the Australian Breastfeeding Association (ABA), then known as Nursing Mothers' Association of Australia, began advocating for including breastfeeding in GDP in 1999. By 2002, its representations to federal parliamentarians would present research evidence of health cost savings from breastfeeding. The following year, this research was cited in Australia's new dietary guidelines on infant feeding (National Health and Medical Research Council).

In 2004 the Association's *National Breastfeeding Leadership Plan* recommended including breastfeeding in national food production statistics and GDP to increase the health policy priority of breastfeeding. ABA's 2006 submission to the Australian Treasury used evidence on health system cost savings (Smith, Thompson and Ellwood) to successfully advocate federal government funding of breastfeeding support measures—the May 2007 Budget announced $8.7 million for a requested national breastfeeding helpline and health professional training.

ABA advocacy citing health system cost savings also triggered a parliamentary inquiry on the benefits of breastfeeding in late 2006. Public submissions highlighted the economic contribution that women make by breastfeeding. The 2007 *Best Start Report* (Commonwealth of Australia, 53-58) urged further research on economic impacts to drive government action and investment in breastfeeding support. The Inquiry also heard evidence on the time costs of breastfeeding, and its Report (54) acknowledged the failure to properly recognize its time-intensity and economic cost to women. It stopped short of recommending paid maternity leave, but meanwhile the Australian government moved towards introducing a new national scheme.

The 2007 Australian Productivity Commission Inquiry into Paid Parental Leave invited evidence on the time costs of breastfeeding and on its economic importance, and in 2009, recommended a publicly funded scheme for 18 weeks paid parental leave. It expected that as a result, "more women will be able to have longer, beneficial interactions in the early phase of their babies' lives and to breastfeed for longer" (Productivity Commission, XX11). The Commission was influenced by the health cost savings from breastfeeding, concluding that the economic costs of not breastfeeding were significant for developed as well as poor countries (Productivity Commission, 4.24).

COUNTING MOTHERS' MILK IN THE UNITED NATIONS' SYSTEM OF NATIONAL ACCOUNTS—PROGRESS IN PRINCIPLE

> Why is it that when we pay for childcare and house-cleaning, when we eat out, when we buy milk for our babies, or when we call in the mechanic or the plumber, these add to GDP and count toward economic growth and progress; but when we look after our own children, clear our own house, cook our own meals, breastfeed our babies, tune up our own cars, and fix our own leaking faucets, these have no value in our current measures of progress? (Collas-Monsod, "Removing the Cloak" 98)

Despite breastfeeding's crucial importance for infant health and survival, national statisticians do not count human milk as a food. Not including breast milk and breastfeeding in GDP is in fact contrary to United Nations' guidelines.

Revised international guidelines were published for National Accounting in 1993 (commonly referred to as SNA93) (Commission of the European Communities). SNA93 was revised to take better account of "subsistence" production; GDP should include all "own account" production of goods by households. This includes agricultural subsistence production such as sowing, planting, tending and harvesting field crops; growing vegetables, fruit and other trees and shrub crops; gathering wild fruits, medicinal and other plants; tending, feeding or hunting animals mainly to obtain meat, milk, hair, skin or other products; and storing or carrying to some basic processing of this produce.

SNA93 also included in GDP any agricultural produce consumed on-farm. The national accounting framework thus included all non-marketed goods, including the production, processing and storage of food by house-holds, within the GDP production boundary.

The Australian Bureau of Statistics (ABS) includes the value of home-grown fruit, vegetables, eggs, beer, wine and meat in estimates of fi-nal private consumption expenditure and therefore GDP. Australian core accounts now include "the own account production of all goods retained by their producers for their own final consumption or gross capital formation" ("Unpaid Work and the Australian Economy", 46), where these are quanti-tatively significant, thereby following the practice set down in SNA93 (para 6.18).

The preferred approach to valuing production in the national accounts system is using market values. The fundamental criteria for inclusion of a good is that it can be traded in a market. The existence of markets in hu-man milk (see above, Section 1) means there are prices of a closely related or analogous product—a shadow price—from which to impute its economic value.

We have shown human is defined as a good within the SNA93 core pro-duction boundary (Smith and Ingham "Mothers' Milk"; Smith and Ing-ham "Breastfeeding") because, in national accounting language, it can be produced, stored, sold on markets, and thus be valued (Commission of the European Communities, para. 6.7).

Demonstrably, the value of human milk production can be estimated using accepted valuation methods for national accounting—an input ba-sed, wage cost approach (replacement wage, opportunity cost), or using the market value of the output (Smith "Human Milk Supply"). Estimated an-nual human milk production in Australia in 1992 was 33 million kg. Using a market value of output approach to valuing production in a national ac-counts framework (i.e. a price of US$50 per litre used for the Norwegian study [Oshaug and Botten]), this had a market value of $2.1 billion a year.

This is qualitatively important compared to other goods produced for own consumption by households which were valued at $1 billion in 1997 and are counted in GDP by the ABS. This means that the production and value of human milk should be included in core account estimates of na-tional food production, consumption and GDP.

Others agree that GDP wrongly excludes breast milk. The 2009

French Presidential Commission on the Measurement of Economic Performance and Social Progress, led by two Nobel Laureates in economics, Joseph Stiglitz and Amartya Sen, cited the example of breastfeeding to illustrate how exclusion from GDP devalued important non-market work and biased policies against unpaid production:

> There is a serious omission in the valuation of home-produced goods – the value of breast milk. This is clearly within the System of National Accounts production boundary, is quantitatively non-trivial and also has important implications for public policy and child and maternal health. (Stiglitz, Sen and Fitoussi, 39)

Including breast milk in GDP is important not only because it acknowledges women's lactation work. It also provides a focus for government actions to promote economic growth and development. For example, if breastfeeding in Australia increased to levels recommended by the World Health Organisation, this would add around $3.7 billion annually (0.7%) to GDP (Smith and Ingham "Breastfeeding and the Measurement").

BARRIERS AND ISSUES

Breast milk is still not included in GDP—why not? In 1990 the Australian Government was advised that unpaid work should continue to be excluded from GDP because the market sector was the primary concern for macroeconomic policy and because unpaid household work was not related to market forces as directly as goods (Australian Bureau of Statistics "Measuring Unpaid Household Work," 6-7).

These arguments do not apply to human milk production. Production levels of human milk are closely related to market activity, with direct competition to breastfeeding from companies selling and profiting from sale of infant feeding products. Labour market participation and breast milk production compete directly (Mandal, Roe and Fein 1-21). It is also questionable as to whether other conventional arguments for excluding unpaid work from GDP apply to human milk production. For example, Collas-Monsod ("Removing the Cloak") has identified arguments that excluding unpaid work is necessary to maintain the usefulness of the accounts to policymakers. It is said to avoid "overburdening or disrupting the central system" (Commission of the European Communities, para. 21.4).

However, excluding human milk production from GDP means that Australia's policymakers focus on promoting the activities of commercial firms producing less than $200 million of infant food products per year, whilst giving no importance to protecting household production of human milk worth $2 billion a year or more. It is difficult to see why disrupting the system by comparing these values is undesirable, or why it overburdens policy analysis to show the large magnitude of non market production of infant food. Likewise, including breastfeeding in GDP would surely enhance monitoring and analysis of long term productivity trends and patterns in the food, nutrition, childcare and health sectors.

Women's work is still not measured in key economic statistics because of the costs involved in changing the collection and use of national accounts (Fraumeni). Experience in the Philippines suggests only "demand driven advocacy" will improve national accounting practices (Virola et al.; Collas-Monsod). Unfortunately, few understand how such statistics can be used for better decision-making, or how to use them for advocacy. Without such pressures, statisticians will do little about introducing them—though "what we don't know could hurt us" (Abraham 3-18, 1).

USING STATISTICS FOR EVIDENCE BASED POLICY—"FLYING BLIND WITH SNA"

Why do statistics matter? In simple terms, they are the evidence on which policies are built. They help to identify needs, set goals and monitor progress. Without good statistics, the development process is blind: policy-makers cannot learn from their mistakes, and the public cannot hold them accountable (World Bank, vii).

National accounts provide a misleading picture of human food production and consumption activities. Present practice has the startling result that increased breastfeeding and human milk production reduces national food output and GDP, because it lowers artificial formula and commercial baby food sales and reduces private and public health expenditures, which are measured. Unmeasured are economic benefits of using more of an environmentally-friendly and high quality food resource, and economic resource savings from reducing illness and disease and lesser use of medical services or products.

An equally questionable corollary of the current GDP measurement practice is that the dramatic worldwide drop in breastfeeding rates during the 1960s and 1970s inaccurately showed higher national output and economic growth from expanded production of formula and higher national health expenditures. This same practice of ignoring the loss of household production now grossly distorts measurement of economic progress in countries like China and India, and overstates economic growth.

The ability of women to breastfeed is a form of national wealth. Yet, the economic returns from this human capital asset are not counted as contributing to GDP or economic well-being. This renders a major national asset invisible to policymakers who use these economic statistics and GDP estimates to determine economic priorities. If it were visible, more policies and programs would be directed at protecting and enhancing breastfeeding knowledge and skills.

As the World Bank reinforces in the above quotation, economic development policies which consider only market activities will be misguided in design and poorly implemented, even counterproductive. Economic waste and lower national productivity, as well as gender inequity result from what is, in effect, "flying blind with SNA."

CONCLUSION

> It is the SNA that threw a cloak over women's contributions, that cloak should and can be removed. (Collas-Monsod, "Integrating Unpaid Work into Macroeconomics")

Counting for Nothing gave impetus to women's push for greater recognition of their productive and reproductive work, and has inspired efforts to give women's work greater visibility as well as improving economic justice for women. Women's lactation work can be shown to at least "count for something" in the public eye. Despite reservations that chasing better economic statistics could be a blind alley for those pursing gender equity, in this case at least, "the accounting project" has helped achieve some economic justice for women.

Breastfeeding illustrates how improving the visibility of women's contribution to well-being using economic statistics has successfully linked to policy measures giving economic recognition to those investing time in caregiving, and helping redistribute the cost of care in Australia.

WORKS CITED

[1] The word "mother" in this chapter includes men who do mothering work as well

[2] "Kvuza" – collective farmstead, precursor of the kibbutz commune.

[3] The documentary *Who Does She Think She Is?* (2008), deals particularly with this tension between motherhood and being an artist. Artist Maye Torres, who appears in the documentary, says, "I had lots of people telling me that I was selfish. Is it selfish to do your own work when you're responsible for the care of others?"

[4] *Sinking Syncing* is a video-artwork (4 min.) featuring photographs and videos of "sink work."

[5] From the video-artwork *Sinking Syncing*

[6] Beterem Safe Kids Israel, an NPO which aims to promote child safety, states that "two thirds of child hospitalizations are due to home accidents... Most of these injuries are due to falls, burns, drowning, poisoning, choking, car accidents, and other 'every-day' causes" (Beterem annual report, 2010).

[7] Isha L'Isha Haifa Feminist Center and the Coalition of Women for Peace

[8] The Second Intifada (the Al-Aqsa uprising) broke out in 2000 and peaked between 2001 and 2003.

[9] In Hebrew the words for hospital and school include the word "house."

WORKS CITED

Abraham, K. G. "What We Don't Know Could Hurt Us: Some Reflections on the Measurement of Economic Activity." *The Journal of Economic Perspectives* 19.3 (2005): 3-18. Print.

Abraham, K. G., and C. D. Mackie. *Beyond the Market: Designing Non-market Accounts for the United States.* National Academies Press, 2005. Print.

Almroth, S., T. Greiner, and M.C. Latham. "Economic Importance of Breastfeeding." *Food Nutr* (Roma) 5.2 (1979): 4-10. Print.

Almroth, Stina, Ted Greiner, and Michael Latham. *The Economic Value of Breastfeeding. Monograph Series.* Vol. Number 6. New York: Cornell University Program on International Nutrition, 1979. Print.

American Academy of Pediatrics, et al. "Breastfeeding and the Use of Human Milk." *Pediatrics* 129.3 (2012): e827-e41. Print.

Australian Breastfeeding Association. "Breastfeeding Leadership." 2004. Web. 13 December 2004.

Australian Bureau of Statistics. "Measuring Unpaid Household Work: Issues and Experimental Estimates." Cat No. 5236.0. Canberra: Australian Bureau of Statistics, 1990. Print.

—. "Unpaid Work and the Australian Economy." Cat No. 5240. Canberra: Australian Bureau of Statistics, 1997. Print.

Baker, M., and K. Milligan. "Maternal Employment, Breastfeeding, and Health: Evidence from Maternity Leave Mandates." *J. Health Econ.* 27.4 (2008): 871-87. Print.

Bartick, Melissa., and Arnold. Reinhold. "The Burden of Suboptimal Breastfeeding in the United States: A Pediatric Cost Analysis." *Pediatrics* 125.5 (2010): e1048. Print.

Benaria, Lourdes. *Gender, Development and Globalisation: Economics as If All People Mattered.* New York: Routledge, 2003. Print.

Berg, Alan. *The Nutrition Factor.* Washington: The Brookings Institution, 1973. Print.

Bhutta, Zulfiqar A., et al. "What Works Interventions for Maternal and Child Undernutrition and Survival." *The Lancet* 371.9610 (2008): 417-40. Print.

Black, Robert E., et al. "Maternal and Child Undernutrition: Global and Regional Exposures and Health Consequences." *The Lancet* 371.9608 (2008): 243-60. Print.

Chatterji, Pinka, and Kevin Frick. "Does Returning to Work after Childbirth Affect Breastfeeding Practices?" *Review of the Economics of the Household* 3.3 (2003): 315-35. Print.

Collas-Monsod, Solita. "Removing the Cloak of Invisibility." *Harvesting Feminist Knowledge for Public Policy: Rebuilding Progress.* 2011. 93. Print.

Commission of the European Communities, International Monetary Fund, Organisation for Economic Cooperation and Development, United Nations and World Bank. System of National Accounts. New York, 1993. Print.

Commonwealth of Australia. *The Best Start.* Report on the Inquiry into the Health Benefits of Breastfeeding. Canberra: House of Representatives Standing Committee on Health and Aging, 2007. Print.

Doyle, Orla, et al. "Investing in Early Human Development: Timing and

Economic Efficiency." *Economics & Human Biology* 7.1 (2009): 1-6. Print.

Drane, Denise. "Breastfeeding and Formula Feeding: A Preliminary Economic Analysis." *Breastfeeding Review* 5.1, May (1997): 7-16. Print.

Elson, Diane. *Progress of the World's Women, 2000.* New York: United Nations Development Program (UNDP), 2000. Print.

—. *The Three R's of Unpaid Work: Recognition, Reduction and Redistribution.* Paper presented at the Expert Group Meeting on Unpaid work, Economic Development and Human Well-Being. 2008. United Nations Development Program (UNDP), New York. Print.

Esquivel, V. "Sixteen Years after Beijing: What Are the New Policy Agendas for Time-Use Data Collection?" *Feminist Economics* 17.4 (2011): 215-38. Print.

Fraumeni, Barbara. M. "Household Production Accounts for Canada, Mexico, and the United States: Methodological Issues, Results and Recommendations." *The Invisible Economy and Gender Inequalities.* Ed. Pan American Health Organisation (PAHO). Washington (DC) PAHO, 2010. 19-30. Print.

Galtry, Judith. "The Impact on Breastfeeding of Labour Market Policy and Practice in Ireland, Sweden, and the USA." *Social Science & Medicine* 57.1 (2003): 167-77. Print.

Hatloy, A., and A. Oshaug. "Human Milk: An Invisible Food Resource." *Journal of Human Lactation* 13.4 (1997): 299-305. Print.

Hawkins, S. S., L. J. Griffiths, and C. Dezateux. "The Impact of Maternal Employment on Breast-Feeding Duration in the UK Millennium Cohort Study." *Public Health Nutr* (2007): 1-6. Print.

Heckman, J. J., D. V. Masterov, and Research National Bureau of Economic. *The Productivity Argument for Investing in Young Children.* National Bureau of Economic Research Cambridge, Mass., USA, 2007. Print.

Kramer, M. S., et al. "Breastfeeding and Child Cognitive Development: New Evidence from a Large Randomized Trial." *Arch Gen Psychiatry* 65.5 (2008): 578-84. Print.

Mandal, B., B. E. Roe, and S. B. Fein. "Work and Breastfeeding Decisions Are Jointly Determined for Higher Socioeconomic Status Us Mothers." *Review of Economics of the Household* published online 28 July (2012): 1-21. Print.

National Health and Medical Research Council. Draft Infant Feeding Guidelines for Health Workers. Canberra: National Health and Medical Research Council, 2011. Print.

Oddy, Wendy H., et al. "Breastfeeding and Early Child Development: A Prospective Cohort Study." *Acta Paediatrica* 100.7 (2011): 992-99. Print.

Oshaug, Arne, and Grete Botten. "Human Milk in Food Supply Statistics." *Food Policy* 19.5 (1994): 479-82. Print.

Productivity Commission. *Paid Parental Leave: Support for Parents with Newborn Children.* Canberra: Productivity Commission, 2009. Print.

Quandt, Sarah. "Sociocultural Aspects of the Lactation Process." *Breastfeeding: Biocultural Perspectives.* Eds. Stuart-Macadam, Patricia and Katherine A Dettwyler. New York: Aldine De Gruyter, 1995. 127-43. Print.

Rippeyoung, Phyllis L. F., "Feeding the State: Breastfeeding and Women's Well-Being in Context." *Journal of the Motherhood Initiative for Research and Community Involvement* 11.1 (2009). Print.

Rippeyoung, Phyllis L. F., and Mary C. Noonan. "Is Breastfeeding Truly Cost Free? Income Consequences of Breastfeeding for Women." *American Sociological Review* 77.2 (2012): 244-67. Print.

Sacker, A., M. A. Quigley, and Y. J. Kelly. "Breastfeeding and Developmental Delay: Findings from the Millennium Cohort Study." *Pediatrics* 118.3 (2006): e682-9. Print.

Sellen, D. W. "Evolution of Infant and Young Child Feeding: Implications for Contemporary Public Health." *Annu Rev Nutr* 27 (2007): 123-48. Print.

Smith, Julie P. "Human Milk Supply in Australia." *Food Policy* 24.1 (1999): 71-91. Print.

Smith, Julie P, and Mark Ellwood. *Where Does a Mothers' Day Go? Preliminary Estimates from the Australian Time Use Survey of New Mothers.* ACERH Research Paper no 1, Canberra.

Smith, Julie P, and Lindy H Ingham. "Breastfeeding and the Measurement of Economic Progress." *Journal of Australian Political Economy* 47.June (2001): 51-72. Print.

Smith, Julie P., and Lindy H. Ingham. "Mothers' Milk and Measures of Economic Output." *Feminist Economics* 11.1 (2005): 41-62. Print.

Smith, Julie P. "Mothers' Milk and Markets." *Australian Feminist Studies* 19.45, November (2004): 369-79. Print.

Smith, Julie P., and Peta J. Harvey. "Chronic Disease and Infant Nutrition: Is It Significant to Public Health?" *Public Health Nutrition* 14.02 (2011): 279-89. Print.

Smith, Julie P., Lindy H. Ingham, and Mark D. Dunstone. *The Economic Value of Breastfeeding in Australia.* Australian National University, Canberra: National Centre for Epidemiology and Population Health, 1998. Print.

Smith, Julie P., Jane F. Thompson, and David A. Ellwood. "Hospital System Costs of Artificial Infant Feeding: Estimates for the Australian Capital Territory." *Australian and New Zealand Journal of Public Health* 26.6 (2002): 543-51. Print.

Stiglitz, Joseph E., Amartya Sen, and Jean-Paul Fitoussi. *The Measurement of Economic Performance and Social Progress Revisited; Reflections and Overview*: Centre de recherche en économie de Sciences Po (OFCE), 2009. Print.

Van Esterik, P., and T. Greiner. "Breastfeeding and Women's Work: Constraints and Opportunities." *Studies in Family Planning* 12.4 (1981): 184-97. Print.

Do Women Contribute Less Than Men to Nation Building? 10th National Convention on Statistics. National Statistical Coordination Board. Philippines. 2007. Print.

Walker, Susan P., et al. "Inequality in Early Childhood: Risk and Protective Factors for Early Child Development." *The Lancet* 378.9799: 1325-38. Print.

Waring, Marilyn. *Counting for Nothing.* Wellington: Allen & Unwin, New Zealand, 1988. Print.

World Bank. World Development Report. Washington DC: World Bank, 2000. Print.

15.

Resilient Feminism

Social Movement Strategy in a Conservative Regnum

MARA FRIDELL & LORNA TURNBULL

INTRODUCTION

IN 1995, THE UN's *Gender and Human Development* report calculated that women's invisible reproductive work contributed $11 trillion in value annually, for free, to the global economy (UNDP). The Fourth World Conference on Women in Beijing, where women from around the world came together to strategize about how to address such systemic inequality, was built on this report. The "Platform for Action" emerged from Beijing, urging states to implement women's equality. The conference and the Platform bolstered the attendees' commitment to tackle the issues at home.

Forty-five women travelled to Beijing from Manitoba, a province of barely one million people in the centre of Canada. They carried home the inspiration, knowledge and perspective to create an organization whose transformative practices and policies would improve the lives of Manitoba women. They were energized by the conference, and informed by the work of women around the world who live the hard realities of colonialism, patriarchy, and Structural Adjustment Policies (SAPs), economic policies which countries must follow in order to qualify for new debt, and to make repayments on previous debts owed to commercial banks, governments and the World Bank. At the expense of women, smallholders, and reproducers, SAP dogmatism reorients states' economic and political commitments strictly to the preferences at the top of the global economic hierarchy, imposing export-led production, capital deregulation, privatization, de-unionization, and the diminishment of democratic participation and the state's broad resource-distribution capacity. Feminist contributions—including the critical recognition of reproduction directly in relation to human flourishing, and a conception of good governance beyond facilitating surplus accumulation—allow us to comprehend the endemic, cascading failures of neoliberal restructuring, and remind us that better relations can be realized.

In advance of the Beijing Conference, the Canadian government affirmed that it was prepared to "strengthen its commitments to equality" (Finestone). Fortified by this position, by global feminists' and Waring's insights, and by a progressive provincial government, the Manitoba feminists carved out a regional feminist agenda, forming coalitions with diverse women, coordinating critical dialogue, and advancing women's understanding of the social good. Recruiting women from all walks of life, they created a strategically-oriented feminist group. The United Nations Platform for Action Committee – Manitoba (UNPAC) was born six months after the Beijing conference. Its core members, the women with the "surplus" time and skills to donate regularly, were mainly professionals with careers in provincial government, communications, and higher education. They were committed to engaging women across social stratifications.

The first UNPAC meeting, in 1996, founded the organization's name and established the structure, including a committee to mobilize community action and monitor the Platform's implementation in the province. Although the Platform envisions a role for civil society, primary responsibility for implementing its program belongs not to unpaid women's collectives, but to states (UN Women). That these women took on the responsibility for disseminating the Platform affirms studies showing that subcommunities often act as political agents where they foresee a probability of coordination failure (Oliver, Marwell, and Teixeira). UNPAC had healthy organizational roots to take on the Platform dissemination task. Muriel Smith, a pioneering feminist politician and UNPAC co-founder had traveled to the Second World Conference on Women in Nairobi a decade earlier as a Provincial Minister, and her leadership was key to mobilizing Manitoba feminists for the Beijing conference and the connected NGOs (nongovernmental organizations) meeting (UNPAC 2012).

In a focus group, UNPAC founders recalled how "electrifying" it was to join together with tens of thousands of women from around the world, how much they learned, and how both the Beijing conference and Waring's feminist outreach model, presented in *Who's Counting*, allowed UNPAC to extend this exceptional experience to Manitoba women. "The global linkages widened our perspective," and were crucial to building their movement. One feminist recalled how her generation's social activism developed, citing a heritage of leadership extending from Eleanor Roosevelt, through Canada's Royal Commission on the Status of Women, to the 1975 UN World Conference on Women in Mexico,

> We evolved from a group of women at home analyzing the global economy. We were part of a family law reform coalition to address discrimination against women that produced women's poverty that prevented women from realizing our human rights. We were inspired to involve rural women. We were inspired by Aboriginal women tackling racial inequality. We needed to be part of bringing together labor and women. We became politicized. We got inspired by the dialogues at the NGOs, the strategizing for women's advancement.

Beijing was galvanizing for these women because it allowed them to both affirm and reflexively modify their own feminist approach, based on the collectively-designed Platform. The Platform is a road-map for equality, aiming at "removing all the obstacles to women's active participation in all spheres of public and private life through a full and equal share in economic, social, cultural and political decision-making." The Platform promotes "a transformed partnership between women and men" to realize the rights and freedoms of women and girls (UN Women). Yet the Platform, while a significant achievement in articulating a global vision of women's equality, also has weaknesses. It is premised on supporting economic growth as a preferred tool for achieving social development and social justice (UN Women) and disregards how strategies of surplus accumulation, codified in biased measures of economic growth (such as GDP or GNP), may conflict with rather than support the distribution of economic resources to ensure women's freedoms.

History shows that social movements are messy, iterative processes of surges and retrenchments, spanning decades to centuries (Turnbull, "Wicked Problem"). Human rights were enshrined in law after World War II, in the context of expanding Keynesian economic surplus distribution, and in the face of a competing communist alternative to the global capitalist order. The Platform was formulated four decades later, when human rights aspirations, and the democratic distribution of economic surplus, were under fire. Recognizing that the concentration of wealth limits the realization of human rights, we are confronted with a choice between abandoning the human rights ideal, or fighting to fortify its material foundation. Beijing and Waring's influence encouraged UNPAC to navigate the latter course.

The territory that UNPAC claimed for the Platform is remote, vast, expensive to traverse, and culturally and socio-economically diverse. It is a region of Canada whose main economic activities include natural resources, agriculture and hydroelectricity. The population is concentrated in the southern capital city of Winnipeg. Many Aboriginal and northern communities are accessible only by air; others are losing their ice roads with the advance of climate change. Transportation across this territory that is nearly three times the size of the United Kingdom can be so expensive, a jug of milk in the north may cost four times what it costs in the south (Lyall).

In the face of these challenges, UNPAC women were propelled by the feminist networks they had in each other, at home, and across the global feminist community from Beijing. UNPAC assessed the issues stymieing women, including debt and political-economic restructuring, through outreach and community conversations (UNPAC 1999). It screened *Who's Counting?* at conferences convened around the province, using the film as a tool for generating local modifications to the Platform, and advocating the Platform to provincial government ministers. An UNPAC founder reports,

> When we came back (from Beijing), we brought in Marilyn Waring, and used *Who's Counting?* to reach out to Manitoba women, get them thinking together with us about how their lives and the lives of so many women around the world are impacted by shared policy systems that determine social priorities.

The film allowed Manitoba women to recognize their own lives within a global context, and motivated them to develop plans of action together in conferences and beyond.

UNPAC's first conference, the 1997 "Marilyn Waring Counting Women's Work" conference, was funded by Status of Women Canada (SWC). The conference engaged rural women's economic knowledge, using Waring's book and the film as resources, along with regional studies on unpaid housework. Keynote topics included uncounted work, the impact of restructuring on women, and the question, "Have women paid the price for the debt?" The conference generated strategies, policy and institutional recommendations, media coverage, and a sense of "urgency for women to be involved in decision-making/policy-making," (UNPAC 1999: 45). Held around Manitoba and focusing on health, violence, and poverty as challenges identified in the regional implementation of the Platform, all of UNPAC's conferences were designed to learn from and inspire the women of the province (UNPAC 2000). The conferences trained local women to be facilitators and lobbyists on political-economic issues, and developed women's action networks. UNPAC's "mobilization methodology" promoted awareness of, and inquiry into, the UN Action Areas. They helped women to assess the effects of Restructuring on women, and to explore connections between poverty and women's economic participation in paid and unpaid labor (UNPAC 1997: 37).

In their focus on Restructuring as an assault on institutions supporting women, UNPAC recognized that the political establishment at the close of the 20th century was becoming much less responsive and accountable to most women and men. These resourceful UNPAC feminists responded with political fluency, both demanding feminist action by the state, and rousing and coalescing diverse women across the province to engage strategically with the government.

EXTENDING AND AMPLIFYING AN INCLUSIVE FRAMEWORK

UNPAC's conferences throughout the province extended knowledge of the Platform, and mobilized rural and urban women. Building on that foundation, UNPAC embarked upon more projects, including their Women & Economy project, Gender Budgeting, Femme Fiscale, and political-economic literacy and leadership curricula. Responding to Waring's thesis that the economy has long been used to intimidate and exclude, the Women & the Economy website was developed by UNPAC as an economic literacy tool. The site provides building blocks to economic literacy showing how fiscal policy affects women, and includes presentations of women's personal stories. Following Waring's model, these building blocks include accessible and critical introductions to economics and the role of government, and banking and debt. It provides interactive material; inspiring quotes from Waring and others; discussions of economic alternatives practical answers to the question, "What can I do?"; and UNPAC's own empowering video, *Banging the Door Down*.

In 2004, UNPAC solicited gender-responsive budgeting policy suggestions from Manitobans, targeting concerns such as recognition of unpaid work, redistribution of wealth, and access to supportive services and revenue generation. Demonstrating the people's capacity for innovation and distinctive leadership, most suggestions related to redirecting the economic surplus to support women and their families. UNPAC also created "Femme Fiscale," a graphic novel-inspired super-heroine dressed colorfully in "Platform-for-Action" boots and cape, combining political theater and a postcard campaign to raise political awareness. The postcards covered topics such as housing, international covenants on human rights, public transport, national childcare, and taxes ("Femme Fiscale Loves Taxes—Here's Why"). UNPAC's media-savvy Femme Fiscale superhero continues to appear on its website and at events, like the release of UNPAC's Equality Report Cards (deGroot and Turnbull).

Coalitions, international and regional, have been at the heart of UNPAC's feminist strategy. "Connection with international movements, the diversity and contiguousness of women's lives and ideas, enriches our community," states one UNPAC founder. "It allowed us to build our advocacy, representing Canadian, including Aboriginal, women." Another member agreed, "We consciously set out to operate in rural Manitoba, to form coalitions and work with indigenous women from small communities in Northern Manitoba." Coalitions with Aboriginal women's organizations have been crucial to developing an informed, effective women's movement; and they have contributed to the development of UNPAC's education projects.

The lives of indigenous people in Canada are still regulated by the Indian Act, colonial legislation enacted in 1876. Portions of the Act relating to the status of First Nation women who married non-Indian men, and to their children, impose even greater burdens upon these women. If women in Canada are still disadvantaged relative to men, Aboriginal women are even more profoundly disadvantaged. Aboriginal women live in deeper poverty, experience more unemployment, are more likely to be single parents, and face far greater rates of violence, and poorer health and educational attainment (Turnbull, "Promise").

Aligning with Aboriginal women's efforts to claim equality and preserve Aboriginal heritage and communities, UNPAC has worked with Aboriginal women leaders, in recent years offering a community-based education program, conducted in Aboriginal organizations, to connect and promote leadership among marginalized Aboriginal women whose lives and communities remain disrupted by colonialism. UNPAC's analysis of the impact of the successive conservative Restructuring and Austerity initiatives, and its critical interventions, have become more incisive, thanks to the ongoing relationship it cultivates with dispossessed women, low-income women, Aboriginal women, and Aboriginal community organizations, internationally, regionally and locally (Cohen 221).

FEMINIST PARKOUR: CONSERVATIVE DIFFUSION, ORGANIZATIONAL ADAPTATION

As Waring's thinking about economic equality was gaining currency across Canada through her speaking tours and film, and UNPAC was building awareness in Manitoba, state support for equality-seeking groups was declining. The women's groups organized under the independent, but federally-funded SWC were compelled to shift from advocating for women's equality and gender wage fairness to condemning the increasing commitment to market fundamentalism. At the same time, unemployment was used to discipline working families in Canada, and new international trade treaties were being signed that abrogated democratically-achieved law (Cohen 221-22).

Canadian feminists were so well organized and incisive in critiquing these attacks and demanding an alternative economic approach that the Conservative Party reacted by slashing Status of Women's funding by fifty percent between 1989 and 1992 (Cohen 224). The Women's Program mandate "to promote policies and programs that take account of gender implications, the diversity of women's perspectives, and enable women to take part in decision-making; to facilitate the involvement of women's organizations in the public policy process; to increase public understanding in order to encourage action on women's equality issues; and to enhance the effectiveness of actions undertaken by women's organizations to improve the situation of women," (Government of Canada) was hobbled by these cuts. By 1997, SWC's "Women's Program," which had provided both core and project funding to organizations like UNPAC since SWC's creation in 1973, reduced its funding model to deliver only project funding. Once core funding was cut, numerous organizations promoting women's equality were forced to shut down. Women found the welfare state institutions that once served and supported them dismantled (National Association of Women and the Law).

In 2004, the federal government reviewed its funding for women's groups, and the accountability mechanisms to ensure that Canada was complying with its international obligations to advance women's equality. Improvements to address the problems with project funding that "made it difficult to sustain a women's movement in Canada and made it increasingly difficult for the women's movement to advocate on behalf of women" were recommended, along with an increase of 25% to the Women's Program budget and a re-introduction of core funding. Despite these recommendations, in 2006 funding was cut again and a reduced mandate only required SWC to facilitate "women's participation in Canadian society by addressing their economic, social and cultural situation through Canadian organizations." Mention of "equality," and "participation in the public policy process" was expunged (Turnbull, "CEDAW"). The year 2006 also saw the demise of the internationally-acclaimed Court Challenges Program (CCP), which provided funds to support test cases of national importance, relating to equality rights. Like the Women's Program of SWC, the CCP had been evaluated to ensure it was achieving its intended purposes, and continued funding was recommended. Conservative critics complained that it promoted feminists and homosexuals and undermined traditional values in Canada, however, and it was cancelled because it did not "provide value for money or meet the priorities of Canadians" and it didn't make sense for the government "to subsidize lawyers to challenge the government's own laws in court" (Turnbull, "CEDAW").

Cuts like these forced women's organizations to concentrate on chasing funding, diminishing their development and human rights focus. The cuts curtailed information sharing among organizations, and reduced the capacity to make connections, undermining women's decision-making and participation. As many other feminist organizations collapsed, the women of UNPAC launched into a muscular "parkour" strategy, twisting their founding objectives to surmount the obstacles raised by an increasingly antagonistic political, legal, and policy environment. With federal SWC funding cut, UNPAC members determined not to break but to bend their mission around new initiatives, to meet charitable status requirements and continue their work despite the constraints of the Conservative federal government.

After much deliberation about how to preserve the spirit of the organization in such a climate, UNPAC succeeded in applying for and securing project funding to develop and deliver educational and career network services to small groups of low-income and Aboriginal women in community centers in the inner city and in rural locations. These educational services took the place of UNPAC's previous economic literacy advocacy. Educational services required UNPAC to hire women as modestly-paid staff, even as the core funding to provide stable work and pay disappeared. The cuts had the effect of re-establishing women's unpaid labor, despite broader, mounting market demands on women's time and energies, requiring UNPAC to navigate the prevalent feminist conflict over exploitation of women's labor. As UNPAC registered for charitable status, and continued applying for grants, the Conservative government began to crack down on charitable organizations that engaged in advocacy. Feminists worldwide feared that conservative mobilization would derail the implementation of the Platform, and UNPAC found that its own trajectory had also been irrevocably transformed by conservative ascendance.

Compared with its earlier initiatives, UNPAC's small, free education and networking programs constituted inefficient mobilization. But where they focused on low-income and Aboriginal women struggling with unsettled lives in the face of welfare state retrenchment, the programs allowed UNPAC as an organization to continue to connect with and learn from society's most vulnerable and excluded women; and where they focused on rural women leaders, the programs continued to facilitate enriching exchanges. Keeping its purpose in mind, UNPAC's adaptations to conservative domination continued to produce successful feminist interventions that sustain feminist aspirations, and hope for the eventual reassertion of broadly-enabling surplus distribution and human rights.

At the core of its resiliency lies UNPAC's resolute respect for both insider and outsider political strategies, and its commitment to fostering insider-outsider strategy as far as possible. UNPAC maintains a strong connection to Manitoba's left-liberal polity, and has advocated directly to political representatives on behalf of women. Over the course of this relationship, UNPAC has supported the development and maintenance of a more favorable state infrastructure, including the maintenance of the provincial Status of Women department. UNPAC's Executive Director relates the strategy behind the organization's support for feminist polity development,

> So many other provinces lost their Status of Women [departments]. UNPAC has always supported the existence of Status of Women. The government needs a women's arm, some-

one who's pushing that agenda. We thought that agenda, the women's agenda would get lost otherwise. We believe that the women's agenda shouldn't be mainstreamed. If no one's responsible, it gets lost (deGroot).

Scholars of challenger politics caution against the corrosive relationship between social movement organizations and elites or the state (McAdam; Piven and Cloward; Domhoff). UNPAC resists this co-optive dynamic. Although UNPAC has been supported by SWC, and has worked directly with the Manitoba Status of Women Division (MSW), it has operated at a distance from the state (the organization was designed as a joint in a bipartite inside-outside political strategy). UNPAC could advance its agenda by strategically supporting, but not overly entwining with progressive polity players. The importance of using both social movement and the polity to attain feminist goals was emphasized in interviews not only by UNPAC leaders, but by MSW as well. MSW states that UNPAC's effective advocacy for the advancement of gender analysis in the Manitoba government is a result of the positive working relationship that UNPAC established with a wide range of actors across the provincial government.

The imprint of an insider-outsider feminist organizational network can be clearly seen in the Government of Manitoba's Gender and Diversity Analysis (GDA) policy origins, located in the international development framework of the Platform, and traced through a 1999 cooperative GDA policy framework introduced at the urging of UNPAC by the Provincial Members of Cabinet responsible for SWM. Echoing its strategy linking a broad array of women's interests and organizations, UNPAC's resourceful strategy—taking advantage of a sympathetic UN polity moment, galvanizing women across the province, and reinforcing a left-liberal government—combined to make feminist institutions and initiatives in the province more robust, more capable of feminist "parkour" action than in regions where conservatism more easily gained hold.

CONCLUSION: CONSERVATIVE ASCENT AND FEMINIST ADAPTATION

Our conservative age has, on one side, advanced the privileges, mobility, freedom, and rights of capital and, on the other side, diminished the political, social, economic, and human rights and freedoms of most women and other smallholders relying upon and fostering the institutions that discount women's and nature's work, obscuring rampant inequality. A steady barrage of offensives have deployed both co-optive strategies and "traumatizing" (Perelman 48-49) frontal attacks dismantling the collective institutions that offer reproductive support to women, their families, and their communities, and commandeering that social wealth to concentrated private accumulation.

We have seen specific forms of these attacks in the contraction of SWC's mandate and budget, and in the constraints this places on women's organizations such as UNPAC. These limits prevent women's organizations from advocating for a distribution of economic and political resources sufficient to allow women to realize their human rights. When asked "What are your regrets?" UNPAC founders decry "Governments that have never incorporated the importance of caregiving. Without incorporating caregiving, we deplete our resources." UNPAC founders regret the withdrawal of funding, the lack of political will "everywhere you look," that socio-economic gaps are much larger today and "women bear the brunt of that gap." Some regretted the expropriation of women's insufficiently-valued time, observing in Waring's spirit, "It's not only financial resources people need, but the time to healthily care for ourselves every day, as well as for our families, our communities, and our environment, that all allow us to thrive."

Despite their regrets, UNPAC founders, members and staff can point to many accomplishments, such as nurturing coalitions, strategic networks and campaigns, and forging an insider-outsider social movement. They frequently cite the connections UNPAC has built: "Rural grassroots contacts are hard to keep. We've maintained rural involvement," including coalitions with Aboriginal women in the North, as well as in the urban core. A few years ago UNPAC established five organizational goals: to keep the global – local connection alive in all its activities; to speak truth to power; to continue to network and gather in celebration; to strengthen the structure of the feminist organization; and to continue to mentor women in economic participation. An unfavorable political climate has forced contradictions amongst these goals, but building on past achievements, UNPAC forges creative ways to allow its goals to continue to guide its work.

In the context of worldwide feminist momentum galvanized by Waring and others, as well as Aboriginal women's efforts to intercede in colonial governance, UNPAC's approaches to making state infrastructure more receptive and accountable to the requirements of women across class and race have been obviously successful in the form of the GDA project. UNPAC has demonstrated that it is radical, democratically-confident, using resources at hand to take theory-coordinated action. Unapologetic, multi-pronged social action has allowed this feminist organization to achieve durable effectiveness.

Through its theoretical commitment, UNPAC was able to reflexively modify its feminist tactics and strategies over time in response to international women's and Aboriginal women's anti-colonial organization, as well as to the deteriorating context of political opportunities. Feminist savvy translated not only into responsiveness and adaptability, but also coherence, robustness, and resistance to cooptation. Our examination has suggested that a feminist organization working in Waring's tradition can reinforce progressivism, and navigate and weather conservative opposition. Doing so requires bringing women together, often in their roles as biological and societal reproducers, both within and outside the halls of the political and legal establishment. Across geographies, across social divides, and across liberation's surges and retrenchments, organizations like UNPAC magnify Waring's work, advancing the visibility, claiming the value, and promoting the fearlessness of women.

WORKS CITED

[1] The word "mother" in this chapter includes men who do mothering work as well

[2] "Kvuza" – collective farmstead, precursor of the kibbutz commune.

[3] The documentary *Who Does She Think She Is?* (2008), deals particularly with this tension between motherhood and being an artist. Artist Maye Torres, who appears in the documentary, says, "I had lots of people telling me that I was selfish. Is it selfish to do your own work when you're responsible for the care of others?"

[4] *Sinking Syncing* is a video-artwork (4 min.) featuring photographs and videos of "sink work."

[5] From the video-artwork *Sinking Syncing*

[6] Beterem Safe Kids Israel, an NPO which aims to promote child safety, states that "two thirds of child hospitalizations are due to home accidents... Most of these injuries are due to falls, burns, drowning, poisoning, choking, car accidents, and other 'every-day' causes" (Beterem annual report, 2010).

[7] Isha L'Isha Haifa Feminist Center and the Coalition of Women for Peace

[8] The Second Intifada (the Al-Aqsa uprising) broke out in 2000 and peaked between 2001 and 2003.

[9] In Hebrew the words for hospital and school include the word "house."

WORKS CITED

Cohen, Marjorie Griffin. "The Canadian Women's Movement and Its Efforts to Influence the Canadian Economy." *Challenging Times: The Women's Movement in Canada and the United States.* Ed. Constance Backhouse and D.H. Flaherty. Montreal: McGill-Queen's, 1992. 215-224. Print.

deGroot, Jennifer. Personal interview. 9 Apr. 2012.

deGroot, Jennifer and Lorna Turnbull. "Femme Fiscale." *Canadian Woman Studies/les cahiers de la femme* 24 (2006): 173. Print.

Domhoff, G. William. *The Power Elite and the State.* New York: Aldine de Guyter, 1990. Print.

Finestone, Sheila. Letter accompanying the report *Setting the Stage for the Next Century: The Federal Plan for Gender Equality.* Ottawa: Status of Women Canada, 1995 n. pag. Web.

Fraser, Nancy. "Feminism, Capitalism and the Cunning of History." *New Left Review* 56 (2009): 97-117. Print.

Government of Canada, "Infosource". Web.

Government of Manitoba. "GDA Training Manual", on file with the authors. n. d. Print.

Lyall, Deborah and the Northern Food Prices Project Steering Committee. Northern Food Prices Report. Healthy Child Committee of Cabinet, Government of Manitoba, 2003. Winnipeg, MB. Print.

McAdam, Doug. *Political Process and the Development of Black Insurgency, 1930-1970.* Chicago: University of Chicago Press, 1982. Print.

National Association of Women and the Law. *The Importance of Funding Women's Groups.* Sept. 2006. Web.

Oliver, Pamela, Gerald Marwell, and Ruy Teixeira. "A Theory of Critical Mass: I. Interdependence, Group Heterogeneity, and the Production of Collective Action." *American Journal of Sociology* 91.3 (1985) 522-56. Print.

Perelman, Michael. *The Invisible Handcuffs of Capitalism: How Market Tyranny Stifles Capitalism by Stunting Workers.* Monthly Review Press, 2011. Print.

Piven, Frances Fox and Richard Cloward. *Poor People's Movements: Why They Succeed, How They Fail.* New York: Pantheon Books, 1977. Print.

Status of Women Canada. *Setting the Stage for the Next Century: The Federal Plan for Gender Equality,* 1995. Print.

Turnbull, Lorna A. "The Promise of Brooks v Canada Safeway Ltd.: those who bear children should not be disadvantaged." *Canadian Journal of Women and the Law* 17.1 (2005) 151-159. Print.

—. "The "Wicked Problem" of Fiscal Equality for Women." *Canadian Journal of Women and the Law* 22.1 (2010): 213-239. Print.

—. "CEDAW For Mother's Equality." *Journal of Motherhood Initiative* 5 (2012): 9. Print.

UN. "UN Report of the World Conference to Review and Appraise the Achievements of the United Nations Decade for Women: Equality, Development and Peace, Nairobi, 15-26 July 1985." United Nations, n.d.: 16-17. Web. 14 Jun 2012.

UNDP. "Human Development Report 1995: Gender and Human Development." 1995. Web. 14 Jun 2012.

UNPAC. 1996. Conference Report – UNPAC (Mb) UN Platform for Action Committee (Manitoba) "Beyond Beijing – Call to Action," March 16, 1996. Web. 14 Jun 2012.

—. 1999. "Counting Women's Work Summary Proceedings." and "Drawing Conclusions from the *Counting Women's Work* Symposium." Brandon, MB. Web. 14 Jun 2012.

—. 2000. "Beijing+5 Report." Web. 14 Jun 2012.

—. 2011 "Gender Budget Project" Women and the Economy. Web. 14 Jun 2012.

—. 2012. Web. 14 Jun 2012.

UNPAC Founding Members Focus Group. Personal interview, 23 Jan. 2012.

UN Women. "The United Nations Fourth World Conference on Women: Platform for Action."

Varoufakis, Yanis. *The Global Minotaur.* London: Zed Books, 2011. Print.

Waring, Marilyn. *Counting for Nothing: What Men Value and What Women are Worth.* University of Toronto Press, 1999. Print.

Who's Counting? Dir. Terre Nash. National Film Board of Canada, 1995. DVD.

AUTHORS' NOTE

The authors thank the members of UNPAC and of Manitoba Status of Women for helping to accurately capture the history of their joint project. We also acknowledge the research assistance of Myra Tait (University of Manitoba, JD 2013) and Rhea Majewski (University of Manitoba, JD 2014).

16.

Counting Embodied Learning

Marilyn Waring and Feminist Pedagogical Practice

JILL EICHHORN

INTRODUCTION

"Engaged pedagogy necessarily values student expression."
bell hooks, *Teaching to Transgress*

MY VAGINA'S FURIOUS and it needs to talk...." So begins a favorite monologue of many women who have seen Eve Ensler's *The Vagina Monologues*. First performed in 1998 as a one-woman show off-Broadway, Ensler's award-winning play resulted from more than 200 interviews she conducted with women from all walks of life around the world. In 2011, more than 5,800 performances were staged in 45 countries as part of VDAY, the fundraising and political organizing arm that offers the script, staging resources and political strategy to college and community groups around the world through the website, vday.org.

For the past ten years, I have used the production of the play as the central component of a Women's Studies course titled *The Vagina Monologues*. Innovative in its pedagogical format, the course requires students to stage and perform the show, connect with the VDAY website and move-ment, and examine political and social conditions for women locally, na-tionally and internationally. Students write weekly journal responses, and the course ends with a research project and presentation on an issue for women, which might be sexual identity, body image, women's represen-tation in the media, or an issue women face in developing countries. In existence for 14 years, VDAY has raised $85 million that has assisted local, regional, and international efforts to launch programs and open shelters where women can heal and transform their lives (vday.org). This interna-tional political dimension is a crucial part of students' experience. In every group I have taught, many students comment about the difference of this educational experience. They report that they feel "connected to something larger than themselves." Through the website and the documentary *VDay: Until the Violence Stops*, students understand from the first day that they are participants in a project with women around the world. But it is the unconventional course requirement of performing the play for a public au-dience that offers students an embodied learning process that includes both rational and emotional dimensions and guides students to reflect on polit-ical frameworks that shape their personal experiences.

Marilyn Waring's *If Women Counted: A New Feminist Economics* guided me to recognize ways that patriarchal social and political structures devalued or erased practices connected to women's lives. As Gloria Steinem points out in the preface to Waring's book, "The states of female beings in general could be transformed by Waring's insistence on making reproduc-tion finally visible as the most basic form of production" (xii). Waring's questions demonstrate how women's second class status becomes embed-ded in everyday practices, resulting in normalizing women's subordination in social and political contexts. Waring's theoretical work has made me vigi-lant to what is invisible or devalued, and led me to consider the implications of that invisibility or devaluation in my classroom practices.

Like any Women's Studies course, *The Vagina Monologues* course makes women's experiences visible. In particular, I count the performance of *The Vagina Monologues* as a substantial portion of the course work. Waring's theoretical work has led me to examine how traditional patriar-chal structures or frameworks frequently prevent us from seeing or valuing what the framework by design makes invisible or subordinate. Her work teaches us, for example, to consider the economic support women's un-paid labor contributes to an economy while denying women any power, status, or recognition for that labor. Focusing on international economic systems, Waring points out how water moving in pipelines has more economic value than water carried by women from wells to homes. This kind of comparison led me to examine the classroom work I assign and how that work is valued and counted. In the case of my course, I came to understand that I had an opportunity to count the production of Ensler's play as part of students' academic development, an embodied exercise distinctive from traditional ways of engaging student development—essays, multiple choice tests, in class presentations or small group discussions—which rarely afford students a context of embodied learning. Performing the play is as legitimate as a paper or test, especially in the case of politically disenfranchised or marginalized groups. If "the institutions we practice in are still dominated by masculinist, Eurocentric norms of 'professional' behavior and accomplishment," as Susan Bordo argues, then when disenfranchised or marginalized groups interact with traditional institutions, only an agenda of transformation will prevent the erasure of their experience (40). Waring's analysis of international economics and the economic value denied women's work inspired me to analyze the work in the classroom and consider what and how I value student work. Through this examination I decided to intervene in structures that privilege individualized learning, perpetuating the invisibility of women's experiences and those of other disenfranchised groups. By integrating the play's production as a major graded component in this course (equivalent to a major writing assignment), I create an opportunity for students to embody stories of women, transforming personal stories into a public narrative, now a counted visible thread in the social fabric.

Perhaps most importantly, performing *The Vagina Monologues* gives students the occasion to say a word in public that is stigmatized. Ensler recounts in her memoir that when she began performing the monologues, she

> realized that just saying the word 'vagina' caused enormous controversy, because 'vagina' is, in fact, the most isolated, reviled word in any language. You can find words like 'nuclear,' 'scud,' or 'plutonium' on the front pages of newspapers and they never cause anywhere near such a stir. (74)

Students report similar experiences talking to friends, family, and teachers about the course. One male professor on our campus told a student that he supported the concept of ending violence against women, but found it problematic that the play's title uses a "dirty" word. In explaining how the cultural taboo around the word "vagina" works, Ensler writes,

> The taboo on the word is no accident. As long as we can-
> not say "vagina," vaginas do not exist. They remain isolated
> and unprotected. Young girls get genitally mutilated and sex-
> trafficked throughout the world. Women get raped, burned
> with acid, and beaten, and no one is held accountable. (75)

Ensler's observations about how the word "vagina" operates in discourse motivate her to transform the value and meaning of the word. While she attempts to intervene in culture through the vehicle of her play, some scholars challenge Ensler's use of the word. It is problematic, one scholar argues, in accepting the identification of woman as linked with the word, "vagina." Kim Hall warns, "The vagina, like the category 'woman,' is a political category" (113). Following the thinking of Monique Wittig, Hall outlines the limitations of reducing the definition of woman to the capacity of giving birth. Hall argues that "to engage in the project of reclaiming the vagina without simultaneously adopting a strategy of disidentification regarding the reality of the vagina does not challenge the social, political, historical, and economic context that imbues the vagina with meaning" (113). However, in middle Tennessee, where some students timidly sign up for Women's Studies courses and whisper about feminist politics, participation in *The Vagina Monologues* is a step in a process of unlearning patriarchal thinking. If the play reinscribes patriarchal concepts about being female, the venue of the theatre and the classroom offer opportunities to discuss the way the play universalizes representations of women's experiences inaccurately. Political analysis aside, the play responds to the experience many students report, that saying the word violates an invisible social contract, and symbolically the word carries connotations of what it means to be female. For student performers and audiences of the play both on and off campus, *The Vagina Monologues* creates a space where women's experiences matter, where their bodies are not sexually objectified and their interests are not narrowly collapsed into sexual objectification, shopping, marriage or children.

   To address the significance of performing the play and of moving from invisibility to visibility, from silence to voice, I frame here three beginnings: Eve Ensler's beginnings with performing the play, students' beginnings with their performances, and my own beginnings in finding my voice. In each story of beginnings, a transformation occurs related to speaking the word "vagina" in a public space. These

stories chronicle the necessary transformation of an individual to recognize her power and begin to use it. As feminist theatre educators Elizabeth Armstrong and Kathleen Juhl comment, "By expanding definitions of pedagogy...we acknowledge that artistic work frequently generates paradigm shifts, creating consciousness-raising that
changes the way we see ourselves and society" (8). Counting the performance of *The Vagina Monologues* as equivalent to an essay or test in the
system of higher education allows female students to feel that their emotional growth matters, students whose experience as females are traditionally marginalized and subordinated in the academic agenda. Through this
act, I expand the range of projects with which students engage and create
the possibility of the paradigm shifts Ensler, my students, and I have experienced.

BEGINNINGS I

Eve Ensler's own transformation fueled by her performance of the play as
a one-woman show is revealed in her introduction to *The Vagina Monologues*:

> Almost 15 years have passed since I first said the word "vagina"
> on a small stage in a little theater called HERE in downtown
> New York City. When I first read these monologues, my most
> pressing concern was being able to get the words out of my ter-
> rified mouth. I certainly could not have conceived then what
> would follow in terms of both a movement to end violence
> against women and girls, and the life of *The Vagina Mono-
> logues* itself. (xi)

More significantly, she explains, "Saying the word I was not supposed to
say is the thing that gave me a voice in the world. Revealing the very personal stories of women and their private parts gave birth to a public, global
movement to end violence against women and girls called V-Day" (xi-xii).
Here Ensler charts how speaking the word "vagina" in public challenges a
social and political framework that subordinates and silences female experiences and perspectives. This transformation Ensler identifies in herself and
the birth of the V-Day movement is connected to the venue of the theater.
She writes,

> Theater...allows us, it encourages us, as a community of stra-
> ngers, to go someplace together and face the issues and realities
> we simply cannot face alone. Alone, we are powerless, trans-
> lating our suffering and struggle into our own private narcis-
> sistic injuries. When we become a group, these issues become
> social or political concerns, responsibilities, a reason for being
> here together. (75)

When Ensler first performed the monologues, women would line up after performances to tell her their stories of abuse and violation. Because of their stories, Ensler gathered a group of celebrities and political activists to ask the question: How do we use this play as a catalyst to end violence against women? Out of that meeting, V-Day was born.

Observing how the word "vagina" was valued and questioning those appraisals, Ensler asked women how they felt about the word. Her questions opened women's silence to voice their experiences of pain, humor, humiliation, joy, and celebration. Just as Waring reveals the subordination of women's work in international economic structures, Ensler asked a question that shows how the word "vagina" is devalued in contrast to other words. Further, she posed the question in a way that generated stories to see and experience a connotation contrary to the mainstream culture's pejorative or embarrassed regard for it. "By saying 'vagina' often enough and loud enough in places where it was not supposed to be said," Ensler writes, "we made the saying of it both political and mystical and gave birth to a worldwide movement to end violence against women" (72). By speaking the word and stories about vaginas, Ensler transformed the culture to value what was once devalued or silenced.

BEGINNINGS II

On the first day of class, I ask students to interview each other to break down the barriers of individualized experience in the classroom and encourage students to connect with each other, but I am also conducting informal research. Students are instructed to ask each other why they are taking this course. Frequently, students report that a friend recommended the course as one that is different and rewarding. In a similar vein, students report that they learn about who they are as women. In other words, their experiences as women carry value as a central component of the course. At the end of the course, these student stories emerged in a format similar to Ensler's through which she generated the material to write her play. My students were asked: Describe your perception of yourself before taking *The Vagina Monologues* course and before performing the play on stage. Secondly, students were prompted: Describe changes, if any, in how you perceive yourself that you attribute to your participation in the course or in the stage production. While the monologues as a whole create necessarily reductive generalizations of women's experience, students' testimonies demonstrate that performing in the play and discussing the issues the play generates constitute a path of agency and voice, as Ensler recounts in her own journey. Performing in the play offers an alternative to sitting in silence and isolation. One student reported, "Before the class, I never participated in discussions." She said she routinely doubted that she had anything significant to add to a conversation. Throughout her life as a student, she listened to classmates speak, judging that her classmates were more "well-spoken" than she. After the course, she reflected that she understood that "everyone has their unique voice," and "every voice is valuable to what needs to be learned." This student transformed from one who sat passively in classroom discussions, perceiving other students as better able to articulate ideas, to feeling the value of adding her voice to any public discussion.

Another student commented that the act of saying aloud the words in the narrative titled "The Flood" taught her "how important words can be and how important a person's experience can be." This student's experience of learning through doing identifies a dimension of performing the show categorized as kinesthetic or embodied learning. The student remarked on a quality of understanding that she did not have before performing the show, and in particular, speaking the story of the flood aloud in public space. In the university environment, reading and writing are privileged as modes of learning over visual and kinesthetic learning. Recognizing a wide range of learning styles is standard practice in the Montessori and Waldorf models, and in the Suzuki method of learning musical instruments. In education courses, future teachers are coached to engage different styles of learning as they plan how to expose their students to new material and ideas. And yet, at the university level, outside the disciplines in the arts, students' self-expression is muted through coaching a disembodied writing voice that is meant to report information or formulate arguments with objective or universal authority. This student's experience shows that speaking words aloud facilitates a kind of understanding that is difficult to quantify.

Evaluating both her professional and emotional development, one student said,

During the first production in 2002, I did not imagine that I would ever be an alumnus of a university, and I did not imagine that I would be faculty, but today, I am both. I used to believe I was a strong woman, that I had my place in the world. Looking back on it now, I learned that I had room to grow, lots of room to grow.

Personally, she described a growth in her voice. "I used to believe I had a voice, but in performing *The Vagina Monologues*, I found a new, stronger voice that I am still getting acquainted with after all this time—singing. I began to sing, and then I began to change for the better." Here the student uses "singing" metaphorically to describe a transformation in the quality of her voice, a stronger voice.

Students recognized their own voices becoming stronger, and they recognized how they might advocate for other women. One student reported that she learned that she could be an advocate for women, but more importantly, she said, "I could be an advocate for myself. I could give myself a voice in a positive, constructive way." She claimed more confidence in herself, and increased comfort in her body image. "I credit 'the monologues' for that transformation," she said. "Getting on stage," she explained, was terrifying, and yet it gave her a sense of "power." Finally, she commented that on stage she felt "a kind of strength that I didn't know I had before." "I surprised myself in what I could actually do," reported another student. Another commented, "I found a part of myself that I didn't know was there." And finally, a student reported that she can now say "vagina" without blushing.

The performers grow, and the audience grows. Following a performance one year, a woman wrote me and thanked me for the opportunity to experience the play. She had been a student at our university for seven years and only this particular year had an opportunity to see the show. At the end of the show, we invite the cast and the audience to stand if they are a survivor of violence so that the audience can honor them. Half of the cast stood up, a few in the audience. The student who wrote me said she summoned the courage to count herself as a survivor and that by standing up she transformed feeling victimized by her experience into feeling that she had survived it, thus embodying her experience. She wrote that she felt "free" of it. This is the alchemy of theatre that Eve Ensler describes, an alchemy that affects both the people in the cast and the audience. To speak the suffering, to take a symbolic stand in public, to acknowledge one's silent or invisible suffering embodies the experience. Through this embodiment, creating the paradigm shift from silence to sound, the experience is transformed.

Performers grow, audience members grow, and students as directors grow. Part of VDay's vision is that *The Vagina Monologues* provides leadership opportunities for women. The VDAY rules offer the script without royalty fees as long as students direct the show and coordinate the publicity. One student story follows her experience of first performing in the show and then directing a show the next year. Before taking the course and performing in the show, she described herself as "terrified completely of talking to two people in a group." However, because "everyone supported each other to have their voice heard in and out of class," this student accomplished taking the stage and delivering her lines. She acknowledged *The Vagina Monologues* course and performance experience as the catalyst that improved her ability to speak in public. In fact, the next year, she took charge of directing an alumni/faculty show. In that performance she chose to read all of the introductions to the monologues. Because of this experience, she said, she had confidence that she could "put something together, get it done, and succeed at it." She concluded that she "cannot think of any other situation where I would have gotten this kind of opportunity."

In the VDay documentary, Jane Fonda says that she believes that "it is fitting that women are transforming through art." More than fitting, the women transform because of the artistic context, where emotions and wholeness of experience inspire women, as Armstrong and Juhl point out, to see themselves in new ways as embodied and empowered.

BEGINNINGS III

In 2001, one of my students, a theatre major, saw *The Vagina Monologues* in San Francisco and returned insisting that we perform the play on campus. I was speechless. Untenured, I was completely unnerved by the prospect of producing this play about women's sexuality. The student talked to a tenured social work professor who taught human sexuality, and a tenured drama professor. They asked me if I wanted to join them in offering a course which we would teach together, bringing in speakers addressing issues the play raised and producing the show as part of the course. The student discovered the College Campaign, V-Day, which offered the script to student groups free of royalties if the play was used to raise money for local agencies that assist women and girls who are survivors of violence. On February 14, 2002, Austin Peay State University was one of 514 campuses in V-Day's College Campaign hosting *The Vagina Monologues.* APSU's 600-seat Clement Auditorium was packed, raising $2000 in two performances.

In 2002, Clarksville's Roxy Regional Theatre produced the show where my student was asked to direct it. I wanted to be brave enough to perform. But, I have to admit that I was intimidated. I wanted to face my fear without letting it paralyze me—and on some level, I did not even understand how paralyzed and frozen I was, just beginning my interior journey of unlocking my personal history of sexual violation. Somewhere around this time, I picked up one of those quotable magnets with words from Eleanor Roosevelt. "You gain strength, courage, and confidence by every experience in which you really stop to look fear in the face … Do the thing you think you cannot do." Part of me did not believe that I could perform those monologues on stage as I had watched my students do without making a fool of myself. And yet, how could I ask them to do what I myself feared?

Their courage inspired me. My voice occasionally quaked. My insides trembled as I sat on stage. Facing my terror, finding my way into the rhythm of the words, sharing the stage with actresses and my colleagues helped me see myself differently. As Armstrong and Juhl suggest about feminist theatre experience, my paradigm shifted, altering my image of myself. My children, who were 12 and 7 at the time, and my partner delighted to hear me swear in public. I delighted to hear myself swear in public. I delighted in the transgressive act, expressing guttural, embodied, "not-taking-shit" swearing. Finding this grounded anger through the words and expressing them in public transformed my anger and feelings of victimization from my own violations. What I have come to understand through teaching this course and other Women's Studies courses is that even for girls and women who have not suffered a personal physical or sexual violation, there is the violation of the media that teaches boys and men to objectify women as it teaches girls and women to objectify themselves. There is no female in the modern world who escapes it. The play, however, offers a public, communal response to the media's efforts to objectify us, for both performers and audience. Women on stage or in the audience learn to transform the way we see ourselves from victims to survivors, from objects to subjects. Our voices join the women's experiences in the play, and together our voices interrupt the silence with sounds and stories women recognize.

That transformation for me has meant that I now teach the course on my own, a professor who has earned tenure. My courage to speak the truths of sexual and physical violation and to listen to students' stories of violation has grown as I have been involved with performing, producing this play and teaching the issues and questions the play generates. Performing in the play is not a substitute for therapy, but, as one woman, Laura, in the V-Day documentary explains, talking about violation in the private space of therapy is a different experience than creating the quilt she made about her own violation and social restrictions in her teens (VDay). Making the quilt and speaking about the experience in public shifts the story from the private domain to the public where the weight of the suffering is at least lessened. In some cases, it disappears. For many women, the shame is so crippling, it silences us. The public ritual of narrating our own experience or a similar one lifts the shame and isolation and frees us to fill the silence with our own sound, our embodied and empowered voices.

I no longer feel fear anticipating my performance at the Roxy. I have performed in three shows each season for ten years. I believe working with this play, with the students, and learning their stories has shown me the importance of embodying the diversity of our experiences. Because of my experience performing the show, I have emphasized in the course work the material of body image, racial and ethnic identities, sexual identities and orientation, birth and menstruation, images of women in the media, particularly Sut Jhally's documentary, *Dreamworlds III*. The study of these subjects deepens the transformation the play stimulates.

Other course components are unconventional as I introduce the structure of the theater process. To value the process of producing the play, I schedule the auditions, one rehearsal, and the final show during class time. I work with a student population that juggles going to school full time, parenting, family obligations and one or two jobs. I use the class time (once a week for three hours) to build in the process they would experience for a dramatic production. Many students have never been on stage before. Frequently students are coming to terms with violations or abusive relationships for the first time, as they are exposed to information that pushes them to examine their personal worlds. On the first day of class, I inform each female student that she will have some part in the show. She only has to say one word, and she doesn't have to be on stage alone, but each female member of the course has to get on stage. I make this requirement after observing for several years students who were reluctant to get on stage, but who challenged themselves to perform. I observed their nervousness and timidity before the show, and then their joy and self-confidence after facing the challenge and transforming through the process. By contrast, I observed students who, fearing to get on stage, were allowed to sit in their fear. Their fear imprisoned them. They still enjoyed the course and the experience, but their relationship to the group and to the experience was different from the experience of those who performed. As Ensler indicates, "the alchemy of theatre," the process and ritual of going through the show, changes each performer. To place the performance of the play as a central project in my course opens a space to see and experience the connotation of the word *vagina* differently. By extension, the connotations of being female in this patriarchal culture expand and allow women to find versions of themselves who demand, for example, as one woman states in the VDay documentary, "rape-free zones."

2001 marked the beginning of my odyssey with teaching a course that created time, space, networking, resources, and critical engagement with the topics generated by Eve Ensler's *The Vagina Monologues*. Many women who have experienced the performance—in the audience or on stage—have reported the transformative potential of the play. There is a deeper transformation when the play is part of an academic course, where the play transforms the traditionally patriarchal paradigm that privileges male experience over female experience. When the play offers participants—directing, performing, or listening—the opportunity to develop confidence, the emotions discovered and expressed create a crucible for women's power. When women embody their voices and experiences, they express their autonomy. When women see themselves as autonomous subjects, they transform their relationship to power.

An exam, a multiple choice test, a personal essay, a research paper— these forms of academic work offer students a particular kind of individualized intellectual experience and growth. As professors and instructors, we evaluate this growth through grades, a ritual that counts and quantifies student progress and learning leading toward an academic degree. These forms of evaluation privilege individualized learning, and this kind of learning context values a particular kind of intellectual ability. Waring's work asks us to count women's contributions in international economic frameworks. Eve Ensler's play asks us to count and value women's gendered experiences. Taking the lead of these two activists who challenge us to imagine and create a world where women's work and experience count, I place the performance of Eve Enlser's *The Vagina Monologues* at the heart of an academic course as a graded component and by doing so I honor the courage female students summon to announce in public space that their experiences as women matter, and their efforts to narrate these stories as a group in a public forum constitutes a legitimate measure of their learning.

WORKS CITED

American Heritage Dictionary. Third Ed. New York: Houghton Mifflin, 1997. Print.

Armstrong, Elizabeth and Kathleen Juhl. Eds. *Radical Acts: Theatre and Feminist Pedagogies of Change.* San Francisco: aunt lute books, 2007. Print.

Bordo, Susan. *Unbearable Weight: Feminism, Western Culture, and the Body.* Berkley, CA: U of California P, 1993. Print.

Ensler, Eve. *The Vagina Monologues.* Tenth Anniversary Edition. New York: Villard, 2008. Print.

Hall, Kim Q. "Queerness, Disability, and The Vagina Monologues." *Hypatia* 20.1 (Winter 2005): 100-116. Literature Resource Center. Web. Oct. 10, 2011.

hooks, bell. *Teaching to Transgress: Education as the Practice of Freedom.* New York: Routledge, 1994. Print.

VDay: Until the Violence Stops. Dir. Abby Epstein. New Video Group, 2005. Film.

VDay: A Global Movement to Stop Violence Against Women and Girls. Web. 25. March 2012.

Waring, Marilyn. *If Women Counted.* New York: Harper Collins, 1988. Print.

17.

Post-graduate Supervision with MJW

KAREN WEBSTER

INTRODUCTION

O N AN EVENING in the third or fourth week of every month, between 15 and 30 postgraduate students, past students and visitors
will gather in the faculty staff room, for Professor Marilyn Waring's infamous pot luck dinner. As the name of the occasion suggests, every
person in the room makes a contribution to the table. They also make a
contribution, throughout the course of the evening, to the sharing of intellectual property that makes these occasions memorable.

Attendance at the gathering is more or less mandatory if you are a post
graduate student of Professor Waring. However, the occasion has more in
common with a whanau (family) gathering than a tutorial or class. Life stories, great joys, moments of sadness and steps along the research pathway
are shared amongst those in the room. What brings this group together is
Marilyn's unerring awhi (mentorship). Under her guidance, the evening
progresses from the shared meal to a more formal sharing of research experiences. This collegial gathering transforms the research journey, which
can be solitary, lonely and long, into one which is convivial, supported and
richly rewarding.

Marilyn joined the Massey University Albany Campus in 1994, and
took up the Chair of Public Policy at AUT University in 2007. By mid-
2011, Marilyn had personally guided 22 masters' students and 18 doctoral

candidates successfully through their research; many of them mature students and many women. They come from almost every corner of the globe and span a wide range of disciplines. Whatever their motivation, they hold Marilyn in high esteem, not only for her personal qualities, but for a professionalism that has her transcend the "good teacher" exemplar. This chapter draws on the contributions of 17 of Marilyn's post graduate researchers. It describes, in many cases using the contributors' own words, how they came to know Marilyn; her teaching and post graduate supervision style and techniques; and the contributions that they are making to the world as a result of knowing her.

HOW WE CAME TO KNOW MARILYN

We come to know Marilyn from her reach into international community development, feminist economics, politics and academia. The group includes post graduate researchers and current masters' and doctoral candidates from Pakistan, Thailand and Canada, who knew of Marilyn's work in international community development.

Amongst those who knew of Marilyn's work in international development are: a social scientist working with NZAID participants in a rural aid projects (Wall); a senior lecturer from the Mekhong Institute, in Khon Kaen University, Northeast Thailand (Suttisa); and a Canadian International Development Agency evaluator of funded education programmes in Fiji, the Gambia and Ghana who was attending the Okanagan University College, Kelowna, Canada (Tucker). The documentary *Who's Counting? Marilyn Waring on Sex, Lies and Global Economics* (Nash) attracted scholars and practitioners in the field of feminist economics, equality and justice.

At home in New Zealand, a group of feminist activists were attracted by Marilyn's work on gender equality, and human rights. Included were feminist activists: a senior lecturer of health and social services at Massey University who explored restorative justice with respect to child sexual abuse (Jülich); a senior lecturer of management and leadership for community organisations at the Unitec (Malcolm); a New Zealand community worker who set out to explore participatory action research with three community groups (Cervin); and an Australian registered psychologist working in New Zealand with women refugee and immigrant survivors of sexual abuse (Mendelsohn).

The third group within Marilyn's post graduate cohort were those who connected with her during her political career. They included a retired politician, diplomat and past mayor of North Shore City, who graduated at the age of 83 years (Gair); a senior AUT lecturer in paramedicine and emergency management, retired dairy farmer and Alliance Party MP, who met Marilyn in the Wellsford Post Office in 1989 (this was after she had left parliament, and was goat farming) (Gillon); and an activist and member of parliament for the New Zealand Green Party (Bradford).

This leads me to the last group, of which I am one. We were drawn to Marilyn's door, at home in New Zealand, by her reputation within academia. We knew of her work in Canada on the Genuine Progress Indicator project, her ability to tease out complex issues surrounding power and gender, and her expertise in national, international and local governance, and wider public policy issues. Our group included: a New Zealand academic pursuing research on homelessness (Mace); a committed central government social and community development worker of Samoan descent, and researcher of sexual abuse (Sumeo); Head of Podiatry from AUT's Akoranga campus who researched the New Zealand drug agency Pharmac's community exceptional circumstances policy (Coyle); a senior lecturer of management at Massey University, who explored power and gender in the world of women's hockey (Edwards); a lecturer from Maharsarakham University in north-east Thailand, researching lifelong learning among rural villagers (Wech-o-sotsakda); and a local government manager researching the roles of elected members in a bicultural context (Webster).

The sections that follow tell stories that highlight Marilyn's teaching and post graduate supervision style. Whether committed to rural community development, feminist economics, politics or academic research and teaching, the stories told by this cohort of Marilyn's post graduate researchers and students have common themes.

MARILYN AS TEACHER AND POST GRADUATE SUPERVISOR

The stories demonstrated that Marilyn's style of teaching and supervision was based on a welcoming, collaborative and facilitative approach. She was empowering and open in her thinking, yet demanding of robustness and rigor in the research process. The spontaneity and creativity that Marilyn encouraged in the academic process and her ongoing awhi created a space for all of her students to question conventional positivist research, and develop new research methodologies.

Marilyn's laugh, and her delight in the research journey and eagerness to meet for supervision, in spite of her crushing schedule of international commitments, is legendary amongst her students, as is her absolute reliability and time management. Regular supervision commitments are scheduled months in advance and considered sacrosanct, alongside sharing the networks that provided her students with a forum to learn from and support each other.

There was no "one way" of supervision with Marilyn. Her highly principled and fun approach, created an environment in which her cohorts charted their own paths to academic success. Marilyn's power as an academic role model was overwhelmingly the influence most acknowledged by those of us who contributed our stories to this chapter. Through her guidance and mentoring Marilyn steered many of us towards full-time or part-time academic careers. The experience of her professional and personal style of respect for and empowering of others had a profound effect on how many of her post graduate cohort communicate with and inspire others.

Welcoming

Marilyn welcomed difference. She recognised that her students came from many parts of the globe, but brought with them a rich blend of professional and life experiences which contributed to their scholarship. Marilyn demonstrated intense interest and excitement in the range of disciplines they brought to her door, many of which were new to her. She did not need to be an expert in the field of knowledge to be an exemplary guide along the research pathway.

From the moment of meeting, Marilyn empowered her students with warm encouragement and an invitation to express their aspirations and share with colleagues and fellow researchers, and to build on their knowledge of the research process. The following quote from Greg emphasises the genuine excitement with which Marilyn greeted each new student to her research family:

> I had just completed my Masters of Public Policy at Victoria University and decided to phone Marilyn and see if there was any possibility of becoming a PhD student of hers. I introduced myself and she immediately said "yes" to my request. I asked her how can you say that when you haven't even met me yet or talked about my proposal. She said "It's Monday morn-

ing. It is five past nine. This is my first day at this university. Yours is the first phone call I have received. I am so impressed that you even know I exist, you will be my first AUT doctoral student" (Coyle).

This enthusiasm was contagious and energised us all, especially those for whom English was a second language. A Thai student, who had taken some time to master English, highlighted how Marilyn made her welcome, irrespective of her broken English, patiently explaining the complexities of the research process and encouraging her to befriend native English speakers (Wech-o-sotsakda).

Green Party politician Sue, acknowledged Marilyn's personalised "women MP in political trauma counseling service," which she encountered on the parliamentary day off, when she first trudged up the stairs to Marilyn's office (Bradford). From that moment, Sue described Marilyn as being with her all the way, encouraging her to seriously consider doing a PhD.

Empowerment

The warm welcome and invitation to join what felt like an exclusive club, was Marilyn's first gesture of empowerment to each of her students. Few of us came from the traditional "A" scholarship background. Instead, we brought a rich tapestry of life experience with some past academic achievement.

Marilyn had a way of tuning in to self doubt and encouraging genuine self-belief in her students' capabilities. Margot, senior management lecturer from Massey University, highlights how many of us were treading the postgraduate path with trepidation and uncertainty:

> I felt nervous of meeting the infamous "MJW," sure that Marilyn would see that I was not smart enough to complete a PhD—however, within three months she had me laughing about the "administrative bullshit" that we had to complete and I simply adored her irreverence. M, in her strong and direct manner, tore up my imposter syndrome and threw it out the window. (Edwards)

In a more gentle approach, this community worker, turned academic described Marilyn as having "walked alongside as I scoped ideas too large for one PhD, scaled them back to an MPhil because that is what felt manageable as a first step, and then encouraged me to upgrade to a PhD" (Malcolm).

Marilyn was quick to recognise her students as the emerging experts in the field of research as they progressed their research. Shirley, who was researching restorative justice for adult survivors of sexual abuse, described how Marilyn kept her moving along the research path:

> I continued reading, re-interviewing survivors when they re-membered something important they wanted to tell me. I in-terviewed community experts, I reflected and thought about what I had learned. I talked to anyone who was prepared to listen, but I did not write. I felt paralysed. Over time it had become much easier to research than make sense of the data I had gathered. I met regularly with Marilyn. She never once suggested that I might not be up to the task. She never once intimated that she was becoming exasperated. She validated everything I was doing. (Jülich)

Marilyn's supervision style resonated with her local and international students, many of whom sought to emulate her approach as part of their own research culture. This included being frank and fearless and telling those above in the hierarchy when they were out of line (Sumeo).

Collaboration and facilitation

While acknowledging the uncertainty of her students, the regular emergence of "imposter syndrome" and various incidences of researcher and writer block, Marilyn clearly established the ground rules. The monthly pot luck meeting was the visible and tangible evidence of Marilyn's collaborative style. It was the vehicle for the cohort to collaborate with and learn from each other. Winifred described this key aspect of the "Waring" research process:

> Being one of Prof Waring's PhD students is not about be-ing a solitary figure studying in a lonely garret, but rather as being part of a community...[the community] does not just happen—but is created through skill and good mod-elling to build an affirmative group from a diverse lot of peo-ple...When Marilyn was stranded overseas, the pot luck con-tinued as though she were there. (Murray)

Many of Marilyn's students stayed with the cohort and continue to share experiences or co-supervise, or simply be present at the pot luck, well after graduating.

In guiding participatory action research, Carmel observed Marilyn to

> [take] on the role of "a companion on the research journey."
> The relationship we shared in many ways modeled the rela-
> tionship that I needed to nurture with the groups I was work-
> ing with. This was one of not dictating the process, of collab-
> orating and openly sharing ideas, supportive personally and
> professionally, sharing a passion and commitment to the jour-
> ney, letting go and trusting in the process ... This was so sub-
> tle and yet so profoundly guiding me in the right direction.
> (Cervin)

Others in the cohort acknowledged a fine distinction between establishing a collaborative research culture, which required their participation
as the researcher, and that of Marilyn herself, as an effective and enthusiastic
facilitator. Marilyn advocated for her students, in a way that was strong, and
protective, without being patronizing. When faced with the challenge of
exploring Maori views of governance and sustainability for my own thesis,
Marilyn facilitated a breakthrough of the cultural barriers holding me back,
by introducing me to the woman who was to become my first Maori awhi
(mentor). This broke the ice with respect to the inadequacy I felt around
Maori tikanga (custom) and kawa (protocol). My new awhi set me on a
path to explore Te Ao Maori (the Maori world view) and indigenous research methods. This profoundly influenced the conduct and findings of
my thesis.

Mentorship and awhi

Marilyn's mentorship and awhi did not stop at creating the collaborative
research environment and facilitating practical connections within our re-
spective research worlds. Carmel described working with Marilyn, as

> like we were discovering and uncovering together. She talked
> of "peeling back the layers of an onion," as we uncovered a
> deeper and deeper understanding of Participatory Action Re-
> search. This dialogue and her collaborative approach were key
> to creating a space for academic reflection. (Cervin)

Jenny accompanied Marilyn to speak at a conference which provided space for sharing inter-cultural dialogue designed to communicate "change" from sharing power to "transforming" power—changing the mechanisms through the merging of local knowledge systems into the development of a new economic model. This experience put her right on track for participating in research in Gambia three weeks later (Tucker).

Greg saw Marilyn

> as a wickedly hard taskmaster who would not tolerate lazy thinking or uninformed comment. She saw straight through a lack of reading.... She told me to give up my doctoral study three times but I equaled her with my stubbornness and my determination grew. At times I was terrified by the depth and strength of her challenge and at times she entirely delighted me with her appreciation of my efforts. She proved an intellectual master when it came to the organisation of ideas and critically examining the essence of social problems.

Greg described Marilyn's inability to treat chapter drafts as imperfect pieces of writing which need shaping, as one of his greatest frustrations. However, he attributes his writing having reached doctoral level, as a testimony to Marilyn's red pen. He testifies that Marilyn "achieved this mostly out of fear, and my desire not to disappoint her" (Coyle).

For others Marilyn was more like a guide than a taskmaster and at times they wished for more direction, though knew they would be told if straying from the path or not making the progress expected. Marilyn urged her students to develop an effective yet compelling writing style that allowed their voices to come through the thesis. She encouraged reflection—and capturing thoughts and ideas at every stage of the research process. Shirley described how:

> At one supervision session [Marilyn] diagnosed that as I was suffering from "researchitis" and urged me to "just write, write anything, and trust the writing process." She asked me what justice meant to me and suggested that I write about this. After she had read this piece she said, "You can see that you have to write about equality now." Actually I hadn't and neither had I thought about equality in any great depth, but I agreed. This exercise was to have a lasting impact on me, on my work.

As it had become easier for me to research than write, so too it became easier to write than pull it all together. Marilyn's task was now to stop me writing, but I was overwhelmed with the amount I had written. This was not a problem in her eyes. She suggested I bring everything I had ever written to her office for our next meeting. Together, we spread it out on the floor, shuffling and reordering the many pieces I had written over the years. By the end of the session I had an almost finished piece of work, we could literally walk through the thesis.

...As a supervised student, then as colleague supervising students with her, I regularly witness Marilyn empowering and enabling students so that they can negotiate their journey of learning. This has had an impact on the way I supervise my students. The lessons learned from having such a guide on my journey translate daily in my interactions with students and I hear myself saying the same things Marilyn said to me: "act like a sponge, read as much as you can" and "trust the process, trust the writing process." (Jülich)

Marilyn's special way of mentoring her students did not stop at degree completion. Her awhi continued with the opportunity to co-supervise new post graduate students. We consider this as "graduating to supervision school" where we role modeled Marilyn's empowering style. Always positive with her students during the supervision, it did not go unnoticed that Marilyn would often leave it to the secondary supervisor in training to provide "constructive" or "corrective" feedback.

Her unique approach, and ongoing mentoring evidenced by this group of Marilyn's post graduate students engendered in them the absolute confidence that they could "count on her to get them to the finish line" and could maintain a critical perspective by simply asking "what would Marilyn have to say about that?" (Edwards).

OUR CONTRIBUTION TO THE WORLD, THROUGH KNOWING MARILYN

Two key themes emerged as we described the contribution we would make to the world, having experienced Marilyn's unique style of post graduate supervision. The first theme concerns the scholarship of her cohort and its influence on practice. The second is Marilyn's influence as a role model.

The scholarship and practice

The examples of applied scholarship that follow demonstrate the breadth of Marilyn's influence through supervision and teaching. In North East Thailand, community development projects now consider social capital, the concept of grounded civil society and collective action in their brief. According to Choopug (Suttisa), the effects of negative government, the poor economic conditions of villagers and the social capital built up around kinship ties is acknowledged as stimulating local people to engage in civil society, in order to address their social issues.

Also in North East Thailand, community learning centres are being established, based on a model established through doctoral research completed under Marilyn's supervision. The research evidenced that rural communities grasped the benefits of information and communication technology (ICT) through the establishment of community learning centres. The model developed by Chanthana (Wech-o-sotsakda) has encouraged economic independence by teaching villagers how ICT can meet their needs, enhance productivity and the reach to markets.

In rural Uzbekistan, serious challenges of technology adoption and agrarian reform, were identified under Marilyn's supervision, and examined through the prism of "Black Feminist" and "Resistance" theories (Wall). Each challenge presented significant difficulties in terms of: perpetuated structures of dependence, the banking system, and in providing a limited margin for experimentation. Whilst the political climate of the time did not allow for radical changes to remove these barriers, there were positive indications of change. The gradual reform process away from the central agro-industrial complex and the reform of state farms into leasehold units hold real potential, indicated a commitment to change that will become increasingly vital for sustained economic and social development.

Additionally, in Auckland, New Zealand, psycho-dramatic group work commenced as part of a research project had been running for 14 years. Delivered by a multicultural team, therapy for women settlers to cope with trauma related to pre-migration and current events had never before been offered in New Zealand. The groups continued to attract NGO funds. Contact from ex-group members who were doing well saw the group as a positive launching pad. One team member, herself an immigrant from Iraq, completed a Masters thesis based on interviews with Iraqi women who attended the groups (Mendelsohn).

Project Restore, initiated in 2004, and funded by the New Zealand

Ministry of Justice, analysed the restorative justice processes used to address sexual violence. The research team led by Dr. Shirley Jülich and Dr. John Buttle from AUT University found that while the negative psychological and social consequences of sexual violence were well-understood and well—documented, an understanding of the economic costs and consequences was more recent. The international literature asserted that the costs to victim-survivors, their families, and the broader society were significant. A costing analysis of crime undertaken by the New Zealand Treasury indicated that one incident of sexual violence cost $72,130. Project Restore is one of the few programmes internationally using restorative justice to address sexual violence (Jülich et al.).

Whakapiri tatou, hei manaaki tangata, hei manaaki whenua: Effective governance for urban sustainability (Webster) examined the role of local government elected members in New Zealand to progress urban sustainability, and the views of Māori (New Zealand indigenous people) leaders' on governance and sustainability. The findings were presented using the "three-housemodel." The Pākehā (NZ European) House established a broader role for elected members to promote urban sustainability by focusing on cross-sector collaboration and multi-level governance, which was notably absent. The Maori House recognised that the Local Government Act 2002 had failed to bring about transformation of Māori participation in local government and proffered two paths to the future: firstly, constitutional change—a new system of local government that recognises the validity of tino rangatiratanga (Māori sovereignty) as an equal authority; and secondly, improvements to the current system of local government were recommended that reflected Te Ao Māori world view, principles and values. The Treaty (of Waitangi) House presented a case for strengthening a partnership approach to governance. The effective inclusion of both Pākehā and Māori communities alike was identified as a prerequisite for further progress towards urban sustainability in Aotearoa New Zealand.

CONCLUSION

Through supervision, Marilyn conveyed to us that we could count on her to be our teacher, guide and mentor, as we overcame the personal challenges of completing a masters or doctorate of philosophy. We shared many unique experiences, not the least of which was the special camaraderie of Marilyn's infamous monthly pot luck dinner. Marilyn's holistic approach and blending of what is professional and what is personal has been fundamental to her academic practice. Through the "good teacher" exemplar, we have each committed to advancing a range of aspirational social conditions including: gender equality, social equity, justice, democracy, good governance, community development, and feminist economics, in the worlds we influence. With her collaborative, facilitative and empowering supervision style Marilyn has become our enduring role model.

WORKS CITED

[1] The word "mother" in this chapter includes men who do mothering work as well

[2] "Kvuza" – collective farmstead, precursor of the kibbutz commune.

[3] The documentary *Who Does She Think She Is?* (2008), deals particularly with this tension between motherhood and being an artist. Artist Maye Torres, who appears in the documentary, says, "I had lots of people telling me that I was selfish. Is it selfish to do your own work when you're responsible for the care of others?"

[4] *Sinking Syncing* is a video-artwork (4 min.) featuring photographs and videos of "sink work."

[5] From the video-artwork *Sinking Syncing*

[6] Beterem Safe Kids Israel, an NPO which aims to promote child safety, states that "two thirds of child hospitalizations are due to home accidents... Most of these injuries are due to falls, burns, drowning, poisoning, choking, car accidents, and other 'every-day' causes" (Beterem annual report, 2010).

[7] Isha L'Isha Haifa Feminist Center and the Coalition of Women for Peace

[8] The Second Intifada (the Al-Aqsa uprising) broke out in 2000 and peaked between 2001 and 2003.

[9] In Hebrew the words for hospital and school include the word "house."

WORKS CITED

Bradford, Sue. "Beneficiary 'Impact' Highlights Poverty of Social Policies." (2012). Web. 26 Dec 2012.

Cervin, Carmel. "Action Research, Power and Responsibility." Doctorate. Massey University, 2001. Print.

Coyle, Greg. "How Does Pharmac's Community Exceptional Circumstances Policy Align with Distributive Justice Principles Described by John Rawls and Amartyr Sen?" Doctorate. AUT University, 2012. Web.

Edwards, Margot. "Gendered Coaching in Women's Hockey." Doctorate. Massey University, 2003. Print.

Gair, George Frederick. "Managing Change as a Minister of the Crown." Masters of Philosophy. AUT University, 2010. Print.

Gillon, Grant Marc. "Formation, Durability and Susceptibility: Coalition Traits That Affected New Zealand's Mmp Governments of 1996-2002." Massey University, 2009. Web. 30 December 2012.

Jülich, Shirley, et al. *Project Restore: An Exploratory Study of Restorative Justice and Sexual Violence.* Auckland: AUT University, 2010. Print.

Jülich, Shirley Jean. "Breaking the Silence: Restorative Justice and Child Sexual Abuse." Doctorate. Massey University, 2001. Print.

Mace, Jenni. F. "Developing Opportunities for Occupational Therapists in Primary Health Organisations in New Zealand." *OT Insight* 29.6 (2008): 1-6. Print.

Malcolm, Margy-Jean. "Nonprofit Management Education as a Site for Collaborative Leadership Learning." Paper presented at the Benchmark 3.5. Conference. Ed. Print.

Mendelsohn, Estelle. "Women Settlers: Groupwork in Resettlement - Psychodrama with Refugee and Immigrant Women Living in Auckland, New Zealand." Massey University, 2002. Print.

Murray, Winifred. "Restorative Justice Facilitation: An Appreciative Inquiry into Effective Practices for Aotearoa/New Zealand Facilitators." Doctorate. AUT University, 2012. Web. 30 December 2012.

Who's Counting? Marilyn Waring on Sex, Lies and Global Economics. Dir. Nash, Terre National Film Board of Canada. 1995. DVD.

Sumeo, Karanina "A Research on Processes Used to Address the Physical and Sexual Abuse of Children in Samoa." Masters in Social Policy. Massey University, 2005. Print.

Suttisa, Choopug. "Civil Society in the Chi River, North East Thailand." Doctorate in Social Work. Massey University, 2005. Print.

Tucker, J.M (1999). Measuring Sustainability of International Development Projects. Canadian International Development Agency.

Wall, Caleb. "Multiple Barriers to Technology Change in Rural Uzbekistan: A Development Perspective." Master of Philosophy in Development Studies. Massey University, 2004. Print.

Webster, Karen. "Whakapiri Tātou, Hei Manaaki Tangata, Hei Manaaki Whenua: Effective Governance for Urban Sustainability." Doctorate in Public Policy. Auckland University of Technology, 2009. Web. 30 December 2012.

Wech-o-sotsakda. "ICT in Community-Based Lifelong Learning Center: Model for Northeast Thailand." Doctorate. AUT University, 2008. Web. 30 December 2012.

Epilogue: Wow!

MARILYN WARING

I READ THE book for the first time from cover to cover in Auckland in early March. The 'Wow' came from my sense that these pages contained a breathtaking arc of alternative ways to run the world. This was a volume where the research/evidence/strategy/action continuum was writ so large — with every chapter redolent with unapologetic passion to change paradigms and practices. I could feel all this quite divorced from the title, but it won't be a surprise that I agreed with almost everything inside!

What I wished more than anything else from *Counting for Nothing* was for it to be of use, and now I see that wish fulfilled. It was a breakthrough book, where what might happen next was dependent on people who shared this understanding of the corruption of what is of value in our world, which still lies at the heart of mainstream economics. I knew it provided those opportunities to change this — but would it even be read?

This initiative from Ailsa and Margunn has had a profound effect on the way in which I understand my life's work. This book fills me with humility and gratitude at being understood. I feel as if even the more subtle messages have been received; that strategies beyond my imagination or skills have been seen and advanced. I have been reminded of words I wrote or said that I had completely forgotten, and others have kept pace with key changes I would make to my original vision of alternatives.

Marilyn Waring
30 March 2014

Contributors' Biographies

Iulie Aslaksen is an ecological economist and senior researcher in the research department of Statistics Norway. Her fields of expertise include ecological economics, biodiversity measurement and policy, sustainable development and precautionary perspectives, feminist economics, and the exploration of the common critical perspectives provided by ecological and feminist philosophy and economics.

Margunn Bjørnholt is director of Policy and Social Research in Norway and holds degrees in sociology and international economics. Her research interests include work-family arrangements and gender equality, alternative financial institutions, public sector reform, and feminist legal theory and social justice.

Torunn Bragstad is an economist, feminist economist and senior researcher in the R&D department of the Norwegian Labour and Welfare Organisation. Her fields of expertise include statistical and econometric analysis of women's income, women's labor market participation, and women's rights to social security, pensions, and sick leave and disability compensations.

Monica J. Casper is Head of Gender and Women's Studies at the University of Arizona. Her interests include bodies, health, sexuality, and trauma. She is author of several books, co-editor of NYU's *Biopolitics* series, publisher and co-editor of *TRIVIA: Voices of Feminism*, and a Managing Editor of *The Feminist Wire*.

Lyn Craig is Associate Professor and an Australian Research Council QEII Fellow at the Social Policy Research Centre at the University of New South Wales. Her research interests include parenthood and the time costs of care, work-family balance and the intra-household effects of work-care policy structures.

Rod Dobell is Professor Emeritus, University of Victoria, Canada. He received his PhD in Economics from MIT and held faculty appointments at Harvard and Toronto. He also served as a senior official in the Government of Canada, at OECD, and as President of Canada's Institute for Research in Public Policy.

Jill Eichhorn coordinates the Women's and Gender Studies Program at Austin Peay State University, where she has taught a course focused on the production of Eve Ensler's *The Vagina Monologues* since 2002.

Jo-Anne Fiske, PhD, is Professor of Women's Studies at the University of Lethbridge. She addresses issues of the state, inequities and policy. She has published widely in *Feminist Studies, Atlantis, BC Studies, American Indian Research and Culture*, and *Journal of Legal Pluralism*. Her current projects relate to health, citizenship, and rural gambling cultures.

Mara Fridell is an Assistant Professor in Sociology and an Affiliate of the Global Political Economy Program at the University of Manitoba. She researches the neoliberal social politics attending conservative social contract reassertion, and is a co-author of the forthcoming book *Fair Trade, Sustainability and Social Change*.

Marty Grace is Professor of Social Work at Victoria University, Melbourne, Australia. She has a longstanding interest in the unpaid work of caring for young children. In addition, she researches and writes in the areas of youth homelessness and women's creativity.

Tagaloatele Peggy Fairbairn-Dunlop is Professor of Pacific Studies at AUT University, New Zealand. She has been researching Pacific development issues for over 30 years, critiquing global models for their appropriateness to Pacific peoples. Publications include "Tamaitai Samoa: Their Stories" and, "Making our Place: Growing up PI in New Zealand."

Dawn Hemingway, MSc, MSW, RSW, is Associate Professor and Chair of the University of Northern BC School of Social Work, adjunct professor in Community Health and Gender Studies, Co-Director of Women North Network/Northern FIRE: UNBC Centre for Women's Health Research and a founding member of Stand Up for the North.

Shirley Jülich, PhD, is a senior lecturer at Massey University, Albany, New Zealand. Her research interests focus on the intersection of recovery and justice from the perspective of adult survivors of child sexual abuse. She is a founding member of Project Restore, a program that uses restorative justice processes to address sexual violence.

Leena M. Kirjavainen is a Docent in Household Economics, University of Helsinki, Finland. Her research has covered economic evaluation of household production time from gender perspective. She has served the Food and Agriculture Organization of the UN in various capacities and continues consulting in international development focusing on rural women and gender issues.

Charlotte Koren is an economist. She worked for several years as senior researcher at Norwegian Social Research (NOVA). Her fields of interests are the economics of unpaid household work, care work, women's pensions, family benefits, child support, and more generally the effects of the National Insurance Scheme on income distribution.

Ailsa McKay is Professor in Economics at Glasgow Caledonian University. She is a founding member of the Scottish Women's Budget Group and a member of the Scottish Governments Equality and Budgets Advisory Group.

Dr. Anit N. Mukherjee is an economist specialising in public finance and social sector policy in education, health and social protection.

Julie A. Nelson is Professor of Economics at the University of Massachusetts Boston. She is the author of *Economics for Humans* (2006) and many other works which examine the relationship of economics to feminism, ecology, and ethics, and was a founding board member of the International Association for Feminist Economics.

Sabine O'Hara is Dean of the College of Agriculture, Urban Sustainability & Environmental Sciences (CAUSES), University of the District of Columbia, Washington, D.C. She is well known for her expertise in sustainable economic development, global education and executive leadership.

Heather Peters, PhD, is an Associate Professor with the School of Social Work at the University of Northern British Columbia (UNBC). Her research interests include social policy and access to services with specific attention to northern and rural contexts, as well as the effects of policy on women, caregivers, and vulnerable populations.

Shira Richter is a multi-inter-disciplinary award winning artist who specializes in articulating the politics of motherhood in large scale projects; film, photography text, performance-lecture. She is an independent researcher, speaker, and activist on the subject of integrating gender studies in the educational system, and teaches at the College of Management Academic Studies, Israel.

Hadara Scheflan Katzav, PhD, is an art scholar and curator, and the head of the art department at the Kibbutzim College of Education in Tel Aviv, Israel, and a lecturer in the Department of Interior Design, the College of Management. Her research interests focus on motherhood in art, critical theory and feminist psychoanalysis.

Meena Shivdas, PhD, is a gender and development expert focusing on women's rights, culture and the law, HIV and social protection.

Julie Smith, PhD, is a Fellow in the Australian Centre for Economic Research on Health, Australian National University. Her research focuses on economic aspects of breastfeeding and human milk, including its valuation in GDP and health cost impacts of premature weaning. She also studies time use and breastfeeding, employment and health.

William Paul Simmons is Associate Professor of Gender and Women's Studies and the Honors College at the University of Arizona. His research applies theoretical, legal, and empirical approaches to social justice and human rights issues. He is the author of *Human Rights Law and the Marginalized Other*.

Lorna Turnbull, JSD, is currently the Dean of the Faculty of Law, University of Manitoba, Canada, and has taught and published in both law and women's studies. She is the author of *Double Jeopardy: Motherwork and the Law*, which is recognized nationally and internationally as "essential reading" on mothers and law.

Anita Vaillancourt, MSW, is an Assistant Professor at Algoma University in the Community Development and Social Work program, and a PhD candidate at the University of Toronto. Her teaching, research, and practice areas include welfare reform, addiction, family violence, social policy and social exclusion in northern rural and non-metropolitan contexts.

Johanna Varjonen, PhD, is an economist of family and consumer sciences and a senior researcher at the National Consumer Research Centre in

Helsinki, Finland. Her research covers various topics of time use and consumption of families, and measurement of unpaid work. She is one of the developers of a satellite account of household production in Europe.

Jodie Walsh is a research coordinator at the Centre for Global Studies, University of Victoria, Canada, working on a range of interdisciplinary projects including management of a science-oriented crowdsourcing initiative, Digital Fishers. She graduated with distinction in history and believes in balancing formal institutional knowledge with the wisdom of experience.

Karen Webster, PhD, works as Principal Advisor for the Auckland Council in Aotearoa New Zealand, is engaged in post-graduate co-supervision with AUT University, and has lectured policy analysis parttime at the University of Auckland. Her research interests focus on Māori and Pākehā governance models, sustainability and the role of local government elected members.

Berit Ås is Professor Emerita of social psychology at the University of Oslo and served as a Member of Parliament in Norway and leader of the Socialist Left Party. She founded the Women's University in Norway, the first feminist university in the world, and she recently re-established it as the Nordic Women's University.